Anti-Bolshevik Communism

Anti-Bolshevik Communism

Paul Mattick

MERLIN PRESS

First published in the UK by The Merlin Press 1978
Reprinted 2007

Merlin Press Ltd.
96 Monnow Street
Monmouth
NP25 3EQ
Wales

www.merlinpress.co.uk

ISBN. 978-0-85036-223-7

British Library Cataloguing in Publication Data
is available from the British Library

Printed in Great Britain by
Lightning Source UK, Milton Keynes

Contents

Introduction

The reprinting of this collection of essays and reviews, which were written during the last 40 years, may find its justification in the current ferment of ideas by which a new left-wing within the socialist movement attempts to derive a theory and practice more adequate to the present situation and the needs of social change. As yet merely of a theoretical nature, this trend has led to a growing interest in the comprehension of past revolutionary movements. However, although its proponents try to differentiate themselves from the old and discredited labour movement, they have not as yet been able to evolve a theory and practice of their own which could be considered superior to those of the past. In fact, the 'lessons of history' seem to be largely wasted on the new generation, which often merely repeats in a more insolent fashion and with less sophistication the proven mistakes of the past. Instead of finding their orientation in the actual social conditions and their possibilities, the new leftists base their concerns mainly on a set of ideologies that have no relevance to the requirements of social change in capitalist nations. They find their inspiration not in the developmental processes of their own society but in the heroes of popular revolution in faraway countries, thereby revealing that their enthusiasm is not as yet a real concern for decisive social change.

Of course, there stands a theory behind this strange aberration, namely, the assumption that anti-imperialist struggles of the 'Third World' will abet the social revolution in capitalist nations, thus leading to world-wide social transformation. Although this theory may only indicate the revolutionaries' present frustration in the given non-revolutionary situation, it was at one time the accepted doctrine of a revolutionary movement which briefly tried, but failed, to extend the Russian into a world revolution. In this respect, the ideas of the new revolutionaries still relate to the old Leninism, which Stalin described as the "Marxism of the period of imperialism".

In Lenin's view, it was not the strongest but the weakest link in the chain of imperialist nations that would, through its own revolution, release a world-revolutionary process. Moreover, as imperialism had become an absolute necessity for capitalism, the anti-imperialist struggle was at once a struggle against world capitalism. He envisioned the world revolution as a kind of repetition of the Russian Revolution on a global scale. Just as the Russian Revolution had been a 'peoples' revolution', embracing workers, peasants and the liberal bourgeoisie, without therefore, in Lenin's mind, losing its socialist character, so the world revolution could be seen as a unitary fight of national-revolutionary movements and working-class struggles in the imperialist nations. And just as, according to Lenin, the existence of the Bolshevik Party in Russia guaranteed the transformation of the 'peoples' revolution' into a communist revolution, so, on the world scale, the Bolshevik International was to transform the national-revolutionary struggles into struggles for international socialism.

More than half a century has passed since this theory was celebrated as a necessary extension of the theories of Marx, who did not emphasise the imperialistic difficulties of capitalism but based his hopes for a socialist revolution on the inherent contradictions of the capitalist system of production. In Marx's view, a fully developed capitalism was a precondition for a socialist revolution, even though he thought it possible that such a revolution may receive its impetus from the outside, that is, from revolutionary occurrences in less developed nations. What Marx had specifically in mind was a revolution in Russia which could conceivably lead to a European revolution. Should the latter succeed, it was reasonable to assume that the character of the international revolution as a whole would be determined by the capitalistically-advanced nations. However, the Russian Revolution did not spread to the West and in its isolation could not realise a socialist society but merely a form of state-capitalism under the authoritarian rule of the Bolshevik Party.

It is of course true that bourgeois revolutions in the traditional sense are no longer possible. The monopolistic control of the world economy by the great capitalist powers and their productive preponderance excludes an independent national capitalistic development in underdeveloped nations. To aspire to this goal nonetheless requires their political liberation from imperialist rule, as well as from their native ruling classes, allied as they are with the foreign oppressors. Because the struggle for liberation has to base itself on the broad masses, it cannot use traditional capitalist ideologies, but must be carried on with anti-imperialist and therefore anti-capitalist ideologies.

These national-revolutionary movements are not signs of an impending world-wide socialist revolution, but just so many attempts at an independent capitalistic development – albeit in a state-capitalist form. To the degree to which the liberated nations succeed in freeing themselves from foreign control, they do increase the difficulties of capitalism and further its dissolution. To that extent, they may also aid the class struggle in the dominating capitalist countries. But this does not alter the fact that the goals of the proletarian revolution in the capitalist nations are necessarily different from those that can be realised in backward countries.

It would be ideal, no doubt, to combine the anti-capitalist and anti-imperialist struggles into one great movement against all forms of exploitation and oppression. Unfortunately, this is only an imaginary possibility; unrealisable because of the actual material and social differences between the various differently developed nations. The history of Russia since 1917, as the prototype of 'socialist revolutions' in backward countries, illuminates the objective limitations to their transformation. Today, we even experience the sorry spectacle of so-called socialist countries, all of them adhering to the Leninist ideology, facing one another in deadly enmity and preparing to destroy one another. It is quite obvious that the national interests of state-capitalist systems – like all national interests – contain in themselves their own imperialistic tendencies. It is thus no longer possible to speak of common needs of the national-revolutionary and the international-socialist movement.

The international socialist movement must of course be an anti-imperialist movement. But it has to actualise its anti-imperialism through the destruction of the capitalist system in the advanced countries. Were this accomplished, anti-imperialism would become meaningless and the social struggles in the underdeveloped part of the world would focus on internal class differences. To be sure, the weakness of anti-capitalist movements in the developed countries is one more reason for the existence of national-revolutionary movements. For the latter cannot wait for the proletarian revolution in the dominating capitalist countries; yet, where they succeed, they can reach at best only partial release from foreign exploitation but not the conditions of socialism. On the other hand, successful proletarian revolutions in the capitalistically developed nations could lead to the internationalisation of all social struggles and progressively hasten the integration of underdeveloped nations into a socialist world system.

That there are national-revolutionary movements in the backward nations but not as yet socialist movements in the imperialist countries is due to the greater and more pressing misery in the former. It is also due to the dissolution of the colonial structure resulting from the second world war and the re-organisation and modification of imperialist rule in the post-war world. Force of circumstances interconnects the national movements with the currently waged imperialist power struggles and 'liberation' from one type of imperialism leads to subordination to another. Under present conditions, in brief, national revolutions remain illusory, with respect both to real national independence and to its apparent socialist ideology. They may, however, be preconditions for future struggles for more realistic goals. But this, too, depends on the course of events in the capitalistically-advanced nations.

The preoccupation with national-revolutionary movements that still characterises left-wing radicalism has led, on an international scale, to a re-dedication to Leninist principles in either a Russian or Chinese garb and dissipates the energies thereby released into meaningless and often grotesque activities. By trying to actualise the Leninist ideas of revolution and its organisation in capitalistically-advanced nations, would-be radicals necessarily hinder the development of a revolutionary consciousness adequate to the tasks of the socialist revolution. Because new revolutionary socialist movements may arise in response to capitalism's increasing social and economic difficulties, it is essential to pay renewed attention to the aspirations and accomplishments of former similar movements and here, in particular, to Bolshevism and its Leninist creed.

In this connection, it is particularly apt to recall another movement which emerged out of the shambles of the Second International and the expectations based on the Russian Revolution. Most of the items in this anthology concern themselves with the problems of the international labour movement at the turn of the century – that is, with the reasons for, and the consequences of, the growth of a labour movement that ceased to be revolutionary because of the resilience of capitalism and its ability to improve the living conditions of the labouring population. Still, the immanent contradictions of capitalism led to the first world war and while leading to the partial collapse of the old labour movement also gave rise to a new radicalism culminating in the Russian and Central European revolutions.

These revolutions involved the organised as well as unorganised masses of workers, which created their own and new form of organisation for action and control in the spontaneously-arising workers' and soldiers' councils. But in both Russia and Central Europe the actual content of the revolution was not equal to its new revolutionary form. Whereas in Russia it was mainly the objective unreadiness for a socialist transformation, in Central Europe, and here particularly in Germany, it was the subjective unwillingness to institute socialism by revolutionary means, which largely accounts for the self-limitation and finally the abdication of the council movement in favour of bourgeois democracy. The ideology of Social Democracy had left its mark; the great mass of workers mistook the political for a social revolution; the socialisation of production was seen as a governmental concern, not as that of the workers themselves. In Russia, it is true, the Bolshevik Party advanced the slogan 'All power to the Soviets,' but only for opportunistic reasons, in order to reach its true goal in the authoritarian rule of the Bolshevik Party.

By itself, the workers' self-initiative and self-organisation offers no guarantee for their emancipation. It has to be realised and maintained through the abolition of the capital-labour relationship in production, through a council system, which destroys the social class divisions and prevents the rise of new ones based on the control of production and distribution by the national state. However difficult this may prove to be, the history of the existing state-capitalist systems leaves no doubt that this is the only way to a socialist society. This had already been recognised by small minorities in the radical movement prior to, during, and after the Russian Revolution and was brought into the open within the communist movement as an opposition to Bolshevism and the theory and practice of the Third International. It is this movement and the ideas it brought forth, which this volume recalls, not, however, to describe a particular part and phase of labour history, but as a warning, which may also serve as a guide for future actions.

The revolutions which succeeded, first of all, in Russia and China, were not proletarian revolutions in the Marxist sense, leading to the 'association of free and equal producers', but state-capitalist revolutions, which were objectively unable to issue into socialism. Marxism served here as a mere ideology to justify the rise of modified capitalist systems, which were no longer determined by market competition but controlled by way of the authoritarian state. Based on the peasantry, but designed with accelerated industrialisation to create an industrial proletariat, they were ready to abolish the traditional bourgeoisie but not capital as a social relationship. This type of capitalism had not been foreseen by Marx and the early Marxists, even though they advocated the capture of state-power to overthrow the bourgeoisie – but only in order to abolish the state itself.

Although designated as socialism, state-control of the economy and over social life generally, exercised by a privileged social layer as a newly emerging ruling class, has perpetuated for the industrial as well as agricultural labouring classes the conditions of exploitation and oppression which had been their lot under the semi-feudal social relations of capitalistically-underdeveloped nations. That this new social system could also be applied in capitalistically more advanced nations was demonstrated after the second world war, through the extension of state-capitalist system into the West by way of imperial conquest. In either case, 'socialism' became quite generally identified with the prevailing state-capitalist systems. Movements exist everywhere whose proclaimed goals are precisely the establishment of similar regimes in additional countries, even though, for opportunistic reasons, these goals may be toned down at times, or even totally disclaimed. There exists then the danger that possible new revolutionary outbreaks may once again be side-tracked into state-capitalist transformations.

This possibility finds its support in the centralising tendencies inherent in capitalism itself. The concentration of capital, its monopolisation, and the rise of corporations in which ownership is separated from direct control, and, finally, the reluctant integration of state and capital in the mixed economy, with its fiscal and monetary manipulations, seem to spell a tendency in the direction of a full-fledged state-capitalism. What once constituted a vague hope on the part of social reformers and what in backward countries became a reality through revolution, appears now as an unavoidable requirement for securing the social relations of capital production.

Although the so-called mixed economy will not automatically transform itself into state-capitalism, new social upheavals may well lead to it in the name of socialism. It is true that 'Marxism-Leninism' presents itself today as a purely reformist movement, which, like the Social Democracy of old, prefers the democratic processes of social change to the revolutionary overthrow of capitalism. In some countries, France and Italy, for instance, relatively strong communist parties offer their services to capitalism to help it overcome its crisis conditions. But should everything fail, and an intensified class struggle pose the question of social revolution, there can be no doubt that these parties will opt for state-capitalism, which in their views, is the only possible form of socialism. Thus, the revolution would be at once a counter-revolution. The end of capitalism demands therefore, first of all, the end of Bolshevik ideology and the rise of an anti-Bolshevik revolutionary movement, such as has been attempted at the earlier revolutionary situation to which this book tries to draw attention.

P.M.

CHAPTER I

Karl Kautsky: From Marx to Hitler

In the fall of 1938, Karl Kautsky died in Amsterdam at the age of 84 years. He was considered the most important theoretician of the Marxist labour movement after the death of its founders, and it may well be said that he was its most representative member. In him were very clearly incorporated both the revolutionary and the reactionary aspects of that movement. But whereas Friedrich Engels could say at Marx's grave that his friend "was first of all a revolutionist", it would be difficult to say the same at the grave of his best-known pupil. "As a theoretician and politician, he will always remain an object of criticism," wrote Friedrich Adler in memory of Kautsky, "but his character lies open, his whole life he remained true to the highest majesty, his own conscience."[1]

Kautsky's conscience was formed during the rise of the German Social Democracy. He was born in Austria, the son of a stage painter of the Imperial Theatre in Vienna. As early as 1875, though not as yet a Marxist, he contributed to German and Austrian labour papers. He became a member of the German Social Democratic Party in 1880, and "only now," he said of himself, "began my development towards a consistent methodical Marxism."[2] He was inspired, like so many others, by Engels' *Anti-Dühring* and was helped in his orientation by Eduard Bernstein, who was then the secretary to the 'millionaire' socialist Hoechberg. His first works were published with Hoechberg's help and he found recognition in the labour movement through his editorship of a number of socialist publications. In 1883 he founded the magazine *Neue Zeit,* which under his direction became the most important theoretical organ of the German Social Democracy.

Kautsky's literary and scientific work is impressive not only because of the scope of his interests but also because of its volume. Even a selected bibliography of his writings would fill many pages. In this work comes to light all that seemed and all that was of importance to the socialist movement during the last 60 years. It reveals Kautsky was first of all a teacher, and that, because he looked upon society from a schoolmaster's perspective, he was well suited to his role as the leading spirit of a movement which aimed at educating workers and capitalists alike. Because he was an educator concerned with the 'theoretical side' of Marxism, he could appear more revolutionary that was consistent with the movement he served. He appeared an 'orthodox' Marxist who tried to safeguard the Marxian inheritance as a treasurer who desires to preserve the funds of his organisation. However, what was 'revolutionary' in Kautsky's teaching appeared revolutionary only in contrast to the general pre-war capitalist ideology. In contrast to the revolutionary theories established by Marx and Engels, it was a reversion to more primitive forms of thinking and to a lesser apperception of the implications of bourgeois society. Thus, though he guarded the treasure-chest of Marxism, he had not beheld all it contained.

In 1862, in a letter to Kugelmann, Marx expressed the hope that his non-popular works attempting to revolutionise economic science would in due time find adequate popularisation, a feat that should be easy after the scientific basis had been laid. "My life work became clear to me in 1883," wrote Kautsky; "it was to be designated to the propagandising and popularisation, and, as far as I am able to, the continuation of the scientific results of Marx's thinking and research."[3] However, not even he, the greatest populariser of Marx, has fulfilled Marx's hope; his simplifications turned out to be new mystifications unable to comprehend the true character of capitalist society. Nevertheless, even in their watered form, Marx's theories remained superior to all the social and economic bourgeois theories and Kautsky's writings gave strength and joy to hundreds of thousands of class conscious workers. He gave expression to their own thoughts and in a language nearer to them than that of the more independent thinker Marx. Though the latter demonstrated more than once his great gift for cogency and clarity, he was not schoolmaster enough to sacrifice to propaganda the enjoyment of his intellectual caprice.

When we said that Kautsky represented also what was 'reactionary' in the old labour movement, we are using that term in a highly specific sense. The reactionary elements in Kautsky and in the old labour movement were objectively conditioned, and only by a long period of exposure to an inimical reality was developed that subjective readiness to turn defenders of the capitalist society. In *Capital* Marx pointed out that "a rise in the price of labour, as a consequence of accumulation of capital, only means, in fact, that the length and weight of the golden chain the wage-worker has already forged for himself, allow of a relaxation of the tension of it."[4] The possibility, under conditions of a progressive capital formation, of improving labour conditions and of raising the price of labour transformed the workers' struggle into a force for capitalist expansion. Like capitalist competition, the workers' struggle served as an incentive for further capital accumulation; it accentuated capitalist 'progress'. All gains of the workers were compensated for by an increasing exploitation, which in turn permitted a still more rapid capital expansion.

Even the class struggle of the workers could serve the needs not of the individual capitalists but of capital. The victories of the workers turned always against the victors. The more the workers gained, the richer capital became. The gap between wages and profits became wider with each increase of the 'workers' share'. The apparently increasing strength of labour was in reality the continuous weakening of its position in relation to that of capital. The 'successes' of the workers, hailed by Eduard Bernstein as a new era of capitalism, could, in this sphere of social action, end only in the eventual defeat of the working class, as soon as capital changed from expansion to stagnation. In the destruction of the old labour movement, the sight of which Kautsky was not spared, became manifest the thousands of defeats suffered during the upswing period of capitalism, and though these defeats were celebrated as victories of gradualism, they were in reality only the gradualism of the workers' defeat in a field of action where the advantage is always with the bourgeoisie. Nevertheless, Bernstein's revisionism, based on the acceptance of appearance for reality and suggested by bourgeois empiricism, though at first denounced by Kautsky, provided the basis for the latter's own success. For without the non-revolutionary practice of the old labour movement, whose theories were formed by Bernstein, Kautsky would not have found a movement and a material basis on which to rise as an important Marxian theoretician.

This objective situation, which, as we have seen, transformed the successes of the labour movement into just so many steps toward its destruction, created a non-revolutionary ideology which was more in harmony with the apparent reality, and which was later denounced as social-reformism, opportunism, social-chauvinism, and outright betrayal. However, this 'betrayal' did not very much bother those who were betrayed. Instead, the majority of the organised workers approved of the change of attitude in the socialist movement, since it conformed to their own aspirations developed in an ascending capitalism. The masses were as little revolutionary as their leaders, and both were satisfied with their *participation* in capitalist progress. Not only were they organising for a greater share of the social product, but also for a greater voice in the political sphere. They learned to think in terms of bourgeois democracy; they began to speak of themselves as consumers; they wanted to take part in all that was good of culture and civilisation. Franz Mehring's *History of the German Social Democracy* typically ends in a chapter on 'Art and the Proletariat'. Science for the workers, literature for the workers, schools for the workers, participation in all the institutions of capitalist society – this and nothing more was the real desire of the movement. Instead of demanding the end of capitalistic science, it asked for labour scientists; instead of abolishing capitalistic law, it trained labour lawyers; in the increasing number of labour historians, poets, economists, journalists, doctors and dentists, as well as parliamentarians and trade-union bureaucrats, it saw the socialisation of society, which therewith became increasingly its own society. That which one can increasingly share in one will soon find defendable. Consciously and unconsciously the old labour movement saw in the capitalist expansion process its own road to greater welfare and recognition. The more capital flourished, the better were the working conditions. Satisfied with action within the framework of capitalism, the workers' organisations became concerned with capitalism's profitability. The competitive national capitalistic rivalries were only verbally opposed. Although the movement was at first striving only for a 'better fatherland', and was later willing to defend what had already been gained, it soon reached the point where it was ready to defend the fatherland 'as it is'.

The tolerance that Marx's 'followers' displayed towards the bourgeois society was not one-sided. The bourgeoisie itself had in its very struggle against the working class learned to 'understand the social question'. Its interpretation of social phenomena became increasingly more materialistic; and soon there was an overlapping of ideologies in both fields of thought, a condition increasing still further the 'harmony' based on the actual disharmony of class frictions within a rising capitalism. However, the 'Marxists' were more eager than the bourgeoisie to 'learn from the enemy'. The revisionist tendencies had developed long before the death of Engels. The latter, and Marx himself, had wavered and displayed moments in which they were carried away by the apparent success of their movement. But what with them was only a temporary modification of their essentially consistent thinking became 'belief' and 'science' for that movement which learned to see progress in larger trade-union treasures and greater election votes.

After 1910 the German social democracy found itself divided into three essential groups. There were the reformists, openly favouring German imperialism; there was the 'left', distinguished by such names as Luxemburg, Liebknecht, Mehring and Pannekoek; and there was the 'centre', trying to follow traditional paths, that is, only in theory, as in practice the whole of the German social democracy could do only what was possible, i.e. what Bernstein wanted them to do. To oppose Bernstein could mean only to oppose the whole of the social democratic practice. The 'left' began to function as such only at the moment it began to attack social democracy as a part of capitalist society. The differences between the two opposing factions could not be solved ideationally; they were solved when the Noske terror murdered the Spartacus group in 1919.

With the outbreak of the war, the 'left' found itself in the capitalist prisons, and the 'right' on the General Staff of the Kaiser. The 'centre', led by Kautsky, simply dispensed with all problems of the socialist movement by declaring that neither the social democracy nor its International could function during periods of war, as both were essentially instruments of peace. "This position," Rosa Luxemburg wrote, "is the position of an eunuch. After Kautsky has supplemented the Communist Manifesto it now reads: Proletarians of all countries unite during peace times, during times of war, cut your throats."[5]

The war and its aftermath destroyed the legend of Kautsky's Marxist "orthodoxy'. Even his most enthusiastic pupil, Lenin, had to turn away from the master. In October 1914 he had to admit that as far as Kautsky was concerned, Rosa Luxemburg had been right. In a letter to Shlyapnikow[6], he wrote, "She saw long ago that Kautsky, the servile theoretician, was cringing to the majority of the Party, to Opportunism. There is nothing in the world at present more harmful and dangerous for the ideological independence of the proletariat than this filthy, smug and disgusting hypocrisy of Kautsky. He wants to hush everything up and smear everything over and by sophistry and pseudo-learned rhetoric lull the awakened consciences of the workers."

What distinguished Kautsky from the general run of intellectuals who flocked to the labour movement as soon as it became more respectable and who were only too eager to foster the trend of class collaboration, was a greater love for theory, a love which refused to compare theory with actuality, like the love of a mother who prevents her child from learning the 'facts of life' too early. Only as a theoretician could Kautsky remain a revolutionist; only too willingly he left the practical affairs of the movement to others. However, he fooled himself. In the role of a mere 'theoretician', he ceased to be a revolutionary theoretician, or rather he could not become a revolutionist. As soon as the scene for a real battle between capitalism and socialism after the war had been laid, his theories collapsed because they had already been divorced in practice from the movement they were supposed to represent.

Though Kautsky was opposed to the unnecessarily enthusiastic chauvinism of his party, though he hesitated to enjoy the war as Ebert, Scheidemann and Hindenburg did, though he was not in favour of an *unconditional* granting of war credits, nevertheless, up to his very end, he was forced to destroy with his own hands the legend of his Marxian orthodoxy that he had earned for himself in 30 years of writing. He who in 1902[7] had pronounced that we have entered a period of proletarian struggles for state power, declared such attempts to be sheer insanity when workers took him seriously. He who had fought so valiantly against the ministerialism of Millerand and Jaurès in France, championed 20 years later the coalition policy of the German social democracy with the arguments of his former opponents. He who concerned himself as early as 1909 with 'The Way to Power', dreamed after the war of a capitalist 'ultra-imperialism' as a way to world peace, and spent the remainder of his life re-interpreting his past to justify his class collaboration ideology. "In the course of its class struggle," he wrote in his last work, "the proletariat becomes more and more the vanguard for the reconstruction of humanity, in which in always greater measure also non-proletarian layers of society become interested. This is no betrayal of the class struggle idea. I had this position already before there was bolshevism, as, for instance, in 1903 in my article on 'Class – Special – and Common Interests' in the *Neue Zeit*, where I came to the conclusion that the proletarian class struggle does not recognise class solidarity but only the solidarity of mankind."[8]

Indeed, it is not possible to regard Kautsky as a 'renegade'. Only a total misunderstanding of the theory and practice of the social democratic movement and of Kautsky's activity could lead to such a view. Kautsky aspired to being a good servant of Marxism; in fact, to please Engels and Marx seemed to be his life profession. He referred to the latter always in the typical social-democratic and philistine manner as the 'great master', the 'Olympian', the 'Thunder God', etc. He felt extremely honoured because Marx "did not receive him in the same cold way in which Goethe received his young colleague Heine".[9] He must have sworn to himself not to disappoint Engels when the latter began to regard him and Bernstein as 'trustworthy representatives of Marxian theory', and during most of his life he was the most ardent defender of 'the word'. He is most honest when he complains to Engels[10] "that nearly all the intellectuals in the party . . . cry for colonies, for national thought, for a resurrection of the Teutonic antiquity, for confidence in the government, for having the power of 'justice' replace the class struggle, and express a decided aversion for the materialistic interpretation of history – Marxian dogma, as they call it". He wanted to argue against them, to uphold against them what had been established by his idols. A good schoolmaster, he was also an excellent pupil.

Engels understood this early 'degeneration' of the movement only too well. In answering Kautsky's complaints, he stated,[11] "that the development of capitalism proved itself to be stronger than the revolutionary counter-pressure. A new upsurge against capitalism would need a violent shock, such as the loss by England of its domination of the world market, or a sudden revolutionary opportunity in France." But neither the one nor the other event occurred. The socialists no longer waited for revolution. Bernstein waited instead for Engels' death, to avoid disappointing the man to whom he owed most – before proclaiming that "the goal meant nothing and the movement everything". It is true that Engels himself had strengthened the forces of reformism during the latter part of his life. However, what in his case could be taken only as the weakening of the individual in his stand against the world, was taken by his epigones as the source of their strength. Time and again Marx and Engels returned to the uncompromising attitude of the *Communist Manifesto* and *Capital* as, for instance, in the *Critique of the Gotha Programme*, which was delayed in its publication in order not to disturb the compromisers in the movement. Its publication was possible only after a struggle with the party bureaucracy, which circumstance led Engels to remark that, "It is in fact a brilliant thought to have German socialist science present, after its emancipation from the Bismarckian socialist laws, its own socialist laws, formulated by the officials of the Social Democratic Party."[12]

Kautsky defended an already emasculated Marxism. The radical, revolutionary, anti-capitalist Marxism had been defeated by capitalist development. At the Congress of the Workers' International in 1872 in The Hague, Marx himself had declared: "Some day the workers must conquer political supremacy, in order to establish the new organisation of labour . . . Of course, I must not be supposed to imply that the means to this end will be the same everywhere . . . and we do not deny that there are certain countries, such as the United States and England in which the workers may hope to secure their ends by peaceful means." This statement allowed even the revisionists to declare themselves Marxists, and the only argument Kautsky could muster against them, as, for instance, during the Social Democratic Party congress in Stuttgart in 1898, was the denial that the democratisation and socialisation process claimed by the revisionists as in progress in England and America, also held good for Germany. He repeated Marx's position as regards the eventuality of a more peaceful transformation of society in some countries, and added to this remark only that he, too, "wishes nothing else but to obtain socialism without a catastrophe." However, he doubted such a possibility.

It is understandable that on the basis of such thinking it was only consistent for Kautsky to assume after the war that with the now possible more rapid development of democratic institutions in Germany and Russia, the more peaceful way to socialism could be realised also in these countries. The peaceful way seemed to him the surer way, as it would better serve that 'solidarity of mankind' that he wished to develop. The socialist intellectuals wished to return the decency with which the bourgeoisie had learned to treat them. After all, we are all gentlemen! The orderly petty-bourgeois life of the intelligentsia, secured by a powerful socialist movement, had led them to emphasise the ethical and cultural aspects of things. Kautsky hated the methods of bolshevism with no less intensity than did the white guardists, though in contrast to the latter, he was in full agreement with the goal of Bolshevism. Behind the aspect of the proletarian revolution the leaders of the socialist movement correctly saw a chaos in which their own position would become no less jeopardised than that of the bourgeoisie proper. Their hatred of 'disorder' was a defence of their own material, social and intellectual position. Socialism was to be developed not illegally, but legally, for under such conditions, existing organisations and leaders would continue to dominate the movement. And their successful interruption of the impending proletarian revolution demonstrated that not only did the 'gains' of the workers in the economic sphere turn against the workers themselves, but that their 'success' in the political field also turned out to be weapons against their emancipation. The strongest bulwark against a radical solution of the social question was the social democracy, in whose growth the workers had learned to measure their growing power.

Nothing shows the revolutionary character of Marx's theories more clearly than the difficulty to maintain them during non-revolutionary times. There was a grain of truth in Kautsky's statement that the socialist movement cannot function during times of war, as times of war temporarily create non-revolutionary situations. The revolutionist becomes isolated, and registers temporary defeat. He must wait till the situation changes, till the subjective readiness to participate in war is broken by the objective impossibility to serve this subjective readiness. A revolutionist cannot help standing 'outside the world' from time to time. To believe that a revolutionary practice, expressed in independent actions of the workers, is always possible means to fall victim to democratic illusions. But it is more difficult to stand 'outside this world', for no one can know when situations change, and no one wishes to be left out when changes do occur. Consistency exists only in theory. It cannot be said that Marx's theories were inconsistent; it can, however, be said, that Marx was not consistent, i.e. that he, too, had to pay deference to a changing reality and, in non-revolutionary times, in order to function at all, had to function in a non-revolutionary manner. His theories were limited to the essentials of the class struggle between bourgeoisie and proletariat, but his practice was continuous, dealing with problems 'as they came up', problems which could not always be solved with essential principles. Unwilling to retire during the upswing period of capitalism, Marxism could not escape functioning in a manner contrary to a theory resulting from the recognition of a real and always present revolutionary class struggle. The theory of the everpresent class struggle has no more justification than the bourgeois concept of progress. There is no automatism keeping things rolling uphill; instead, there is combat with changing fortunes; there is the deathlock of the struggle and the utter defeat. Mere numbers of workers opposed to the powerful capitalist state at times when history still favours capitalism do not represent the giant on whose back the capitalist parasites rest, but rather the bull who has to move in the directions his nose-stick forces him to go. During the non-revolutionary period of the ascending capitalism, revolutionary Marxism could exist only as ideology, serving an entirely different practice. In this latter form it was again limited by actual occurrences. As a mere ideology it had to cease existing as soon as great social upheavals demanded a change from an indirect to a direct class collaboration ideology for capitalistic purposes.

Marx developed his theories during revolutionary times. The most advanced of the bourgeois revolutionists, he was the closest to the proletariat. The defeat of the bourgeoisie as revolutionists, their success within the counter-revolution, convinced Marx that the modern revolutionary class can be only the working class, and he developed the socio-economic theory of their revolution. Like many of his contemporaries, he underestimated the strength and flexibility of capitalism, and expected too soon the end of bourgeois society. Two alternatives opened themselves to him: he could either stand outside the actual development, restricting himself to inapplicable radical thinking, or participate under the given conditions in the actual struggles, and reserve the revolutionary theories for 'better times'. This latter alternative was rationalised into the 'proper balance of theory and practice', and the defeat or success of proletarian activities became therewith the result of 'right' or 'wrong' tactics once more; the question of the proper organisation and of correct leadership. It was not so much Marx's earlier connection with the bourgeois revolution that led to the further development of the Jacobinic aspect of the labour movement called by his name, but the non-revolutionary practice of this movement, because of the non-revolutionary times.

The Marxism of Kautsky, then, was a Marxism in the form of a mere ideology, and it was therewith fated to return in the course of time into idealistic channels. Kautsky's 'orthodoxy' was in truth the artificial preservation of ideas opposed to an actual practice, and was therewith forced into retreat, as reality is always stronger than ideology. A real Marxian 'orthodoxy' could be possible only with a return of real revolutionary situations, and then such 'orthodoxy' would concern itself not with 'the word', but with the principle of the class struggle between bourgeoisie and proletariat applied to new and changed situations. The retreat of theory before practice can be followed with utmost clarity in Kautsky's writings.

The many books and articles written by Kautsky deal with almost all social problems, in addition to specific questions concerning the labour movement. However, his writings can be classified into Economy, History and Philosophy. In the field of political economy, not much can be said about his contribution. He was the populariser of the first volume of Marx's *Capital* and the editor of Marx's "Theories of Surplus Value", published during the years from 1904 to 1910. His popularisations of Marx's economic theories do not distinguish themselves from the generally accepted interpretation of economic phenomena in the socialist movement – the revisionists included. As a matter of fact, parts of his famous book "The Economic Doctrines of Karl Marx" were written by Eduard Bernstein. In the heated discussion waged at the turn of the century concerning the meaning of Marx's theories in the second and third volume of *Capital*, Kautsky took very small part. For him the first volume of *Capital* contained all that was of importance to the workers and their movement. It dealt with the process of production, the factory and exploitation, and contained all that was needed to support a workers' movement against capitalism. The other two volumes dealing in greater detail with capitalist tendencies towards crises and collapse did not correspond to immediate reality and found little interest not only by Kautsky but by all Marxian theoreticians of the upswing period of capitalism. In a review of the second volume of *Capital*, written in 1886, Kautsky expressed the opinion that this volume is of less interest to the workers, as it deals largely with the problem of the realisation of surplus value, which after all should be rather the concern of the capitalists. When Bernstein, in the course of his attack upon Marx's economic theories, rejected the latter's theory of collapse, Kautsky defended Marxism by simply denying that Marx ever had developed a special theory pointing to an objective end of capitalism, and that such a concept was merely an invention of Bernstein. The difficulties and contradictions of capitalism he searched for in the sphere of circulation. Consumption could not grow so rapidly as production and a permanent over-production would lead to the political necessity of introducing socialism. Against Tugan-Baranowsky's theory of an unhampered capitalist development proceeding from the fact that capital creates its own markets and can overcome developing disproportionalities, a theory which influenced the whole reformist movement, Kautsky[13] set his underconsumption theory to explain the unavoidability of capitalist crises, crises which helped to create the subjective conditions for a transformation from capitalism to socialism. However, 25 years later, he openly admitted that he had been wrong in his evaluation of the economic possibilities of capitalism, as "from an economic viewpoint, capital is much livelier today than it was 50 years ago".[14]

The theoretical unclarity and inconsistency that Kautsky[15] displayed on economic questions, were only climaxed by his acceptance of the once denounced views of Tugan-Baranowsky. They were only a reflection of his changing general attitude towards bourgeois thought and capitalist society. In his book "The Materialistic Conception of History", which he himself declares to be the best and final product of his whole life's work, dealing as it does in nearly 2000 pages with the development of nature, society and the state, he demonstrates not only his pedantic method of exposition and his far-reaching knowledge of theories and facts, but also his many misconceptions as regards Marxism and his final break with Marxian science. Here he openly declares "that at times revisions of Marxism are unavoidable".[16] Here he now accepts all that during his whole life he had apparently struggled against. He is no longer solely interested in the interpretation of Marxism, but is ready to accept responsibility for his own thoughts, presenting his main work as his own conception of history, not totally removed but independent from Marx and Engels. His masters, he now contends, have restricted the materialistic conception of history by neglecting too much the natural factors in history. He, however, starting not from Hegel but from Darwin, "will now extend the scope of historical materialism till it merges with biology".[17] But his furthering of historical materialism turns out to be no more than a reversion to the crude naturalistic materialism of Marx's forerunners, a return to the position of the revolutionary bourgeoisie, which Marx had overcome with his rejection of Feuerbach. On the basis of this naturalistic materialism, Kautsky, like the bourgeois philosophers before him, cannot help adopting an idealistic concept of social development, which, then, when it deals with the state, turns openly and completely into the old bourgeois conceptions of the history of mankind as the history of states. Ending in the bourgeois democratic state, Kautsky holds that "there is no room any longer for violent class conflict. Peacefully, by way of propaganda and the voting system can conflicts be ended, decisions be made."[18]

Though we cannot possibly review in detail at this place this tremendous book of Kautsky,[19] we must say that it demonstrates throughout the doubtful character of Kautsky's 'Marxism'. His connection with the labour movement, seen retrospectively, was never more than his participation in some form of bourgeois social work. There can be no doubt that he never understood the real position of Marx and Engels, or at least never dreamed that theories could have an immediate connection with reality. This apparently serious Marxist student had actually never taken Marx seriously. Like many pious priests engaging in a practice contrary to their teaching, he might not even have been aware of the duality of his own thought and action. Undoubtedly he would have sincerely liked being in reality the bourgeois of whom Marx once said, he is "a capitalist solely in the interest of the proletariat". But even such a change of affairs he would reject, unless it were atainable in the 'peaceful' bourgeois, democratic manner. Kautsky, "repudiates the Bolshevik melody that is unpleasant to his ear," wrote Trotsky, "but does not seek another. The solution is simple: the old musician refuses altogether to play on the instrument of the revolution."[20]

Recognising at the close of his life that the reforms of capitalism that he wished to achieve could not be realised by democratic, peaceful means, Kautsky turned against his own practical policy, and just as he was in former times the proponent of a Marxian ideology which, altogether divorced from reality, could serve only its opponents, he now became the proponent of bourgeois *laissez faire* ideology, just as much removed from the actual conditions of the developing fascistic capitalist society, and just as much serving this society as his Marxian ideology had served the democratic stage of capitalism. "People love today to speak disdainfully about the liberalistic economy," he wrote in his last work; "however, the theories founded by Quesnay, Adam Smith and Ricardo are not at all obsolete. In their essentials Marx had accepted their theories and developed them further, and he has never denied that the liberal freedom of commodity production constituted the best basis for its development. Marx distinguishes himself from the Classicists therein, that when the latter saw in commodity production of private producers the only possible form of production, Marx saw the highest form of commodity production leading through its own development to conditions allowing for a still better form of production, social production, where society, identical with the whole of the working population, controls the means of production, producing no longer for profit but to satisfy needs. The socialist mode of production has its own rules, in many respects different from the laws of commodity production. However, as long as commodity production prevails, it will best function if those laws of motion discovered in the era of liberalism are respected."[21]

These ideas are quite surprising in a man who had edited Marx's "Theories of Surplus Value", a work which proved exhaustively "that Marx at no time in his life countenanced the opinion that the new contents of his socialist and communist theory could be derived, as a mere logical consequence, from the utterly bourgeois theories of Quesnay, Smith and Ricardo."[22] However, this position of Kautsky's gives the necessary qualifications to our previous statement that he was an excellent pupil of Marx and Engels. He was such only to the extent that Marxism could be fitted into his own limited concepts of social development and of capitalist society. For Kautsky, the 'socialist society', or the logical consequence of capitalist development of commodity production, is in truth only a state-capitalist system. When once he mistook Marx's value concept as a law of socialist economics if only applied consciously instead of being left to the 'blind' operations of the Market, Engels pointed out to him[23] that for Marx, value is a strictly historical category; that neither before nor after capitalism did there exist or could there exist a value production which differed only in form from that of capitalism. And Kautsky accepted Engels' statement, as is manifested in his work "The Economic Doctrines of Karl Marx" (1887), where he also saw value as a historical category. Later, however, in reaction to bourgeois criticism of socialist economic theory, he re-introduced in his book "The Proletarian Revolution and its Programme" (1922) the value concept, the market and money economy, commodity production, into his scheme of a socialist society. What was once historical became eternal; Engels had talked in vain. Kautsky had returned from where he had sprung, from the *petite-bourgeoisie,* who hate with equal force both monopoly control and socialism, and hope for a purely quantitative change of society, an enlarged reproduction of the *status quo*, a better and bigger capitalism, a better and more comprehensive democracy – as against a capitalism climaxing in fascism or changing into communism.

The maintenance of liberal commodity production and its political expression were preferred by Kautsky to the 'economics' of fascism because the former system determined his long grandeur and his short misery. Just as he had shielded bourgeois democracy with Marxian phraseology, so he now obscured the fascist reality with democratic phraseology. For now, by turning their thoughts backward instead of forward, he made his followers mentally incapacitated for revolutionary action. The man who shortly before his death was driven from Berlin to Vienna by marching fascism, and from Vienna to Prague, and from Prague to Amsterdam, published in 1937 a book[24] which shows explicitly that once a 'Marxist' makes the step from a materialistic to an idealistic concept of social development, he is sure to arrive sooner or later at that borderline of thought where idealism turns into insanity. There is a report current in Germany that when Hindenburg was watching a Nazi demonstration of storm troops he turned to a General standing beside him saying, "I did not know we had taken so many Russian prisoners." Kautsky, too, in this his last book, is mentally still at 'Tannenberg'. His work is a faithful description of the different attitudes taken by socialists and their forerunners to the question of war since the beginning of the fifteenth century up to the present time. It shows, although not to Kautsky, how ridiculous Marxism can become when it associates the proletarian with the bourgeois needs and necessities.

Kautsky wrote his last book, as he said, "to determine which position should be taken by socialists and democrats in case a new war breaks out despite all our opposition to it".[25] However, he continued, "There is no direct answer to this question before the war is actually here and we are all able to see who caused the war and for what purpose it is fought." He advocates that "if war breaks out, socialists should try to maintain their unity, to bring their organisation safely through the war, so that they may reap the fruit wherever unpopular political regimes collapse. In 1914 this unity was lost and we still suffer from this calamity. But today things are much clearer than they were then; the opposition between democratic and anti-democratic states is much sharper; and it can be expected that if it comes to the new world war, all socialists will stand on the side of democracy." After the experiences of the last war and the history since then, there is no need to search for the black sheep that causes wars, nor is it a secret any longer why wars are fought. However, to pose such questions is not stupidity as one may believe. Behind this apparent naïvete lies the determination to serve capitalism in one form by fighting capitalism in another. It serves to prepare the workers for the coming war, in exchange for the right to organise in labour organisations, vote in elections, and assemble in formations which serve both capital and capitalistic labour organisations. It is the old policy of Kautsky, which demands concessions from the bourgeoisie in exchange for millions of dead workers in the coming capitalistic battles. In reality, just as the wars of capitalism, regardless of the political differences of the participating states and the various slogans used, can only be wars for capitalist profits and wars against the working class, so, too, the war excludes the possibility of choosing between conditional or unconditional participation in the war by the workers. Rather, the war, and even the period preceding the war, will be marked by a general and complete military dictatorship in fascist and anti-fascist countries alike. The war will wipe out the last distinction between the democratic and the anti-democratic nations. And workers will serve Hitler as they served the Kaiser; they will serve Roosevelt as they served Wilson; they will die for Stalin as they died for the Tsar.

Kautsky was not disturbed by the reality of fascism, since for him, democracy was the natural form of capitalism. The new situation was only a sickness, a temporary insanity, a thing actually foreign to capitalism. He really believed in a war for democracy, to allow capitalism to proceed in its logical course towards a real commonwealth. And his 1937 predictions incorporated sentences like the following: "The time has arrived where it is finally possible to do away with wars as a means of solving political conflicts between the states."[26] Or, "The policy of conquest of the Japanese in China, the Italians in Ethiopia, is a last echo of a passing time, the period of imperialism. More wars of such a character can hardly be expected."[27] There are hundreds of similar sentences in Kautsky's book, and it seems at times that his whole world must have consisted of no more than the four walls of his library, to which he neglected to add the newest volumes on recent history. Kautsky is convinced that even without a war fascism will be defeated, the rise of democracy recur, and the period return for a peaceful development towards socialism, like the period in the days before fascism. The essential weakness of fascism he illustrated with the remark that "the personal character of the dictatorships indicates already that it limits its own existence to the length of a human life."[28] He believed that after fascism there would be the return to the 'normal' life on an increasingly socialistic abstract democracy to continue the reforms begun in the glorious time of the social democratic coalition policy. However, it is obvious now that the only capitalistic reform objectively possible today is the fascistic reform. And as a matter of fact, the larger part of the 'socialisation programme' of the social democracy, which it never dared to put into practice, has meanwhile been realised by fascism. Just as the demands of the German bourgeoisie were met not in 1848 but in the ensuing period of the counter-revolution, so, too, the reform programme of the social democracy, which it could not inaugurate during the time of its own reign, was put into practice by Hitler. Thus, to mention just a few facts, not the social democracy but Hitler fulfilled the long desire of the socialists, the *Anschluss* of Austria; not social democracy but fascism established the wished-for state control of industry and banking; not social democracy but Hitler declared the first of May a legal holiday. A careful analysis of what the socialists actually wanted to do and never did, compared with actual policies since 1933, will reveal to any objective observer that Hitler realised no more than the programme of social democracy, but without the socialists. Like Hitler, the social democracy and Kautsky were opposed to both bolshevism and communism. Even a complete state-capitalist system as the Russian was rejected by both in favour of mere state control. And what is necessary in order to realise such a programme was not dared by the socialists but undertaken by the fascists. The anti-fascism of Kautsky illustrated no more than the fact that just as he once could not imagine that Marxist theory could be supplemented by a Marxist practice, he later could not see that a capitalist reform policy demanded a capitalist reform practice, which turned out to be the fascist practice. The life of Kautsky can teach the workers that in the struggle against fascistic capitalism is necessarily incorporated the struggle against bourgeois democracy, the struggle against Kautskyism. The life of Kautsky can, in all truth and without malicious intent, be summed up in the words: From Marx to Hitler.

1939

1 *Der Sozialistische Kampf.* Paris, November 5, 1938, p.271.
2 K. Kautsky, *Aus der Frühzeit des Marxismus.* Prague, 1935, p.20.
3 *Ibid.*, p.93.

4 *Capital.* Vol.I, p.677 (Kerr ed.).
5 *Die Internationale.* Spring 1915.
6 *The Letters of Lenin.* London 1937, p.342.
7 *The Social Revolution.*
8 K. Kautsky, *Sozialisten und Krieg.* Prague, 1937, p.673.
9 *Aus der Frühzeit des Marxismus,* p.50.
10 *Ibid.,* p.112.
11 *Ibid.,* p.155.
12 *Ibid.,* p.273.
13 *Neue Zeit,* 1902, No.5.
14 K. Kautsky, *Die Materialistische Geschichtsauffassung.* Berlin, 1927. Vol.II, p.623.
15 The limitations of Kautsky's economic theories and their transformations in the course of his activities are excellently described and criticised by Henryk Grossman in his book *Das Akkumulations- und Zusammenbruchsgesetz des kapitalistischen Systems* (Leipzig, 1929), to which the interested reader is referred.
16 K. Kautsky, *Die Materialistische Geschichtsauffassung.* Vol.II, p.630.
17 *Ibid.,* p.629.
18 *Ibid.,* p.431.
19 The reader is referred to Karl Korsch's extensive criticism of Kautsky's work, *Die Materialistische Geschichtsauffassung. Eine Auseinandersetzung mit Karl Kautsky.* Leipzig, 1929.
20 L. Trotsky, *Dictatorship vs. Democracy.*
21 *Sozialisten und Krieg.* p.665.
22 K. Korsch, *Karl Marx.* New York, 1938, p.92. See also: Engels' Preface to the German edition of *The Poverty of Philosophy,* 1884; and to the second volume of *Capital,* 1895.
23 *Aus der Frühzeit des Marxismus,* p.145.
24 *Sozialisten und Krieg.*
25 *Ibid.,* p.VIII.
26 *Ibid.,* p.265.
27 *Ibid.,* p.656.
28 *Ibid.,* p.646.

CHAPTER II

Luxemburg versus Lenin

Rosa Luxemburg as well as Lenin developed from the Social Democracy, in which both played important roles. Their work influenced not only the Russian, Polish and German labour movement, but was of world-wide significance. Both symbolised the movement opposed to the revisionism and reformism of the Second International. Their names are inseparably entwined with the re-organisation of the labour movement during and after the World War, and both were Marxists to whom theory was at the same time actual practice. Energetic human beings, they were – to use a favourite expression of Rosa Luxemburg's – 'candles that burned at both ends'.

Though Luxemburg and Lenin had set themselves the same task – the revolutionary revival of the labour movement sunk in the swamps of reformism, and the overthrow of capitalist society on a world-wide scale – still in their striving toward this goal their ways diverged; and although they always retained respect for each other, they nevertheless remained at odds on decisive questions of revolutionary tactics and on many questions of revolutionary principle. It may be stated here in advance that on many essential points the conceptions of Luxemburg differ from those of Lenin as day from night, or – the same thing – as the problems of the bourgeois revolution from those of the proletarian. All attempts of inconsistent Leninists, from political considerations, to reconcile Lenin with Luxemburg now that both are dead and to erase the opposition between them, in order to derive advantage from both of them, is merely a silly falsification of history which serves no one but the falsifiers and them only temporarily.

The thing that united Luxemburg and Lenin was their common struggle against the reformism of pre-war time and the chauvinism of the Social Democracy during the war. But this struggle was at the same time accompanied by the dispute between the two regarding the road which leads to revolution; and since tactic is inseparable from principle, by a dispute regarding the content and form of the new labour movement. Even though it is well known that both were mortal enemies of revisionism, and for this reason their names are often mentioned in the same breath, on the other hand it is extremely difficult today to form a real picture of the differences between them. To be sure, the Third International has, in the course of the last decade, in connection with its inner political crises, frequently used and abused the name of Rosa Luxemburg, especially in its campaigns against what it refers to as 'counter-revolutionary Luxemburgism', but neither has Luxemburg's work become better known thereby, nor have the differences which she had with Lenin been clarified. In general, it is regarded as better to let the past lie buried; and just as the German Social Democracy once refused – "for lack of money"[1] – to publish the works of Luxemburg, so also has the promise (through Clara Zetkin) of the Third International to publish those works been broken.[2] Still, wherever competition arises against the Third International, Rosa Luxemburg comes into favour. Even the Social Democracy is often tasteless enough to speak lovingly and sorrowfully of the 'erring' revolutionary, who is mourned rather as a victim of her "impetuous nature"[3] than of the bestial brutality of the mercenaries of party-comrade Noske. And even where, after the experience with both Internationals, people profess to be concerned not only with building a new and really revolutionary movement but also at the same time want to profit by the lessons of the past, the concern with Luxemburg and Lenin goes no farther than the reduction of their oppositions to the dispute over the national question and even here almost exclusively to the tactical problems with reference to Polish independence. In this enterprise, pains are taken to make this opposition as mild as possible, to isolate it, and to close with the assertion, contradicting all the facts, that Lenin emerged victorious from this conflict.

The dispute between Luxemburg and Lenin on the national question cannot be dissociated from the other problems on which the two were at odds. This question is bound up in the closest manner with all others affecting the world revolution and is but a single illustration of the fundamental difference between Luxemburg and Lenin, or of the difference between jacobinical and the truly proletarian idea of the world revolution. If, like Max Shachtman[4], one holds Luxemburg's conception to be confirmed as against the nationalistic adventures of the Stalin period of the Third International, it must also be regarded as justified in opposition to Lenin. However much the policy of the Third International may have changed since Lenin's death, on the national question it has remained truly Leninist. A Leninist must of necessity take a position opposed to Luxemburg; he is not only her theoretical opponent, but her mortal enemy. The Luxemburg position involves the destruction of Leninist Bolshevism, and therefore no one who appeals for authority to Lenin can at the same time lay claim to Rosa Luxemburg.

Opposition to Reformism

The development of world capitalism, the imperialistic expansion, the advancing monopolisation of economy and the super-profits with which it was bound up, made possible the transitory formation of an aristocracy within the labour movement, the enactment of social legislation and a general improvement of the workers' standard of living, and all this in turn led to the spread of revisionism and to the development of reformism in the labour movement. Revolutionary Marxism was rejected as opposed to the facts of capitalist development, and in its place the theory of the slow growth of socialism by way of democracy was accepted. With the growth of the legal labour movement, thus rendered possible, the allegiance of great numbers of the petty-bourgeoisie was secured, who soon took over the intellectual leadership of the movement and shared with the upstart workers in the material advantages of the salaried positions which it offered. Around the turn of the century, reformism had triumphed all along the line. The resistance to this development on the part of the so-called 'orthodox' Marxists, headed by Kautsky, was never more than a matter of phrases and even that was soon given up. Among the better known theoreticians of that time, Luxemburg and Lenin are to be mentioned particularly as carrying their struggle ruthlessly through to the end, not only against established reformism but soon also against the 'orthodox', in the interest of a truly Marxist labour movement.

Of all the attacks on revisionism, one may venture to say that those of Rosa Luxemburg were the most powerful. In her polemic directed against Bernstein[5] she pointed out once more, in opposition to the nonsense of pure legalism, that "the exploitation of the working class as an economic process cannot be abolished or softened through legislation in the framework of bourgeois society".[6] Social reform, she insisted, "does not constitute an invasion, into capitalist exploitation, but a regulating, an ordering of this exploitation in the interest of capitalist society itself".[6] Capital, says Rosa Luxemburg, is not heading for socialism, but collapse, and it is this collapse to which the workers must be adjusted – not to reform, but to revolution. This is not to say, however, that we have to renounce the questions of the present; revolutionary Marxism, too, fights to improve the workers' situation within capitalist society. But, in contrast to revisionism, it is interested far more in how the fight is conducted than in the immediate objectives. To Marxism the matter of moment in the trade-union and political struggle is the development of the subjective factors of the working class revolution, the promotion of revolutionary class consciousness. The blunt setting of reform over against revolution is a false statement of the question; these oppositions must be given their proper place in the whole of the social process. We must avoid losing sight of the final goal, the proletarian revolution, through the struggle for everyday demands.[6] In a similar manner, revisionism was attacked somewhat later by Lenin. To him also, reforms were only a by-product of the struggle directed to the conquest of political power. Both were at one in their struggle against the emasculation of the Marxist movement and took their stand on the platform of the revolutionary struggle for power. They came out for the first time in opposition to each other when Russian conditions before, during and after the revolution of 1905 made the revolutionary struggle for power a vital issue which had to be met in a concrete manner. Thus the conflict which flared up between Luxemburg and Lenin turned first on tactical problems, matters of organisation and the national question.

On the National Question

Lenin, strongly influenced by Kautsky, believed like him that movements for national independence were to be regarded as progressive because "the national State assures the best conditions for the development of capitalism". In his polemic against Rosa Luxemburg he asserts that the demand for the right of self-determination of nations is revolutionary for the reason that "this demand is a democratic one which is not at all different from the other democratic demands". Yes, "in the spirit of bourgeois nationalism of each oppressed nation," he asserts, "there is contained a democratic protest against oppression, and we support this protest unreservedly."[7]

Lenin's attitude on the right of self-determination was, as may be seen from other of his works, like his attitude toward democracy,[8] and one must know this attitude toward democracy in order to understand his attitude toward the national question and the right of self-determination of nations. In his theses on "The Socialist Revolution and the Right of Self-Determination of Nations" he states: "It would be utterly false to think that the fight for democracy diverts the proletariat from the socialist revolution. To the contrary: just as victorious socialism which does not bring about complete democracy is impossible, so also the proletariat which fails to conduct an all-sided, consistent and revolutionary struggle for democracy cannot prepare itself for victory over the bourgeoisie." Thus it becomes clear that to Lenin nationalist movements and wars were nothing other than movements and wars for democracy, in which the proletariat is obliged to participate, since to him the struggle for democracy was of course the necessary precondition of the struggle for socialism. "If the struggle for democracy is possible, war for democracy is also possible."[9] And to him, for that matter, "the words 'defence of the fatherland', in a truly national war, are by no means a form of deception"[9], and in such a case Lenin favours defence. "In so far as the bourgeois of the oppressed nation is fighting against the oppressor," he writes, "so far are we in all cases, more decisively than any others, in favour of it, because we are the undaunted and consistent enemies of all oppression."[10]

To this position Lenin remained true to the end, and Leninism has been true to it down to this day – so long as it did not endanger bolshevik rule itself. Only one slight change was undertaken. While to Lenin prior to the Russian Revolution national wars and movements for liberation were a part of the general democratic movement, after the revolution they became a part of the proletarian world-revolutionary process.

Lenin's position, as here summarised, appeared to Rosa Luxemburg as thoroughly false. In her *Junius Pamphlet* which came out during the War, she states her own standpoint briefly as follows: "So long as capitalist States endure, particularly so long as imperialist world-politics determines and gives form to the inner and outer life of the States, the national right of self-determination has not the least thing in common with their practice either in war or in peace . . . In the present-day imperialistic milieu there can be no national wars of defence, and any socialist policy which fails to take account of this definite historical level and which in the midst of the world vortex lets itself be governed merely by the isolated viewpoints of a single country is doomed in advance."

To this opinion Rosa Luxemburg held fast to the very end, unable to make the least concession in this respect to Lenin; and after the Russian Revolution when the policy of the national right of self-determination became practice she asks why is it that the Bolsheviks held so stubbornly and with such unwavering consistency to the slogan of the right of self-determination, since after all such a policy "stands in the most glaring contradiction to their outspoken centralism in other respects as well as to the conduct they have displayed with respect to the other democratic principles . . . The contradiction yawning here is the more puzzling for in the case of the democratic forms of political life we have to do with most valuable, indeed indispensable foundations of socialist policy, while the famous 'right of self-determination of nations' is nothing but empty petty-bourgeois phraseology and humbug."[11]

Rosa Luxemburg accounts for this false national policy of Lenin's as a "variety of opportunism" calculated to "bind the many foreign nationalities present in the Russian Empire to the cause of the revolution"; like the opportunism with respect to the peasants, "whose land hunger was satisfied by the liberty to seize the estates of the nobility and who in this way were to be kept loyal to the revolution."[11]

"The calculation turned out, alas, to be quite unjustified. Contrary to what the Bolsheviks expected, one after another the (liberated) 'nations' took advantage of the freshly granted freedom to take a position of deadly enmity to the Russian Revolution, combining against it with German Imperialism, under whose protection they carried the banner of counter-revolution to Russia itself . . . Of course it is not the 'nations' by whom that reactionary policy is carried on, but only the bourgeois and petty-bourgeois classes . . . who have converted the national right of self-determination into an instrument of their counter-revolutionary class policy. But . . . it is precisely here that we have the utopian and petty-bourgeois character of this nationalistic phrase, that in the raw reality of class society . . . it simply becomes converted into a means of bourgeois class rule."[12]

This injection by the Bolsheviks of the question of national strivings and separatist tendencies into the midst of the revolutionary struggle was regarded by Rosa Luxemburg as having "thrown the greatest confusion into the ranks of socialism". She goes on to state: "The Bolsheviks have supplied the ideology which has masked the campaign of counter-revolution; they have strengthened the position of the bourgeoisie and weakened that of the proletariat . . . With the phrase about the self-determination of nations the Bolsheviks furnished water for the mills of counter-revolution and thus furnished an ideology not only for the strangling of the Russian Revolution itself, but for the planned counter-revolutionary liquidation of the entire World War."[12]

Why did Lenin insist so stubbornly – we may enquire with Rosa Luxemburg once more – on the slogan of the self-determination of nations and that of the liberation of oppressed peoples? There is no doubt that this slogan stands in contradiction to the demand for the world revolution, and Lenin as well as Luxemburg was interested in the outbreak of the world revolution, since, like all Marxists of that time, he did not believe that Russia could hold out in the revolutionary struggle if thrown upon her own resources. He agreed with Engels that "if a Russian revolution gives rise at the same time to a European proletarian revolution, the present joint-ownership (Gemeineigentum) in Russia may serve as the starting point of a communist development." Hence it was not only clear to Lenin that the Bolsheviks in Russia had to seize the power, but also that the Russian revolution must be made a European and hence a world revolution if it was to lead to socialism. On the basis of the objective situation resulting from the World War, Lenin was no more able than Luxemburg to conceive that Russia could hold out against the capitalist powers if the revolution failed to spread into Western Europe. To Rosa Luxemburg it was very improbable that "the Russians will be able to hold out in this witches' sabbath"[13] – a view which was based not merely on her experience with and her mistrust of people like Lenin and Trotsky who mouthed their silly phrases about the right of self-determination of nations, their policy of making concessions to the peasants, etc.; nor was it because of the imperialistic attacks against the Russian Revolution, nor did it flow from a standpoint propagated by the Social Democracy, which proved statistically that the backward economic development of Russia neither justified the revolution nor allowed for socialism. She believed this primarily because, as she wrote while in jail, "the Social Democracy in the highly developed West is made up of wretched cowards and will look calmly on while the Russians bleed".[13] She was in favour of the bolshevik revolution, however much she criticised the Bolsheviks from the viewpoint of the needs of the world revolution, and she sought constantly to trace their economic retreats back to the failure on the part of the proletariat of Western Europe to aid them. "Yes," she writes, "naturally I am not much pleased with the Bolsheviks even now in their peace fanaticism [Brest-Litovsk – P.M.]. But after all . . . they are not to blame. They are in a jam, have only the choice between two evils and choose the lesser. Others are responsible for the fact that the Russian Revolution turns out to the devil's advantage".[13] And again she writes: "The German government-socialists may shout that the rule of the Bolsheviks is a caricature of the dictatorship of the proletariat. If it was or is, then only for the reason that it is a product of the conduct of the German proletariat, conduct which was a caricature of socialist class struggle."[14]

Rosa Luxemburg died too early to see that the bolshevik policy, even though it ceased to further the world-revolutionary movement, was yet capable of assuring the rule of the Bolsheviks in the framework of state capitalism. As Liebknecht, in harmony with Rosa Luxemburg, wrote from jail: "If the German revolution fails to take place, there remain for the Russian revolution the alternatives: to go down fighting or to present a mere wretched appearance of life."[15]

The Bolsheviks chose the latter. "There are communists in Russia," wrote Eugen Varga when he was still a Marxist, "who have grown tired of waiting so long for the European revolution and who want to adjust themselves definitely to Russian isolation. With a Russia which would regard the social revolution of the other countries as a matter with which it had no concern . . . the capitalist countries would at any rate be able to live as peaceful neighbours . . . Such a bottling up of revolutionary Russia . . . would slow down the pace of the world revolution."[16]

The national policy of Lenin has not proved fatal to bolshevik rule. It is true that large areas have remained separate from Russia and become reactionary States, but the power of the bolshevik State is firmer than ever. Apparently the Leninist line has been confirmed, and apparently Rosa Luxemburg's warnings have turned out to be unjustified. But this belief is true only in so far as it relates to the powerful position of the bolshevik state apparatus; it is by no means valid, however, from the standpoint of the world revolution, the standpoint at stake in the dispute between Luxemburg and Lenin. Bolshevik Russia still exists, to be sure; but not as what it was at the beginning, not as the starting point of the world revolution, but as a bulwark against it. The Russia which was hailed by Rosa Luxemburg, and every revolutionist along with her, has lost its original promise; what remains is a Russia about which Rosa Luxemburg as early as 1918 expressed the following fear: "Like a terrifying spectre there approaches . . . an alliance of the Bolsheviks with Germany. A bolshevik alliance with German imperialism would be the most frightful moral blow for international socialism . . . With the grotesque 'mating' between Lenin and Hindenburg the moral source of light in the East would be extinguished . . . Socialist revolution . . . under the patronage of German imperialism, . . . that would be the most monstrous thing that we could still experience. And furthermore, it would be . . . pure utopia . . . Any political downfall of the Bolsheviks in noble struggle against the superior force and unkindness of the historical situation would be preferable to this moral downfall."[17]

Though the long friendship of Leninist Russia with Hindenburg Germany has for the moment grown cool and the bolshevik dictatorship today prefers to rest on French bayonets in particular and the League of Nations in general, it nevertheless practises openly today the thing for which it has always stood in principle and to which Bukharin at the fourth world congress of the Comintern gave clear expression in the following manner: "There is no difference of principle between a loan and a military alliance . . . We are already big enough to conclude a military alliance with another bourgeoisie, in order by means of this bourgeois State to crush another bourgeoisie. This form of national defence, of the military alliance with bourgeois States, makes it the duty of the comrades of one country to help this bloc to victory."

In the grotesque mating between Lenin and Hindenburg, between capitalist interests and those of the bolshevist rulers, is illustrated, for that matter, the decline of the world-revolutionary wave, a decline which has still not reached the bottom. The labour movement flocking around the name of Lenin is a football of capitalistic politics, absolutely incapable of any revolutionary action. Lenin's tactic – the utilisation of nationalist movements for world revolutionary purposes – has in historical perspective proved mistaken. The warnings of Rosa Luxemburg were more justified than she could ever have cared to believe.

The 'liberated' nations form a fascist ring around Russia. 'Liberated' Turkey shoots down the communists with arms supplied to her by Russia. China, supported in its national struggle for freedom by Russia and the Third International, throttles its labour movement in a manner reminiscent of the Paris Commune. Thousands and thousands of workers' corpses are testimony of the correctness of Rosa Luxemburg's view that the phrase about the right of self-determination of nations is nothing but "petty-bourgeois humbug". The extent to which the "struggle for national liberation is a struggle for democracy" is surely revealed by the nationalistic adventures of the Third International in Germany, adventures which contributed their share to the preconditions for the victory of fascism. Ten years of competition with Hitler for the title to real nationalism turned the workers themselves into fascists. And Litvinov celebrated in the League of Nations the victory of the Leninist idea of the self-determination of peoples on the occasion of the Saar plebiscite. Truly, in view of this development, one must indeed wonder at people like Max Shachtman who still today are capable of saying: "Despite the sharp criticism levelled by Rosa at the Bolsheviks for their national policy after the revolution, the latter was nevertheless confirmed by the results."[18]

It must further be noted in this connection that Lenin's attitude on the national question was by no means a definitely consistent one, but always subordinated to the needs of the Bolsheviks. Moreover, it was thoroughly contradictory. Lenin writes: "Revolutionary actions in war time against the government of one's own country indicate surely not only the desire for its defeat, but also the actual promotion of such a defeat."[19] On pursuing this thought we come to the following absurd contradiction. Since the warring countries are not equally affected by defeatism and at the same time by the proletarian revolution, this tactic facilitates the victory of that country which is least affected thereby and also the oppression of the vanquished country. During an imperialist war the proletariat must, according to Lenin, be for the defeat of its own country. If that defeat has come about, the workers must then turn around and support their bourgeoisie in its struggle for national liberation. And if then the 'oppressed nation' with the aid of the proletariat has again taken its place in the family of nations, the workers must once more cast aside national defence. A false interpretation of the Leninist thought? Just a moment: let us take a look at the actual practice. In 1914–18 Lenin and the Bolsheviks in their position on Germany were opposed to national defence. In 1919–23 they were for the national defence and for the national liberation of Germany. Today when, thanks to the aid of the proletariat, Germany has again become an imperialist power, they are once more opposed to national defence. And tomorrow – what they are for or against tomorrow depends on the constellations of power for the next world war, which will see Russia as the ally of this or that group. The defeatist tactic represented by Lenin during the late war stands in complete contradiction to the right of self-determination of nations and to national wars of liberation. It is a mere moving about in a circle; the proletariat plays the part of compensatory justice between the capitalist rivals. Rosa Luxemburg took pains to point out that this has nothing to do with Marxist class struggle.

Lenin was a practical politician. It was essentially only as a tactician that he distinguished himself from the theoreticians of the Second International. What they sought to attain along democratic ways, he attempted to win by revolutionary means. Not with speeches in parliament, but with force on the real field of the class struggle, he wanted to realise socialism *for* the workers. By means of his party, he wanted to make the revolution *for* the masses, in that the party won the masses to itself. The power had to come into the hands of the Bolsheviks, in order that the exploited of Russia might be liberated. The power had to be in the hands of the Bolsheviks in order that world capitalism might be overcome by revolution. The appropriation of political power through the party was the beginning and end of the Leninist policy – a policy which has often been acclaimed as clever and flexible, but in reality was purely opportunistic.

At the outbreak of the revolution, the Russian bourgeoisie was not in a position itself to take over and hold power, since it was not in a position to solve the agrarian problem. This was left to the Bolsheviks. "The democratic-bourgeois revolution has been carried through to the end by us as by no one else," Lenin declared on the fourth anniversary of the October revolution, and this revolution was carried through with the aid of the peasantry. The Bolsheviks had power, and they constantly balanced the opposition between peasants and workers in such manner that power could be kept. In order to retain this power the familiar zig-zag policy was conducted both on a Russian and on an international scale; it was this policy which made the history of the Third International a history of its crises and of its downfall.

The very first concession to the peasants enabled Rosa Luxemburg to foresee in rough outline the necessary development of bolshevik Russia, unless the reactive force of this 'transgression' were suppressed by the world revolution. "The proclamation for immediate seizure and distribution of land by the peasants," she wrote, "had necessarily to work in the very opposite direction to that intended. It is not only not a socialist measure, but it bars the way to such."[20] Rosa Luxemburg was not aware (being in jail at the time) that the peasants had divided up the land even before the Bolsheviks had authorised it, and that the latter merely legalised what was already practically in effect. The spontaneity of the peasant masses was quicker than the word of the 'bearers of revolutionary consciousness', as the Bolsheviks regarded themselves.

The Bolsheviks wanted, however, to carry the bourgeois revolution consistently to its end, and for this purpose there was required also the conversion of the peasants into country wage-workers: the capitalisation of agriculture. This process is still in full swing, and is celebrated throughout the world as collectivisation; it is by no means completed, nor can it be without giving rise to new revolutionary conflicts. Apparently, however, the Leninists can maintain that Luxemburg was wrong in assuming that without the world revolution Bolshevism had to capitulate on the peasant question. Still, such a contention involves proving also that Bolshevism has actually led to socialism. What exists in Russia, however, is not socialism but state capitalism. Even though it may be called socialism, it still remains state capitalism exploiting wage-labour, and hence the Luxemburg fear, however much modified, has after all been confirmed.

The peasant movements during the first years of the Russian Revolution forced the Bolsheviks, in order to remain in power, to accept a course which necessarily hindered the world revolution and which in Russia itself permitted nothing more than a state capitalism which later on must be revolutionarily overthrown by the proletariat if it wants to arrive at socialism. At this point, however, we are interested merely in the fact that with the aid of the peasant movement the Bolsheviks were able to come to power, and, furthermore, that they believed it sufficient to be in possession of the political and economic command posts in order, with a correct policy, to arrive at socialism. The course that was forced upon the Bolsheviks by reason of backward conditions – the most thorough-going centralisation of all authority and the concessions to the peasants – appeared to them as their own shrewd and successful policy, which they sought to employ also on the international field.

The laws of motion of the Russian Revolution had been foreseen by Lenin with remarkable clarity long before its outbreak, and his whole theory and practice was cut to fit these Russian conditions. This is the explanation of his super-centralism, his definite conception of the role of the party, his acceptance of Hilferding's ideas of socialisation, and also his position on the national question. Even though Rosa Luxemburg, from her familiarity with Russian conditions, was very well able to understand the Leninist policy and to analyse the basis for it as no other Marxist could do, and though she was able, so long as the Bolsheviks actually appeared as a world-revolutionary force, to take all this as unavoidable into the bargain, she nevertheless came out with full force against the design to form from this special Russian situation a recipe for the solution of the revolutionary tasks of the workers throughout the world. "The danger begins," she says of the Leninist policy, "when the Bolsheviks make a virtue out of necessity and seek to establish this tactic, forced upon them by these fatal conditions, as something applicable for all time to come and to recommend it to the international proletariat as the model of socialist tactic to be universally imitated."[21]

Since the alliance between peasants and workers had conformed to Lenin's expectations in putting the power into the hands of the Bolsheviks, he conceived the course of the world revolution as a similar process, even though on a larger scale. The oppressed peoples were mainly agrarian nations, and in its peasant policy the Communist International as a matter of fact sought to combine agrarian and proletarian interests on a world scale in order to place them in opposition to capital, after the Russian manner, and to defeat it throughout the world. The national liberation movements in the colonies and those of the national minorities in the capitalist countries, were supported by the bolsheviks, because in this way imperialist intervention of the capitalist countries in Russia was weakened.

However, the world revolution refused to be treated as an enlarged copy of the Russian. The adventures of the Communist International in its endeavours to make of itself a worker *and peasant* international are recognised as blunders; instead of furthering, they disintegrated the revolutionary movement against capitalism. All that could be attained in this way was the consolidation of Bolshevik state power in Russia through the winning of a long historical breathing spell which led to the development of a Russian and international situation such as confronts us still today.

While Lenin's position on the national question was on the one hand determined by the social-democratic standpoint of pre-war time, which he had not completely overcome, and on the other appeared to him as a means of setting up and consolidating bolshevik mastery in Russia and its eventual extension on a world-wide scale, for Rosa Luxemburg it had no other meaning than that of a false policy which would be dearly paid for.

In contradistinction to Lenin, for whom, quite in keeping with his general position, organisation and the conquest of power for the party was the necessary presupposition for the victory of socialism, Rosa Luxemburg's glance was directed to the class needs of the proletariat. Furthermore, while Lenin's theory and practice were tied up mainly with the backward conditions of Russia, Rosa Luxemburg constantly took as her starting point the more highly developed capitalist countries and hence was incapable of seeing in the 'historical mission' of the working class a party-and-leadership problem. She laid more weight upon the spontaneous mass movements and the self-initiative of the workers than upon the growth of the organisation and the quality of the leaders. Thus she differed fundamentally from Lenin in her appraisal of the factor of spontaneity in history and hence also as regards the role of organisation in the class struggle. Before entering into these differences, however, we should like to contrast briefly the views of Luxemburg and Lenin on the Marxian theory of accumulation, since this question is very closely bound up with all the others.

The Collapse of Capitalism

In her campaign against the revisionists, Rosa Luxemburg had already emphasised that the labour movement must be prepared to face the question of revolution, not that of reform, since capitalism is inevitably heading toward collapse. In opposition to revisionism, which strove to impute to capitalism an endless duration, she maintained that "with the assumption that capitalist accumulation has no economic limit, socialism loses its granite foundation of objective historical necessity. We then take flight into the mist of pre-Marxist systems and schools which sought to deduce socialism from the mere injustice and badness of the present-day world and from the mere revolutionary determination of the working class".[22]

Her principal literary work, conceived as part of her struggle against reformism, was designed to demonstrate an objective limit to capitalist development, and was at the same time a critique of the Marxian theory of accumulation.[23]

In her opinion, Marx had merely raised the question of accumulation of the total capital, but left it unanswered. His *Capital* appeared to her 'incomplete', a 'torso'; it contained 'gaps' which were to be filled in. Marx had "represented the process of capital accumulation in a society consisting merely of capitalists and workers"; in his system he "passed over foreign trade" so that it is "just as necessary as at the same time it is impossible, in his system to realise surplus value outside the two existing social classes". In Marx, the accumulation of capital "has become involved in a vicious circle"; his work contains "glaring contradictions", which she set about to overcome.

She herself based the necessity of capitalist collapse on "the dialectical contradiction that capitalist accumulation requires for its movement to be surrounded by non-capitalist areas . . . and can continue only so long as it is provided with such a milieu".[24]

She looked for the difficulties of accumulation in the sphere of circulation, in the question of turnover and that of the realisation of surplus value, while to Marx these difficulties are already present in the sphere of production, since to him accumulation is a question of capital expansion (Kapitalverwertung). The *production* of surplus value, not its realisation, is to him the real problem. It appeared to Rosa Luxemburg, however, that a part of the surplus value could not be disposed of in a capitalism such as that represented by Marx; its conversion into new capital was possible only by way of foreign trade with non-capitalist countries. Here is the way she put the matter: "The process of accumulation tends everywhere to set in the place of natural economy simple commodity economy, in the place of simple commodity economy the capitalist economy, to bring capitalist production as the one and exclusive mode of production to absolute dominance in all countries and branches of industry. Once the final result is attained – though this remains merely a theoretical construction – accumulation becomes an impossibility. The realisation and capitalisation of surplus value is transformed into an insoluble task . . . The impossibility of accumulation means, capitalistically, the impossibility of further unfolding of the productive forces and thus the objective historical necessity of the decline of capitalism."[25]

These reflections of Rosa Luxemburg's were not new; all that was original about them was the foundation she gave them. She attempted to demonstrate their correctness by reference to Marx's scheme of reproduction in the second volume of *Capital*. According to Marx, capital must accumulate. A definite relation must exist between the different branches of production, in order that the capitalists may find on the market the means of production, the workers and the means of consumption for reproduction. This relation, which is not controlled by human beings, asserts itself blindly by way of the market. Marx reduced it to two comprehensive departments: the production of means of production, and the production of means of consumption. The exchange between the two departments he illustrated by arbitrarily chosen figures. On the basis of this Marxian schema, accumulation proceeds apparently without disturbances. The exchange between the two departments goes on smoothly. "If we take the schema literally," says Rosa Luxemburg, "it would appear as if capitalist production exclusively realised its total surplus value and employed the capitalised surplus value for its own needs. If capitalist production, however, is itself exclusively the purchaser of its surplus product, no limit to accumulation is discoverable . . . Under the Marxian presuppositions, the schema permits of no other interpretation than limitless production for the sake of production."[26]

But that, says Rosa Luxemburg, can after all not be the 'purpose' of accumulation. Such a production as that suggested by the schema is "from the capitalist standpoint quite senseless". "The Marxian diagram of accumulation gives no answer to the question: for whom the expanded production really takes place . . . To be sure, in the course of accumulation, the workers' consumption mounts, as does that of the capitalists; still, the personal consumption of the capitalists comes under the heading of simple reproduction, and for *whom* do the capitalists produce when they do not consume the entire surplus value, but voluntarily practise abstinence, i.e. accumulate? . . . Still less can the purpose of uninterrupted capital accumulation be the maintenance of an ever greater army of workers, since the consumption of the workers is capitalistically a consequence of accumulation, but never its purpose and its presupposition . . . If the Marxian schema of expanded reproduction were to conform to reality, it would indicate the end of capitalist production."[27]

But the frictionless exchange relation between the two great departments of production, their equilibrium, is in the Marxian schema simply impossible, according to Rosa Luxemburg. "The assumption of a rising organic composition of capital would show that the maintenance of the necessary quantitative proportion is precluded; that is, the impossibility of long-continued accumulation is demonstrable schematically in purely quantitative terms. An exchange between the two departments is impossible, there remains an unsaleable surplus in the department of consumption goods, an over-production of surplus value which can be realised only in non-capitalist countries."[28] With this theory Rosa Luxemburg explained also the imperialistic necessities of the capitalist countries.

This theory of Rosa Luxemburg's stands in direct contradiction to Lenin's view of the matter, as may be seen from all his works dealing with economics. In complete accord with Marx, he looked for the contradictions which pointed to the historical limitations of capitalism, not like Rosa Luxemburg in the sphere of circulation, but in that of production. Lenin took his stand uncritically and unreservedly on the Marxian economic theories, because he regarded them as incapable of being supplemented. In his own theoretical works he confined himself to employing the Marxian doctrines in investigating the development of capitalism in general and of Russian capitalism in particular. There is a special, though still untranslated, work of Lenin's against Rosa Luxemburg's theory of accumulation, but it merely repeats the viewpoint which he has set down in all his other works on the subject and which we have merely to become acquainted with here in order completely to grasp the full force of the contradiction between the two conceptions.

In his writings against the Narodniki, Lenin had already anticipated many of his arguments against Rosa Luxemburg's conception. The Narodniki asserted that the domestic capitalist market was insufficient for the expansion of capitalist economy and moreover that it continually diminished with the accompanying impoverishment of the masses. Like Rosa Luxemburg later, they also could not grant that the capitalist surplus value could be realised without foreign markets. According to Lenin, however, the question of the realisation of surplus value has nothing to do with this problem; "the lugging in of foreign trade does not solve the problem, but merely shifts it".[29]

To him the necessity of the foreign market for a capitalist country is "not at all explained by the laws of the realisation of the social product (and of surplus value in particular), but by the fact that capitalism arises only as the result of a highly developed commodity circulation which goes beyond the boundaries of the State".[30] The disposal of the product on the foreign market explains nothing, "but itself demands an explanation, that is, the finding of its equivalent . . . When one speaks of the 'difficulties' of realisation," says Lenin, "one must also realise that these 'difficulties' are not only possible but also unavoidable, and in fact with regard to all parts of the capitalist product and not to the surplus value alone. The difficulties of this sort, which originate in the unproportional distribution of the different branches of production, arise constantly not only in connection with the realisation of surplus value, but also in connection with the realisation of the variable and constant capital; not only in connection with the realisation of the product in the form of consumption goods, but also in the form of means of production."[31]

"As we know," writes Lenin in his *Characterisation of Economic Romanticism,* 1899, "the law of capitalist production consists in the fact that the constant capital increases faster than the variable; that is, an ever greater part of the newly formed capital flows to that department of social production which turns out means of production. Consequently, this department must unconditionally grow more rapidly than the one which turns out means of consumption. Consequently, the means of consumption come to occupy a less and less prominent part in the total mass of capitalist production. And that is in full harmony with the historical mission of capitalism and its specific social structure: the former consists, that is, in the development of the productive forces of society; the latter precludes the utilisation thereof by the mass of the population."

Nothing is to Lenin "more senseless than to deduce from this contradiction between production and consumption that Marx had contested the possibilities of realising surplus value in capitalist society, or had explained crises as resulting from insufficient consumption . . . The different branches of industry which serve each other as a 'market' do not develop uniformly, they overtake each other and the more developed industry seeks foreign markets. This circumstance does not by any means indicate that it is impossible for the capitalist nation to realise surplus value . . . It merely points to the unproportionality in the development of the various industries. With a different distribution of the national capital, the same quantity of products could be realised within the country."[32]

So far as Lenin was concerned, Marx with his scheme of reproduction had "completely cleared up the process of the realisation of the product in general and of surplus value in particular, and revealed that there was no justification whatever for lugging the foreign market into the question".[33] Capitalism's susceptibility to crisis and its expansionist tendencies are explained for Lenin by the lack of uniformity in the development of the various branches of industry. It is from the monopolist character of capitalism that he derives the constant colonial expansion and the imperialistic partition of the world. By means of capital export and the control over sources of raw materials, the bourgeoisie of the leading capitalist countries derives enormous extra profits. The imperialist expansion, in his view, does not serve so much for the realisation of surplus value as for increasing the mass of profits.[34]

There is no doubt that Lenin's conception is much closer to the Marxian than is Rosa Luxemburg's. It is true that the latter was quite correct in recognising in the Marxian theory of accumulation the law of collapse of capitalism; she overlooked, however, the Marxian basis for this view and produced her own theory of realisation, which Lenin correctly rejected as unmarxist and false. It is interesting to note in this connection, however, that in the bibliography appended to his biography of Marx, Lenin referred to the "analysis of the (Luxemburgian) false interpretation of the Marxist theory by Otto Bauer".[35]

Now Bauer's critique[36] of Rosa Luxemburg's theory of accumulation had rightly been denoted by the latter in her *Anti-Critique*, as a "disgrace for the official Marxism"; for Bauer repeated in his attacks nothing but the revisionist conception that capitalism is without objective limits. To his mind, "capitalism is conceivable even without expansion" . . . It is "not on the mechanical impossibility of realising surplus value" that capitalism will go down, he says, but "on the indignation to which it drives the masses of the people . . . It will receive its death blow from the constantly growing working class, schooled, united and organised through the mechanism of capitalist production itself."[37]

By means of a modified schema of reproduction which avoided many of the defects deplored by Rosa Luxemburg in that of Marx, Bauer endeavoured to furnish proof that even on the assumption of a rising organic composition of capital, a frictionless exchange between the two departments in the schema of capitalist reproduction was still possible. Rosa Luxemburg demonstrated to him, however, that even in his modified schema an unsaleable surplus remains over in the department of consumption, and that in order to be realised it compels to the conquest of new markets. To this, Bauer had nothing more to say. And nevertheless Lenin referred to him as the "analyst of Rosa Luxemburg's false theory".

Not only did Bauer's argument leave Rosa Luxemburg unscathed;

there is also the fact that the conclusions which he drew from his schema, indicating unlimited accumulation (independently of the question of the exchange relation between the two departments), could be demonstrated with reference to this same schema as wholly unfounded. Henryk Grossman proved that if Bauer's schema were expanded to cover a longer period of time, the result was not Bauer's frictionless expansion of capitalism, but the collapse of capital expansion. The struggle against Rosa Luxemburg's theory of collapse had led merely to a new one.[38]

The dispute between Luxemburg and Bauer, which found Lenin's sympathies on the side of the latter, was a dispute over nothing, and again it is not without interest to note that the senselessness of the whole discussion was not observed by Lenin. This discussion turned on the impossibility or possibility of a frictionless exchange relation between the two departments of the Marxian reproduction schema, on which depended the full realisation of surplus value. In the Marxian system, the schema was thought of merely as an aid to theoretical analysis and was not conceived as having any objective basis in reality. Henryk Grossman, in his convincing reconstruction of the plan of Marx's *Capital*[39] as well as in other works, has revealed the real meaning of the reproduction schema, and thus set the discussion with reference to Marx's theory of accumulation on a new and more fruitful basis. The entire criticism directed at Marx by Luxemburg on the basis of this schema was posited on the assumption that the reproduction schema had an objective basis.

But, says Grossman, "the schema, in itself, lays no claim to presenting a picture of concrete capitalist reality. It is only a link in the Marxian process of approximation, one which forms with other simplifying assumptions, on which the schema is grounded, and with the later modifications by which the matter is made progressively a more concrete inseparable whole. Thus any one of these three parts without the two others becomes completely meaningless for the recognition of the truth, and can have no further significance than a preliminary stage of knowledge, the first step in the process of approaching concrete reality (Annäherungsverfahren)".[40]

The Marxian schema deals with the exchange values, but in reality the commodities are not exchanged at their values but at production prices. "In a reproduction schema built on values, different rates of profit must arise in each department of the schema. There is in reality, however, a tendency for the different rates of profit to be equalised to average rates, a circumstance which is already embraced in the concept of production prices. So that if one wants to take the schema as a basis for criticising or granting the possibility of realising surplus value, it would first have to be transformed into a price schema."[41]

Even if Rosa Luxemburg had been successful in demonstrating that in the Marxian schema the full turnover of the commodities is impossible, that with each year an increasing superfluity of means of consumption must arise, what would she have proved? "Merely the circumstance that the 'indisposable remainder' in the consumption department arises within the schema of value, that is, on the presupposition that the commodities are exchanged at their values."[42] But this presupposition does not exist in reality. The schema of value on which Luxemburg's analysis is based has different rates of profit in the various branches of production, and these rates are not equated to average rates, since the schema takes no account of competition. What do Luxemburg's conclusions amount to then as regards reality, when they are derived from a schema having no objective validity?

"Since competition gives rise to the transformation of values into production prices and thereby the redistribution of the surplus value among the branches of industry (in the schema), whereby there necessarily occurs also a change in the previous proportionality relation of the spheres of the schema, it is quite possible and even probable that a 'consumption balance' in the value schema subsequently vanishes in the production-price schema and, inversely, an original equilibrium of the value schema is subsequently transformed in the production-price schema into a disproportionality."[43]

The theoretical confusion of Rosa Luxemburg is best illustrated in the fact that on the one hand she sees in the average rate of profit the governing factor which "actually treats each individual capital only as part of the total social capital, accords it profit as a part of the surplus value to which it is entitled in accordance with its magnitude without regard to the quantity which it has actually won",[44] and that she nevertheless examines the question as to whether a complete exchange is possible; and that on the basis of a schema which knows no average rate of profit. If one takes into account this average rate of profit, Rosa Luxemburg's disproportionality argument loses all value, since one department sells above and the other under value and on the basis of the production price the undisposable part of the surplus value may vanish.

Marx's law of accumulation is identical with that of the fall of the rate of profit. The fall of the rate of profit can be compensated by the growth of the mass of profit for only a limited time, due to the continuous compulsion to accumulation. It is not from an excess of surplus value incapable of being realised that capitalism goes under according to Marx, but from *lack* of surplus value. Rosa Luxemburg completely overlooked the consequences of the fall of the rate of profit; and for this reason, she also had to raise the question, meaningless from the Marxian standpoint, as to the 'purpose' of accumulation.

"It is said," she writes, "that capitalism will go under because of the fall of the rate of profit . . . This comfort is unfortunately quite dissipated by a single sentence from Marx, namely, the statement that for large capitals the fall of the rate of profit is counterbalanced by mass of profit. The decline of capitalism from the fall of the rate of profit is therefore still a good way off, somewhat like the time required for the sun's extinction."[45] She failed to see that while Marx had, to be sure, set forth such a fact, he had also at the same time suggested its limit, and that the fall of the rate of profit results in the fall of the mass of profit; in fact, that the former gives expression to what is at first the relative, and then the absolute fall of the actual mass of profit, in relation to capital's needs for accumulation.

It is true that Lenin had found it inconceivable that "the rate of profit has a tendency to sink",[46] and he referred to the fact that "Marx had analysed this tendency and a number of circumstances by which it was concealed or which operated to counteract it".[47] But the full importance of this law in the Marxian system he too failed to grasp clearly; a fact which explains, on the one hand, his acceptance of Bauer's rejoinder to Rosa Luxemburg, and on the other the restriction of his own explanation of crisis to the disproportional development of the various spheres of production. And, for that matter, it may explain also his contradictory conceptions, by which at one time he believed in an unavoidable end of capitalism, and at another time emphasised that there were absolutely no situations from which capitalism could not find a way out. There is not to be found in his works any convincing economic argument for the end of capitalism, and yet at the same time he has the firmest conviction that the system is unavoidably heading toward its fall. This may be explained by the fact that while he did not believe with Bauer and the Social Democracy in the possibility of the reformist transformation of capitalism to socialism, he nevertheless assumed with them that the overthrow of capitalism was exclusively a question of the development of the revolutionary consciousness of the working class or, more precisely stated, a question of organisation and its leadership.

Spontaneity and the Role of Organisation

We have previously seen that Rosa Luxemburg correctly emphasised that for Marx the law of accumulation was at the same time the law of collapse of capitalism. Her reasoning was false; the conclusions nevertheless were correct. Though in her explanation of the law of collapse she diverged completely from Marx, she yet recognised the existence of that law. Lenin's arguments against the Luxemburgian conception were sound, and, *so far as they went*, completely in harmony with Marx; nevertheless, he evaded the question as to whether capitalism is faced with an objective limit. His own doctrine of crisis is inadequate and inconsistent. His theory, while more correct, did not lead to truly revolutionary conclusions. Rosa Luxemburg's argument, even though false, still remained revolutionary. For the question is one of emphasising and demonstrating capitalism's tendency to collapse.

Lenin, who still stood much nearer than Rosa Luxemburg to the Social Democracy, saw the collapse of capitalism more as a conscious political act than as an economic necessity. He failed to see that the question of whether the economic or the political factor predominates with reference to the proletarian revolution is not one of abstract theory but of the concrete situation of the moment. The two factors are in reality inseparable in other than a purely conceptual sense. Lenin had accepted much of Hilferding's speculations regarding capitalist development, which according to the latter tended toward a so-called 'general cartel'.[48] That is to say, it was not only that, as at first, he had to set out from the bourgeois character of the coming Russian revolution and thus consciously adapted himself to its bourgeois manifestations and necessities, but he was also later burdened with the Hilferdingian attitude in relation to the more highly developed capitalist countries, and thus arrived at his over-estimation of the 'political side' of the proletarian revolution.

According to Lenin, it was also false to assume (and this held for the *international* scene) that we are living in the age of the pure proletarian revolution; in fact, to him such a revolution can never be. The *true* revolution is for him the dialectical conversion of the bourgeois revolution into the proletarian. The demands of the bourgeois revolution which are still on the order of the day can henceforth be actualised only within the framework of the proletarian revolution; but this proletarian revolution is proletarian only in the leadership; it embraces *all the oppressed* who must become the allies of the proletariat: the peasants, the middle classes, the colonial peoples, oppressed nations, etc. This genuine revolution takes place in the age of imperialism, which, developed by the monopolisation of economy, is for Lenin a 'parasitical', a 'stagnating' capitalism, 'the last stage of capitalist development' immediately before the outbreak of the social revolution.[49] Imperialism leads, in Lenin's conception, "very near to complete socialisation of production; it drags, as it were, the capitalist against his will and without his being aware of the fact, into a social order which offers a transition from complete freedom of competition to complete socialisation".[50]

Monopoly capitalism has, according to Lenin, already made production ripe for socialisation; the only remaining question is to take the control over economy out of the hands of the capitalists and put it in the hands of the State, and then also to regulate distribution according to socialist principles. The whole question of socialism is one of the conquest of political power for the proletarian party, which would then actualise socialism for the workers. Between Lenin and the Social Democracy there were no differences so far as concerned socialist construction and its organisational problems. The only difference had reference to the manner in which control over production was to be acquired: by parliamentary or by revolutionary means. The possession of political power, the control over the complete monopoly, were in both conceptions a sufficient solution of the problem of socialist economy. For this reason also Lenin is not alarmed at the prospect of state capitalism, against the opponents of which he says at the eleventh party congress of the Bolsheviks: "State capitalism is that form of capitalism which we shall be in a position to restrict, to establish its limits; this capitalism is bound up with the State, and the State – that is the workers, the most advanced part of the workers, the vanguard, is us. And it is we on whom the nature of this state capitalism will depend."

While for Otto Bauer the proletarian revolution depended alone on the attitude of the class-conscious, organised workers, on the *political will* (which from a single glance at the social-democratic organisation, by which its members were completely dominated, practically meant that it depended on Otto Bauer & Company), so here for Lenin the fate of the state capitalism depends on the attitude of the party, which in turn is determined by the bureaucracy, and the whole of history is again the history of the magnanimity, the selflessness and the gallantry of a group of people who are trained in these virtues by the most supremely virtuous.

But with this position of Lenin's on state capitalism, which for him is determined in accordance with will and not by economic laws, in spite of the fact that the laws of state capitalism are no other than those of monopoly capitalism, Lenin had only remained true to himself, for to him in the last analysis the revolution also depended on the quality of the party and of its leadership. In harmony with

Kautsky, for whom the revolutionary consciousness, indispensably necessary to the revolution (a consciousness which for Kautsky was ideology and nothing else) could only be brought to the workers from the outside, since the workers were incapable of developing it out of themselves, Lenin also asserted that "the working class, exclusively by its own efforts, is able to develop only trade-union consciousness; that is, it may realise the necessity for combining in unions, to fight against the employers and to strive to compel the government to pass necessary labour legislation, etc. The social doctrine, however, has proceeded from the philosophical, historical and economic theories which originated with educated representatives of the owning classes, the intellectuals".[51] A political consciousness, the necessary pre-supposition of the socialist victory, the workers, according to Lenin, were incapable of developing. Thus socialism had again ceased to be the 'work of the working class', as Marx viewed it; socialism now depended on the revolutionary ideology of the bourgeoisie; and no doubt the religious 'Marxist' J. Middleton Murry is today merely following in the traces of Kautsky and Lenin when he comes to the logical conclusion that the whole of socialism is nothing more than "substantially a movement of converted bourgeois".[52]

Certainly, Lenin stands on Marxist ground when he asserts that the workers are incapable of developing a political consciousness. In his polemic against Arnold Ruge, who so sadly deplored the lack of political consciousness, and was puzzled by this lack because after all such consciousness ought to have been developed by the impoverishment existing at the time, Marx said: "It is false to say that social distress creates political understanding. The truth is rather the reverse: social well-being creates political understanding. Political understanding is an intellectual quality and is given to him who already has, who lives in clover."[53]

But Lenin has no further connection with Marx, and sinks to the level of the bourgeois revolutionist *à la* Ruge, when he cannot conceive of a proletarian revolution without this intellect-consciousness, when he makes the revolution a matter of the conscious intervention of the 'knowing ones', or of the professional revolutionists. Against this Ruge-Lenin conception, Marx said: "The more cultivated and general the political understanding of a people, the more does the proletariat . . . dissipate its energies in irrational, useless and brutally suppressed revolts. Because the proletariat thinks along political lines, it perceives the cause of all evils in the wills of men and all remedies to lie in force and the overthrow of a *particular form of the State* . . . Political understanding conceals from it the roots of social distress; distorts its insight into its real aims, deceives its social instinct."[54]

To Ruge's assertion (and Lenin's position) that a revolution without the 'political soul' is impossible, Marx answers: "A revolution of political souls organises a ruling clique in society, in accordance with the limited and doubly-cleft nature of these souls, at the cost of society."[55] But Lenin had never aimed at more than a change of mastery over the means of production, since this seemed to him to suffice for socialism. Hence also his over-emphasis on the subjective, political factor – a circumstance by which he was led to view the organisational work of socialism as a political act. According to Marx there is indeed no socialism without revolution, and this revolution is the political act of the proletariat. But the proletariat "requires this political act only insofar as it has need of the process of destruction and dissolution. Where the organising activity begins, where its proper aim, its soul emerges, there socialism casts away the political hull."[56]

The bourgeois elements in Lenin's thought, which in the first place make the end of capitalism dependent on certain political presuppositions which are not necessarily present; which, furthermore, fancied that increasing monopolisation was identical with the socialisation of production (a thing which today it is obvious to anyone is not the case), which made the whole matter of socialism dependent on the taking over of the monopolies by the State and the replacing of an old by a new bureaucracy, and for which the revolution was reduced to a contest between the revolutionists and the bourgeoisie for winning the masses: such a position had necessarily to minimise the revolutionary element of the spontaneous mass movement and its power and clarity of goal in order to be able to magnify correspondingly the individual role and that of socialist consciousness which has become congealed to an ideology.

Lenin cannot, to be sure, deny the element of spontaneity, but for him it is "essentially nothing other than the germinal form of consciousness",[57] which is brought to completion in the organisation and only then is truly revolutionary because completely conscious. The spontaneous awakening of the masses does not satisfy him; it does not suffice for socialist victory. "The fact that the masses are spontaneously entering the movement," he writes, "does not make the organisation of this struggle less necessary. On the contrary, it makes it more necessary."[58]

The mistake inherent in the spontaneity theory, he says, is that "it belittles the role of the conscious element" and that it "refuses strong individual leadership", which for Lenin is "essential to class success". The weaknesses of organisation are to him the weaknesses of the labour movement itself. The struggle must be organised, the organisation planned; all depends on that and the correct leadership. This latter must have influence over the masses, and this influence counts more than the masses. Where and how the masses are organised, whether in soviets or in trade unions, is, to him, a matter of indifference. The important thing is that they be led by the Bolsheviks.

Rosa Luxemburg sees these matters in a quite different light. She does not confuse revolutionary consciousness with the intellect-consciousness of the Leninist professional revolutionists, but for her it is the act-consciousness of the masses themselves, growing from the constraint of necessity. The masses act revolutionarily because they cannot act otherwise, and because they must act. Marxism to her is not only ideology which crystallises in the organisation, but the living and struggling proletariat which actualises Marxism not because it wants to, but because it cannot do otherwise. While for Lenin the masses are only the material which the conscious revolutionists work, just as to the streetcar motorman the streetcar serves only for travelling, in Rosa Luxemburg's writings the conscious revolutionists spring not only from growing insight but more still from the mass in its actual revolutionary activity. It is not only that she rejects on principle the over-emphasis on the role of organisation and leadership; she demonstrates from experience that "during the revolution it is extremely difficult for any directing organ of the proletarian movement to foresee and calculate which occasions and factors can lead to explosions and which cannot . . . The rigid, mechanical, bureaucratic conception," she says, "cannot conceive of the struggle save as the product of organisation at a certain stage of its strength. On the contrary, the living, dialectical explanation makes the organisation arise as a product of the struggle."[59]

With reference to the Russian mass-strike movement of 1905 she says: "There was no predetermined plan, no organised action, because the appeals of the parties could scarcely keep in pace with the spontaneous rising of the masses; the leaders had scarcely time to formulate the watchwords of the on-rushing crowd." And generalising, she continues: "If the situation should lead to mass strikes in Germany, it will almost certainly not be the best organised workers who will develop the greatest capacity for action, but the worst organised or totally unorganised."[60]

"Revolutions," she expressly emphasises, "cannot be made at command. Nor is this at all the task of the party. Our duty is only at all times to speak out plainly without fear or trembling; that is, to hold clearly before the masses their tasks in the given historical moment, and to proclaim the political programme of action and the slogans which result from the situation. The concern with whether and when the revolutionary mass movement takes up with them must be left confidently to history itself. Even though socialism may at first appear as a voice crying in the wilderness, it yet provides for itself a moral and political position the fruits of which it later, when the hour of historical fulfillment strikes, garners with compound interest."[61]

Rosa Luxemburg's spontaneity conception has often been denounced, the usual thing being to denominate it as a 'catastrophe policy' as directed against the organisation of the labour movement itself. She frequently found it necessary to emphasise that her conception was not "pour la désorganisation".[62] "The Social Democrats," she wrote, "are the most enlightened, most class-conscious vanguard of the proletariat. They cannot and dare not wait in a fatalistic fashion, with folded arms, for the advent of the revolutionary situation; wait for that which, in every spontaneous movement, falls from the clouds. On the contrary, they must now, as always, hasten the development of things and endeavour to accelerate events."[63]

This role of the organisation she regards as possible and therefore welcome and a matter of course, while Lenin regards it as absolutely necessary and makes the whole revolution dependent on the fulfillment of this necessity. This difference regarding the significance of organisation for the revolution involves also two different conceptions regarding form and content of the organisation itself. According to Lenin, "the only serious principle of organisation for our movement is the most absolute secrecy, the strictest selection of members,[64] the forming of professional revolutionists. Once these qualities are present, something more still is assured than 'democracy', namely, complete comradely confidence among the revolutionists. And this 'more' is for us unconditionally necessary, for with us . . . there can be no question of replacing it by democratic control. It is a great mistake to believe that the impossibility of a real democratic control makes the members of the revolutionary organisation uncontrollable. They have no time to think of puppet-like forms of democracy, but they feel their responsibility very keenly."[65]

By means of the rules of organisation (which, so long as they were democratic, meant nothing) Lenin wanted to "forge a more or less sharp weapon against opportunism. The deeper the source of opportunism lies, the sharper must be this weapon."[66] This weapon was 'centralism', the strictest discipline in the party, the complete subordination of all activity to the instructions of the central committee. Of course, Rosa Luxemburg was admirably capable of tracing this "nightwatchman spirit"[67] of Lenin's to the special situation of the Russian intellectuals;

but "it is false to think," (she writes against Lenin) "that the still impracticable majority rule of the workers within their party-organisation may be replaced by a sole-mastery on the part of the central authority of the party, and that the lacking public control on the part of the working masses over the acts and omissions of the party organs would be just as well replaced by the inverted control of a central committee over the activity of the revolutionary workers."[67] And even though the self-leadership of the workers should lead to blunders and false steps, Rosa Luxemburg is nevertheless ready to take all this into the bargain, for she is convinced that "even mistakes which a truly revolutionary labour movement commits are, in historical perspective, immeasurably more fruitful and valuable than the infallibility of the very best 'central committee' ".[67]

The differences between Luxemburg and Lenin which we have here pointed out have in part already been more or less surpassed by history. Many of the things which gave substance to this dispute are of no moment today. Nevertheless, the essential factor in their debates, whether the revolution depends on the organised labour movement or on the spontaneous movement of the workers, is of the most pressing significance. But here also history has already decided in favour of Rosa Luxemburg. Leninism is buried under the ruins of the Third International. A new labour movement which has no concern with the social-democratic remains which were still recognisable in Lenin and Luxemburg, nor yet has any intention of renouncing the lessons of the past, is arising. To separate itself from the deadly traditional influences of the old labour movement has become its first prerequisite, and here Rosa Luxemburg is as great an aid as Leninism has been a hindrance. This new movement of the workers with its inseparable nucleus of conscious revolutionists can do more with Luxemburg's revolutionary theory, in spite of its many weaknesses, and derive from it more hope, than from the total accomplishment of the Leninist International. And as Rosa Luxemburg once said, in the midst of the World War and collapse of the Second International, so the present-day revolutionists can say in view of the collapse of the Third International: "But we are not lost, and we shall conquer if we have not unlearned how to learn."

1935

1 Cf. Letter of the editorial board of *Neue Zeit* to Rosa Luxemburg, Jan.6, 1916.

2 Cf. C. Zetkin: 'Rosa Luxemburg's Position on the Russian Revolution'. Published by the Communist International, 1922.

3 In innumerable articles in the social democratic press.
4 Cf. Max Shachtman's article 'Lenin and Rosa Luxemburg' in *The New International*, March 1935.
5 R. Luxemburg: *Social Reform or Revolution*. We refrain hereafter from giving more precise references for the quotations (volume, page, etc.) since we translate from the German or Russian text, and it is an easy matter to look them up, in so far as the works are available in English.
6 Cf. R. Luxemburg: *Social Reform or Revolution.*
7 Cf. Lenin: *On the Right of Self-Determination of Nations* (1916), in the Collected Works.
8 Cf. Lenin: *On the Caricature of Marxism and on Imperialistic Economism* (1916), in the Collected Works.
9 *Ibid.*
10 Lenin: *On the Right of Self-Determination of Nations.*
11 Cf. R. Luxemburg: *The Russian Revolution.*
12 *Ibid.*
13 R. Luxemburg in *Letters* to Luise Kautsky, November-December 1917.
14 R. Luxemburg: *The Russian Revolution.*
15 K. Liebknecht: *Politische Aufzeichnungen aus dem Nachlass*, Berlin 1921.
16 E. Varga: *Die wirtschaftspolitischen Probleme der proletariaschen Diktatur,* Hamburg 1921.
17 R. Luxemburg: *Spartacus.*
18 Max Shachtman in *The New International,* March 1935.
19 Lenin and Zinoviev: *Gegen den Strom,* Hamburg, 1921. Articles of 1914–1916.
20 R. Luxemburg: *The Russian Revolution.*
21 *Ibid.*
22 R. Luxemburg: *Anti-Critique.*
23 R. Luxemburg: *The Accumulation of Capital.*
24 *Ibid.*
25 *Ibid.*
26 *Ibid.*
27 *Ibid.*
28 *Ibid.*
29 Lenin: *The development of Capitalism in Russia,* 1899.
30 *Ibid.*
31 *Ibid.*
32 *Ibid.*
33 *Ibid.*
34 Cf. Lenin: *Imperialism as the Last Phase in the Development of Capitalism,* 1915.
35 Lenin: *Bibliography of Marxism*, in the Collected Works.
36 O. Bauer: *Die Akkumulation des Kapitals,* Neue Zeit, 1913.
37 *Ibid.*
38 H. Grossman: *Das Akkumulations- und Zusammenbruchsgesetz des kapitalistischen Systems.*
39 H. Grossman: *Die Aenderung des Aufbauplans des Marxschen Kapitals.*
40 H. Grossman: *Die Wert-Preis-Transformation bei Marx und das Krisenproblem.*
41 *Ibid.*
42 *Ibid.*
43 *Ibid.*

44 R. Luxemburg: *The Accumulation of Capital.*
45 R. Luxemburg: *Anti-Critique.*
46 Lenin: *Karl Marx*, in the Collected Works.
47 *Ibid.*
48 R. Hilferding: *Das FinanzKapital.*
49 Lenin: *Address to the First Congress of the Soviets 1917.*
50 Lenin: *Imperialism.*
51 Lenin: *What is to be Done?*
52 *Marxism* – a symposium, London 1935.
53 K. Marx: *On the King of Prussia and Social Reform.*
54 *Ibid.*
55 *Ibid.*
56 K. Marx: *Selected Essays.*
57 Lenin: *On Trade Unions*, in the Collected Works.
58 Lenin: *What is to be Done?*
59 R. Luxemburg: *The Mass Strike.*
60 *Ibid.*
61 R. Luxemburg: *Spartacus.*
62 R. Luxemburg: *Brief an Kautsky*, 1905.
63 R. Luxemburg: *The Mass Strike.*
64 This 'principle' was dropped by Lenin whenever such a course appeared opportune. Thus he once threw away the 50,000 revolutionary workers of the German Communist Labour Party (K.A.P.D.) in order not to be deprived of the five million votes of the reformist Independent Socialist Party (U.S.P.D.) of Germany.
65 Lenin: *What is to be Done?* Lenin's idealism comes to light in this formulation as well. Instead of actually and materially assuring control through organising that control within the organisation, he replaces it by 'something better', by the phrases 'comradely confidence' and 'feeling of responsibility'. Practically, however, this meant: mechanical obedience, order from above, conformity below.
66 Lenin: *One Step Forward, Two Steps Backward*, 1904.
67 R. Luxemburg: *Organisational Questions of the Russian Social Democracy*, Neue Zeit 1905.

CHAPTER III

The Lenin Legend

The yellower and more leathery the skin of the mummified Lenin grows, and the higher the statistically determined number of visitors to the Lenin Mausoleum climbs, the less are people concerned about the real Lenin and his historical significance. More and more monuments are erected to his memory, more and more motion pictures turned out in which he is the central figure, more and more books written about him, and the Russian confectioners mould sweetmeats in forms which bear his features. And yet the fadedness of the faces on the chocolate Lenins is matched by the unclarity and the improbability of the stories which are told about him. Though the Lenin Institute in Moscow may publish his collected works, they no longer have any meaning beside the fantastic legends which have formed around his name. As soon as people began to concern themselves with Lenin's collar-buttons, they also ceased to bother about his ideas. Everyone then fashions his own Lenin, and if not after his own image, at any rate after his own desires. What the Napoleonic legend is to France and the legend of Fredricus Rex to Germany, the Lenin legend is to the new Russia. Just as people once absolutely refused to believe in the death of Napoleon, and just as they hoped for the resurrection of Fredricus Rex, so in Russia still today there are peasants to whom the new 'little father Czar' has not died but continues to indulge his insatiable appetite in demanding from them ever fresh tribute. Others light eternal lamps under the picture of Lenin: to them he is a saint, a redeemer to whom one prays for aid. Millions of eyes stare at millions of these pictures, and see in Lenin the Russian Moses, St. George, Ulysses, Hercules, God or Devil. The Lenin cult has become a new religion before which even the atheistic communists gladly bend the knee: it makes life easier in every respect. Lenin appears to them as the father of the Soviet Republic, the man who made victory possible for the revolution, the great leader without whom they themselves would not exist. But not only in Russia and not only in popular legend, but also to a large part of the Marxist intelligentsia throughout the world, the Russian Revolution has become a world event so closely bound up with the genius of Lenin that one gets the impression that without him that revolution and hence also world history might possibly have taken an essentially different course. A truly objective analysis of the Russian Revolution, however, will at once reveal the untenability of such an idea.

"The assertion that history is made by great men is from a theoretical standpoint wholly unfounded." Such are the words in which Lenin himself turns on the legend which insists on making him alone responsible for the 'success' or the 'crime' of the Russian Revolution. He considered the world war determining as regards the direct cause of its outbreak and for the time of its occurrence. Yes, without the war, he says, "the revolution would possibly have been postponed for decades longer." The idea that the outbreak and the course of the Russian Revolution depended in very large measure on Lenin necessarily implies a complete identification of the revolution with the taking over of power by the Bolsheviks. Trotsky has made a remark to the effect that the entire credit for the success of the October uprising belongs to Lenin; against the opposition of almost all his party friends, the resolution for insurrection was carried by him alone. But the seizure of power by the Bolsheviks did not give to the revolution the spirit of Lenin; on the contrary, Lenin had so completely adapted himself to the necessities of the revolution that practically he fulfilled the task of that class which he ostensibly combatted. Of course it is often asserted that with the taking over of state power by the Bolsheviks the originally bourgeois-democratic revolution was forthwith converted into the socialist-proletarian one. But is it really possible for anyone seriously to believe that a single political act is capable of taking the place of a whole historical development; that seven months – from February to October – sufficed to form the economic presuppositions of a socialist revolution in a country which was just engaged in getting rid of its feudal and absolutistic fetters, in order to give freer play to the forces of modern capitalism?

Up until the Revolution, and in very large measure even yet today, the decisive role in the economic and social development of Russia was played by the agrarian question. Of the 174 million inhabitants prior to the war, only 24 million lived in cities. In each thousand of the gainfully employed, 719 were engaged in agriculture. In spite of their enormous economic importance, the majority of the peasants still led a wretched existence. The cause of their deplorable situation was the insufficiency of soil. State, nobility and large landed proprietors assured to themselves with asiatic brutality an unconscionable exploitation of the population.

Since the abolition of serfdom (1861) the scarcity of land for the peasant masses had constantly been the question around which all others revolved in Russian domestic politics. It formed the main object of all reform endeavours, which saw in it the driving power of the approaching revolution, which had to be turned aside. The financial policy of the czarist regime, with its ever new levies of indirect taxes, worsened the situation of the peasants still more. The expenditures for the army, the fleet, the state apparatus, attained gigantic proportions. The greater part of the State budget went for unproductive purposes, which totally ruined the economic foundation of agriculture.

' Freedom and Land' was thus the necessary revolutionary demand of the peasants. Under this watchword occurred a series of peasant uprisings which soon, in the period from 1902 to 1906, assumed significant scope. In combination with the mass strike movements of the workers taking place at the same time, they produced such a violent commotion in the heart of Czarism that that period may in truth be denoted as a 'dress rehearsal' for the revolution of 1917. The way in which Czarism reacted to these rebellions is best illustrated by the expression of the then vice-governor of Tambiovsk, Bogdanovitch: "Few arrested, the more shot." And one of the officers who had taken part in the suppression of the insurrections wrote: "All around us, bloodshed; everything going up in flames; we shoot, strike down, stab." It was in this sea of blood and flames that the revolution of 1917 was born.

Notwithstanding the defeats, the pressure of the peasants grew more and more menacing. It lead to the Stolypin reforms, which, however, were only empty gestures, stopped short with promises and in reality brought the agrarian question not a single step forward. But once the little finger has had to be extended, there will soon be snatching for the whole hand. The further worsening of the peasants' situation during the war, the defeat of the czarist armies on the fronts, the growing revolt in the cities, the chaotic czarist policy in which all reason was thrown overboard, the general dilemma resulting to all classes of society, led to the February revolution, which first of all finally brought about the violent solution of the agrarian question, which had been a burning one during the past half century. Its political character, however, was not impressed upon this revolution by the peasant movement; this movement merely gave it its great power. In the first announcements of the central executive committee of the Petersburg workers' and soldiers' councils the agrarian question was not even mentioned. But the peasants soon forced themselves upon the attention of the new government. Tired of waiting for it to take action in the agrarian question, in April and May of 1917 the disappointed peasant masses began to appropriate the land for themselves. The soldiers on the fronts, fearful of failing to get their proper share in the new distribution, abandoned the trenches and hurried back to their villages. They took their weapons with them, however, and thus offered the new government no possibility of restraining them. All its appeals to the sentiment of nationality and the sacredness of Russian interests were of no avail against the urge of the masses to provide at last for their own economic needs. And those needs were embraced in peace and land. It was related at the time that peasants who were implored to remain on the front, as otherwise the Germans would occupy Moscow, were quite puzzled and answered the government emissaries: "And what's that to us? Why, we're from the Tamboff Government."

Lenin and the Bolsheviks did not invent the winning slogan 'Land to the Peasants' ; rather, they accepted the real peasant revolution going on independently of them. Taking advantage of the vacillating attitude of the Kerensky regime, which still hoped to be able to settle the agrarian question by way of peaceful discussion, the Bolsheviks won the goodwill of the peasants and were thus enabled to drive the Kerensky government out and take over the power themselves. But this was possible for them only as agents of the peasants' will, by sanctioning their appropriation of land, and it was only through their support that the Bolsheviks were able to maintain themselves in power.

The slogan 'Land to the peasants' has nothing to do with communist principles. The cutting up of the large estates into a great number of small independent farming enterprises was a measure directly opposed to socialism, and which could be justified only on the ground of tactical necessity. The subsequent changes in the peasant policy of Lenin and the Bolsheviks were powerless to effect any change in the necessary consequences of this original opportunistic policy. In spite of all the collectivising, which up to now is largely limited to the technical side of the productive process, Russian agriculture is still today basically determined by private economic interests and motives. And this involves the impossibility, in the industrial field as well, of arriving at more than a state-capitalist economy. Even though this state capitalism aims at transforming the farming population completely into exploitable agricultural wage workers, this goal is not at all likely to be attained in view of the new revolutionary encounters bound up with such a venture. The present collectivising cannot be regarded as the fulfillment of socialism. This becomes clear when one considers that observers of the Russian scene such as Maurice Hindus hold it possible that "even if the Soviets were to collapse, Russian agriculture would remain collectivised, with control more perhaps in the hands of the peasants than of the government". However, even if the bolshevik agricultural policy were to lead to the desired end, even a state capitalism extending to all branches of national economy, the situation of the workers would still remain unchanged. Nor could such a consummation be regarded as a transition to real socialism, since those elements of the population now privileged by the state capitalism would defend their privileges against all changes in exactly the same way as did the private owners previously at the time of the 1917 revolution.

The industrial workers still formed a very small minority of the population, and were accordingly unable to impress upon the Russian Revolution a character in keeping with their own needs. The bourgeois elements which likewise were combatting Czarism soon recoiled before the nature of their own tasks. They could not accede to the revolutionary solution of the agrarian question, since a general expropriation of land might all too easily bring in its train the expropriation of industry. Neither the peasants nor the workers followed them, and the fate of the bourgeoisie was decided by the temporary alliance between these latter groups. It was not the bourgeoisie but the workers who brought the bourgeois revolution to its conclusion; the place of the capitalists was taken over by the bolshevik state apparatus under the Leninist slogan: 'If capitalism anyhow, then let's make it.' Of course the workers in the cities had overthrown capitalism, but only in order now to convert the Bolshevik party apparatus into their new masters. In the industrial cities the workers' struggle went on under socialist demands, seemingly independent of the peasant revolution under way at the same time and yet in a decisive sense determined by this latter. The original revolutionary demands of the workers were objectively incapable of being carried through. To be sure, the workers were able, with the aid of the peasants, to win the state power for their party, but this new State soon took a position directly opposed to the workers' interests. An opposition which even today has assumed forms which actually make it possible to speak of a 'Red Czarism': suppression of strikes, deportations, mass executions, and hence also the coming to life of new illegal organisations which are conducting a communist revolt against the present bogus socialism. The talk just now about an extension of democracy in Russia, the thought of introducing a sort of parliamentarianism, the resolution at the last soviet congress about dismantling the dictatorship, all this is merely a tactical manoeuvre designed to compensate for the government's latest acts of violence against the opposition. These promises are not to be taken seriously, but are an outgrowth of the Leninist practice, which was always well calculated to work both ways at the same time in the interest of its own stability and security. The zigzag course of the Leninist policy springs from the necessity of conforming constantly to the shiftings of class forces in Russia in such manner that the government may always remain master of the situation. And so there is accepted today what was rejected the day before, or vice versa; unprincipledness has been elevated into a principle, and the Leninist party is concerned with only one thing, namely, the exercise of state power at any price.

At this place, however, we are interested only in making clear that the Russian Revolution was not dependent on Lenin or on the Bolsheviks, but that the decisive element in it was the revolt of the peasants. And, for that matter, Zinoviev, still in power at the time and on Lenin's side, had stated as late as the 11th Bolshevik Party Congress (March-April 1921): "It was not the proletarian vanguard on our side, but the coming over to us of the army, because we demanded peace, which was the decisive factor in our victory. The army, however consisted of peasants. If we had not been supported by the millions of peasant soldiers, our victory over the bourgeoisie would have been out of the question." The great interest of the peasants in the matter of land, the slight interest with reference to the question of government, enabled the Bolsheviks to conduct a victorious struggle for the government. The peasants were quite willing to leave the Kremlin to the Bolsheviks, provided only that they themselves were not interfered with in their own struggle against the large estate owners.

But even in the cities, Lenin was not the decisive factor in the conflicts between capital and labour. On the contrary, he was helplessly drawn along in the wake of the workers, who in their demands and actual measures went far beyond the Bolsheviks. It was not Lenin who conducted the revolution, but the revolution conducted him. Though as late as the October uprising Lenin restricted his earlier and more thorough-going demands to that of control of production, and wished to stop short with the socialisation of the banks and transportation facilities, without the general abolition of private ownership, the workers paid no further attention to his views and expropriated all enterprises. It is interesting to recall that the first decree of the Bolshevik government was directed against the wild, unauthorised expropriations of factories through the workers' councils. But these soviets were still stronger than the party apparatus, and they compelled Lenin to issue the decree for the nationalisation of all industrial enterprises. It was only under the pressure brought to bear by the workers that the Bolsheviks consented to this change in their own plans. Gradually, through the extension of state power, the influence of the soviets became weakened, until today they no longer serve more than decorative purposes.

During the first years of the revolution, up to the introduction of the New Economic Policy (1921), there was actually of course some experimentation in Russia in the communist sense. This is not, however, to be set down to the account of Lenin, but of those forces which made of him a political chameleon who at one time assumed a reactionary and at another a revolutionary colour. New peasant uprisings against the Bolsheviks first drive Lenin to a more radical policy, a stronger emphasis upon the interests of the workers and the poor peasants who had come off short-handed in connection with the first distribution of land. But then this policy proves a failure, since the poor peasants whose interests are thus preferred refuse to support the Bolsheviks and Lenin 'turns the face again to the middle peasants'. In such a case Lenin has no scruples about strengthening the private-capitalist elements anew, and the earlier allies, who have now grown uncomfortable, are shot down with cannon, as was the case in Kronstadt.

The power, and nothing but the power: it is to this that the whole political wisdom of Lenin finally reduces. The fact that the paths along which it is attained, the means which lead to it, determine in their turn the manner in which that power is applied, was a matter with which he had very little concern. Socialism, to him, was in the last instance merely a kind of state capitalism, after the "model of the German postal service". And this state capitalism he overtook on his way, for in fact there was nothing else to be overtaken. It was merely a question of who was to be the beneficiary of the state capitalism, and here Lenin gave precedence to none. And so George Bernard Shaw, returning from Russia, was quite correct when, in a lecture before the Fabian Society in London, he stated that "the Russian communism is nothing more than the putting into practice of the Fabian programme which we have been preaching the last forty years".

No one, however, has yet suspected the Fabians of containing a world-revolutionary force. And Lenin is of course first of all acclaimed as a world revolutionary, notwithstanding the fact that the present Russian government by which his 'estate' is administered issues emphatic denial when the press publishes reports of Russian toasts to the world revolution. The legend of the world-revolutionary significance of Lenin receives its nourishment from his consistent international position during the world war. It was quite impossible for Lenin at that time to conceive that a Russian revolution would have no further repercussions and be abandoned to itself. There were two reasons for this view: first, because such a thought was in contradiction with the objective situation resulting from the world war; and secondly, he assumed that the onslaught of the imperialist nations against the Bolsheviks would break the back of the Russian Revolution if the proletariat of Western Europe failed to come to the rescue. Lenin's call for the world revolution was primarily a call for support and maintenance of Bolshevik power. The proof that it was not much more than this is furnished by his inconsistency in this question: in addition to making his demands for world revolution, he at the same time came out for the 'right of self-determination of all oppressed peoples', for their national liberation. Yet this double-entry bookkeeping sprang likewise from the jacobinical need of the Bolsheviks to hold on to power. With both slogans the forces of intervention of the capitalist countries in Russian affairs were weakened, since their attention was thus diverted to their own territories and colonies. That meant a respite for the Bolsheviks. In order to make it as long as possible, Lenin established his International. It set for itself a double task: on the one hand, to subordinate the workers of Western Europe and America to the will of Moscow; on the other, to strengthen the influence of Moscow upon the peoples of Eastern Asia. Work on the international field was modelled after the course of the Russian Revolution. The goal was that of combining the interests of the workers and peasants on a worldwide scale and control of them through the Bolsheviks, by means of the Communist International. In this way at least the Bolshevist state power in Russia received support; and in case the world revolution should really spread, the power over the world was to be won. Though the first design was attended with success, at the same time the second was not accomplished. The world revolution was unable to make headway as an enlarged imitation of the Russian, and the national limitations of the victory in Russia necessarily made of the Bolsheviks a counter-revolutionary force on the international plane. Hence also the demand for the 'world revolution' was converted into the 'theory of the building of socialism in one country'. And this is not a perversion of the Leninist standpoint – as Trotsky, for example, asserts today – but the direct consequence of the pseudo world-revolutionary policy pursued by Lenin himself.

It was clear at that time, even to many Bolsheviks, that the restriction of the revolution to Russia would make of the Russian Revolution itself a factor by which the world revolution would be impeded. Thus, for example, Eugene Varga wrote in his book 'Economic Problems of the Proletarian Dictatorship', published by the Communist International (1921): "The danger exists that Russia may be cut out as the motive power of the international revolution. . . . There are Communists in Russia who have grown tired of waiting for the European revolution and wish to make the best of their national isolation. . . . With a Russia which would regard the social revolution of the other countries as a matter with which it had no concern, the capitalist countries would at any rate be able to live in peaceful neighbourliness. I am far from believing that such a bottling up of revolutionary Russia would be able to stop the progress of the world revolution. But that progress would be slowed down." And with the sharpening domestic crises in Russia around that time, it was not long before almost all communists, including Varga himself, had the feeling of which Varga here complains. In fact, still earlier, even in 1920, Lenin and Trotsky took pains to stem the revolutionary forces of Europe. Peace throughout the world was required in order to assure the building of state capitalism in Russia under the auspices of the Bolsheviks. It was inadvisable to have this peace disturbed either by way of war or new revolutions, for in either case a country like Russia was sure to be drawn in. Accordingly, Lenin imposed, through splitting and intrigue, a neo-reformist course upon the labour movement of Western Europe, a course which led to its total dissolution. It was with sharp words indeed that Trotsky, with the approval of Lenin, turned on the uprising in Central Germany (1921): "We must flatly say to the German workers that we regard this philosophy of the offensive as the greatest danger and in its practical application as the greatest political crime." And in another revolutionary situation, in 1923, Trotsky declared to the correspondent of the Manchester Guardian, again with the approval of Lenin: "We are of course interested in the victory of the working classes, but it is not at all to our interest to have the revolution break out in a Europe which is bled and exhausted and to have the proletariat receive from the hands of the bourgeoisie nothing but ruins. We are interested in the maintenance of peace." And ten years later, when Hitler seized power, the Communist International did not move a finger to prevent him. Trotsky is not only in error, but reveals a failure of memory resulting no doubt from the loss of his uniform, when today he characterises Stalin's failure to help the German communists as a betrayal of the principles of Leninism. This betrayal was constantly practised by Lenin, and by Trotsky himself. But according to a dictum of Trotsky's, the important thing is of course not *what* is done, but *who* does it. Stalin is, as a matter of fact, the best disciple of Lenin, in so far as concerns his attitude to German fascism. The Bolsheviks have also of course not refrained from entering into alliances with Turkey and lending political and economic support to the government of that country even at a time when the sharpest measures were being taken there against the communists – measures which frequently eclipsed even the actions of a Hitler.

In view of the fact that the Communist International in so far as it continues to function is merely an agency for the Russian tourist trade, in view of the collapse in all countries of the communist movements controlled from Moscow, the legend of Lenin the world-revolutionist, is no doubt sufficiently weakened that one may count on its disappearance in the near future. And of course even today the hangers-on of the Communist International are no longer operating with the concept of the world revolution, but speak of the 'Workers Fatherland', from which they draw their enthusiasm so long as they are not forced to live in it as workers. Those who continue to acclaim Lenin as the world revolutionary par excellence are as a matter of fact getting excited about nothing more than Lenin's political dreams of worldwide power, dreams which faded to nothingness in the light of day.

The contradiction existing between the real historical significance of Lenin and that which is generally ascribed to him is greater and at the same time more inscrutable than in the case of any other personage acting on modern history. We have shown that he can not be made responsible for the success of the Russian Revolution, and also that his theory and practice can not, as is so often done, be appraised as of world-revolutionary importance. Neither, in spite of all assertions to the contrary, can he be regarded as having extended or supplemented Marxism. In the work of Thomas B.. Brameld entitled 'A Philosophical Approach to Communism', recently published by the University of Chicago, communism is still defined as "a synthesis of the doctrines of Marx, Engels and Lenin". It is not only in this book, but also generally, and quite particularly in the party-communist press, that Lenin is placed in such a relation to Marx and Engels. Stalin has denoted 'Leninism' as 'Marxism in the period of imperialism'. Such a position, however, derives its only justification from an unfounded overestimation of Lenin. Lenin has not added to Marxism a single element which could be rated as new and independent. Lenin's philosophical outlook is dialectical materialism as developed by Marx, Engels and Plekhanov. It is to it that he refers in connection with all important problems: it is his criterion in everything and the final court of appeal. In his main philosophical work, 'Materialism and Empiro-criticism', he merely repeats Engels in tracing the oppositions of the different philosophical points of view back to the one great contradiction: Materialism vs. Idealism. While for the first position, Nature is primary and Mind secondary, exactly the opposite holds of the other. This previously known formulation is documented by Lenin with additional material from the various fields of knowledge. And so there can be no thought of any essential enrichment of the Marxian dialectic on the part of Lenin. In the field of philosophy, to speak of a Leninist school is impossible.

In the field of economic theory, also, no such independent significance can be ascribed to Lenin. Lenin's economic writings are more Marxist than those of any of his contemporaries, but they are only brilliant applications of the already existing economic doctrines associated with Marxism. Lenin had absolutely no thought of being an independent theoretician in matters of economics; to him, Marx had already said everything fundamental in this field. Since, to his mind, it was quite impossible to go beyond Marx, he concerned himself with nothing further than proving that the Marxist postulates were in accord with the actual development. His principal work on economics, 'The Development of Capitalism in Russia', is eloquent testimony on this point. Lenin never wanted to be more than Marx's disciple, and so it is only in legend that one can speak of a theory of 'Leninism'.

Lenin wanted above all else to be a practical politician. His theoretical works are almost exclusively of a polemic nature. They combat the theoretical and other enemies of Marxism, which Lenin identifies with his own political strivings and those of the Bolsheviks generally. To Marxism, practice decides regarding the truth of a theory. As a practician endeavouring to actualise the doctrines of Marx, Lenin may have actually rendered Marxism an enormous service. However, as regards Marxism again, every practice is a social one, which can be modified and influenced by individuals only in very limited measure, never decisively. There is no doubt that the union of theory and practice, of final goal and concrete questions of the moment, with which Lenin was constantly concerned, may be acclaimed as a great accomplishment. But the criterion for this accomplishment is again the success which attends it, and that success, as we have already said, was denied to Lenin. His work not only failed to advance the world revolutionary movement; it also failed to form the preconditions for a truly socialist society in Russia. The success (such as it was) did not bring him nearer to his goal, but pushed it father into the distance.

The actual condition in Russia and the present situation of the workers throughout the world ought really to be sufficient proof to any communist observer that the present 'Leninist' policy is just the opposite of that expressed by its phraseology. And in the long run such a condition must without doubt destroy the artificially constructed Lenin Legend, so that history itself will finally set Lenin in his proper historical place.

1935

CHAPTER IV

Bolshevism and Stalinism

The alleged purpose of Trotsky's biography of Stalin[1] is to show "how a personality of this sort was formed, and how it came to power by usurpation of the right to such an exceptional role". The real purpose of the book, however, is to show why Trotsky lost the power position he temporarily occupied and why his rather than Stalin's name should follow Lenin's. Prior to Lenin's death it had always been 'Lenin *and* Trotsky' ; Stalin's name had invariably been near or at the end of any list of prominent Bolsheviks. On one occasion Lenin even suggested that he put his own signature second to Trotsky's. In brief, the book helps to explain why Trotsky was of the opinion "that he was the natural successor to Lenin" and in effect is a biography of both Stalin and Trotsky.

All beginnings are small, of course, and the Bolshevism of Lenin and Trotsky differs from present-day Stalinism just as Hitler's brown terror of 1933 differed from the Nazism of World War II. That there is nothing in the arsenal of Stalinism that cannot also be found in that of Lenin and Trotsky is attested to by the earlier writings of Trotsky himself.[2] For example Trotsky, like Stalin, introduced *compulsory labour service* as a 'socialist principle' . He, too, was convinced "that not one serious socialist will begin to deny to the Labour State the right to lay its hands upon the worker who refuses to execute his labour power". It was Trotsky who hurried to stress the 'socialistic character ' of inequality, for, as he said, "those workers who do more for the general interest than others receive the right to a greater quantity of the social product than the lazy, the careless, and the disorganisers". It was his opinion that everything must be done to "assist the development of rivalry in the sphere of production".

Of course, all this was conceived as the 'socialist principle' of the ' transformation period' . It was dictated by objective difficulties in the way of full socialisation. There was not the desire but the need to strengthen party dictatorship until it led to the abolishment of even those freedoms of activity which, in one fashion or another, had been granted by the bourgeois state. However, Stalin, too, can offer the excuse of necessity.

In order to find other arguments against Stalinism than his personal dislike for a competitor in intra-party struggles, Trotsky must discover and construct political differences between himself and Stalin, and between Stalin and Lenin in order to support his assertion that without Stalin things would have been different in Russia and elsewhere.

There could not have been any 'theoretical' differences between Lenin and Stalin, as the only theoretical work bearing the name of the latter had been inspired and supervised by Lenin. And if Stalin's 'nature craved' the centralised party machine, it was Lenin who constructed the perfect machine for him, so that on that score, too, no differences could arise. In fact, as long as Lenin was active, Stalin was no trouble to him, however troublesome he may have been to 'The Number Two Bolshevik'.

Still, in order for Trotsky to explain the 'Soviet Thermidor', there must be a difference between Leninism and Stalinism, provided, of course, there was such a Thermidor. On this point, Trotsky has brought forth various ideas as to when it took place, but in his Stalin biography he ignores the question of time in favour of the simple statement that it had something to do with the "increasing privileges for the bureaucracy". However, this only brings us back to the early period of the Bolshevik dictatorship which found Lenin and Trotsky engaged in creating the state bureaucracy and increasing its efficiency by increasing its privileges.

Competitors for Power

The fact that the relentless struggle for position came into the open only after Lenin's death suggests something other than the Soviet Thermidor. It simply indicates that by that time the Bolshevik state was of sufficient strength, or was in a position, to disregard to a certain degree both the Russian masses and the international bourgeoisie. The developing bureaucracy began to feel sure that Russia was theirs for keeps; the fight for the plums of the Revolution entered its more general and more serious stage.

All adversaries in this struggle stressed the need of dictatorship in view of the unsolved internal frictions between 'workers' and 'peasants', the economic and technological backwardness of the country as a whole, and the constant danger of attack from the outside.

But within this setting of dictatorship, all sorts of arguments could be raised. The power-struggle within the developing ruling class expressed itself in policy-proposals either for or against the interests of the peasants, either for or against the limitation of factory councils, either for or against an offensive policy on the international front. High-sounding theories were expounded with regard to the estimation of the peasantry, the relationship between bureaucracy and revolution, the question of party generations, etc. and reached their climax in the Trotsky-Stalin controversy on the 'Permanent Revolution' and the theory of 'Socialism in one Country'.

It is quite possible that the debaters believed their own phrases; yet, despite their theoretical differentiations, whenever they acted upon a real situation they all acted alike. In order to suit their own needs, they naturally expressed identical things in different terms. If Trotsky rushes to the front – to all fronts in fact – he merely defends the fatherland. But Stalin "is attracted by the front, because here for the first time he could work with the most finished of all the administrative machines, the military machine" for which, by the way, Trotsky claims all credit. If Trotsky pleads for discipline, he shows his 'iron hand'; if Stalin does the same, he deals with a 'heavy hand'. If Trotsky's bloody suppression of the Kronstadt Rebellion was a 'tragic necessity', Stalin's suppression of the Georgian independence movement is in the manner of a "great-Russian Russifier, riding roughshod over the rights of his own people as a nation". And *vice versa*: suggestions made by Trotsky are called false and counter-revolutionary by Stalin's henchmen; when carried out under Stalin's auspices, they become additional proof of the great leader's wisdom.

To understand Bolshevism, and in a narrower sense Stalinism, it is not enough to follow the superficial and often silly controversies between Stalinists and Trotskyites. After all, the Russian Revolution embraces more than just the Bolshevik Party. It was not even initiated by organised political groups but by spontaneous reactions of the masses to the breakdown of an already precarious economic system in the wake of military defeat. The February upheavals 'started' with hunger riots in market places, protest strikes in factories, and the spontaneous declaration of solidarity with the rioters on the part of the soldiers. But all spontaneous movements in modern history have been accompanied by organised forces. As soon as the collapse of Czarism was imminent, organisations came to the fore with directives and definite political goals.

If prior to the Revolution Lenin had stressed organisation rather than spontaneity, it was because of the retarded Russian conditions, which gave the spontaneous movements a backward character. Even the politically advanced groups offered only limited programmes. The industrial workers desired capitalistic reforms similar to those enjoyed by the workers in more capitalistically advanced countries. The petty-bourgeoisie and important layers of the capitalist class wanted a Western bourgeois democracy. The peasants desired land in a capitalist agriculture. Though progressive for Czarist Russia, these demands were of the essence of bourgeois revolution.

The new liberalistic February government attempted to continue the war. But it was the conditions of war against which the masses were rebelling. All promised reforms within the Russian setting of that time and within the existing imperialistic power relationships were doomed to remain empty phrases; there was no way of directing the spontaneous movements into those channels desired by the government. In new upsurges the Bolsheviks came into power not by way of a *second revolution* but by a forced change of government. This seizure of power was made easy by the lack of interest that the restless masses were showing in the existing government. The October *coup*, as Lenin said, "was easier than lifting a feather". The final victory was "practically achieved by default . . . Not a single regiment rose to defend Russian democracy . . . The struggle for supreme power over an empire that comprised one-sixth of the terrestrial globe was decided between amazingly small forces on both sides in the provinces as well as in the two capital cities."

The Bolsheviks did not try to restore the old conditions in order to reform them, but declared themselves in favour of the *concrete results* of the conceptually backward spontaneous movements: the ending of the war, the workers' control of industry, the expropriation of the ruling classes and the division of land. And so they stayed in power.

The pre-revolutionary demands of the Russian masses had been backward for two reasons: they had long been realised in the main capitalist nations, and they could no longer be realised in view of existing world conditions. At a time when the concentration and centralisation process of world capitalism had brought about the decline of bourgeois democracy almost everywhere, it was no longer possible to initiate it afresh in Russia. If *laissez faire* democracy was out of the question, so were all those reforms in capital-labour relations usually related to social legislation and trade-unionism. Capitalist agriculture, too, had passed beyond the breaking up of feudal estates and production for a capitalist market to the industrialisation of agriculture and its consequent incorporation into the concentration process of capital.

The Bolsheviks and Mass Spontaneity

The Bolsheviks did not claim responsibility for the Revolution. They gave full credit to the spontaneous movements. Of course, they underlined the obvious fact that Russia's previous history, which included the Bolshevik party, had lent some kind of vague revolutionary consciousness to the unorganised masses and they were not backward about asserting that without their leadership the course of the Revolution would have been different and most probably would have led to a counter-revolution. "Had the Bolsheviks not seized power," writes Trotsky, "the world would have had a Russian name for Fascism five years before the March on Rome."

But counter-revolutionary attempts on the part of the traditional powers failed not because of any conscious direction of the spontaneous movements, not because of Lenin's "sharp eyes, which surveyed the situation correctly", but because of the fact that these movements could not be diverted from their *own* course. If one wants to use the term at all, the 'counter-revolution' possible in the Russia of 1917 was that inherent in the Revolution itself, that is, in the opportunity it offered the Bolsheviks to restore a centrally-directed social order for the perpetuation of the capitalistic divorce of the workers from the means of production and the consequent restoration of Russia as a competing imperialist power.

During the revolution, the interests of the rebelling masses and of the Bolsheviks merged to a remarkable degree. Beyond the temporary merger, there also existed a deep unity between the socialising concepts of the Bolsheviks and the *consequences* of the spontaneous movements. Too 'backward' for socialism but also too 'advanced' for liberal capitalism, the Revolution could end only in that consistent form of capitalism which the Bolsheviks considered a pre-condition of socialism, namely, state-capitalism.

By identifying themselves with the spontaneous movement they could not control, the Bolsheviks gained control over this movement as soon as it had spent itself in the realisation of its immediate goals. There were many such goals differently reached in different territories. Various layers of the peasantry satisfied, or failed to satisfy, divergent needs and desires. Their interests, however, had no real connection with those of the proletariat. The working class itself was split into various groups with a variety of specific needs and general plans. The petty-bourgeoisie had still other problems to solve. In brief, there was a spontaneous unity against the conditions of Czarism and war, but there was no unity in regard to immediate goals and future policy. It was not too difficult for the Bolsheviks to utilise this social division for building up their own power, which finally became stronger than the whole of society because it never faced society as a whole.

Like the other groups which asserted themselves within the revolution, the Bolsheviks, too, pressed forward to gain their particular end: the control of government. This goal reached farther than those aspired to by the others. It involved a never-ending struggle, a continuous winning and re-winning of power positions. Peasant groups settled down after dividing the land, workers returned to the factories as wage-labourers, soldiers, unable to roam the countrysides forever, returned to the life of peasant and worker, but for the Bolsheviks the struggle only really began with the success of the Revolution. Like all governments, the Bolshevik regime involves submission of all existing social layers to its authority. Slowly centralising all power and control into their hands, the Bolsheviks were soon able to dictate policy. Once more Russia became thoroughly organised in the interests of a special class – the class of privilege in the emerging system of state-capitalism.

The Party 'Machine'

All this has nothing to do with Stalinism and 'Thermidor' but represents Lenin's and Trotsky's policy from the very day they came to power. Reporting to the Sixth Congress of Soviets in 1918, Trotsky complained that "Not all Soviet workers have understood that our administration has been centralised and that all orders issued from above must be final . . . We shall be pitiless with those Soviet workers who have not yet understood; we will remove them, cast them out of our ranks, pull them up with repressions." Trotsky now claims that these words were aimed at Stalin who did not co-ordinate his war-activity properly and we are willing to believe him. But how much more directly must they have been aimed at all those who were not even 'second-rate' but had no rating at all in the Soviet hierarchy. There already existed, as Trotsky relates, "a sharp cleavage between the classes in motion and the interests of the party machines. Even the Bolshevik Party cadres, who enjoyed the benefit of exceptional revolutionary training were definitely inclined to disregard the masses and to identify their own special interests with the interests of the machine on the very day after the monarchy was overthrown."

Trotsky holds, of course, that the dangers implied in this situation were averted by Lenin's vigilance and by objective conditions which made the "masses more revolutionary than the Party, and the Party more revolutionary than its machine". But the machine was headed by Lenin. Even before the Revolution, Trotsky points out, the Central Committee of the Party "functioned almost regularly and was entirely in the hands of Lenin". And even more so after the Revolution. In the spring of 1918 the "ideal of 'democratic centralism' suffered further reverses, for in effect the power within both the government and the Party became concentrated in the hands of Lenin and the immediate retinue of Bolshevik leaders who did not openly disagree with him and carried out his wishes". As the bureaucracy made headway nevertheless, the emerging Stalinist machine must have been the result of an oversight on the part of Lenin.

To distinguish between the ruler of the machine and the machine on the one hand, and between the machine and the masses on the other implies that only the masses and its top-leader were truly revolutionary, and that both Lenin and the revolutionary masses were later betrayed by Stalin's machine which, so to speak, made itself independent. Although Trotsky needs such distinctions to satisfy his own political interests, they have no basis in fact. Until his death – disregarding occasional remarks against the dangers of bureaucratisation, which for the Bolsheviks are the equivalent of the bourgeois politicians' occasional crusades for a balanced budget – Lenin never once came out against the Bolshevik party machine and its leadership, that is, against himself. Whatever policy was decided upon received Lenin's blessing as long as he was at the helm of the machine; and he died holding that position.

Lenin's 'democratic' notions are legendary. Of course state-capitalism under Lenin was different from state-capitalism under Stalin because the dictatorial powers of the latter were greater – thanks to Lenin's attempt to build up his own. That Lenin's rule was less terroristic than Stalin's is debatable. Like Stalin, Lenin catalogued *all* his victims under the heading 'counter-revolutionary'. Without comparing the statistics of those tortured and killed under both regimes, we will admit that the Bolshevik regime under Lenin and Trotsky was not strong enough to carry through such Stalinist measures as enforced collectivisation and slave-labour camps as a main economic and political policy. It was not design but weakness which forced Lenin and Trotsky to the so-called *New Economic Policy,* that is, to concessions to private-property interests and to a greater lip-service to 'democracy'.

Bolshevik 'toleration' of such non-bolshevik organisations as the Social Revolutionists in the early phase of Lenin's rule did not spring, as Trotsky asserts, from Lenin's 'democratic' inclinations but from inability to destroy all non-bolshevik organisations at once. The totalitarian features of Lenin's Bolshevism were accumulating at the same rate at which its control and police power grew. That they were forced upon the Bolsheviks by the 'counter-revolutionary' activity of all non-bolshevik labour organisations, as Trotsky maintains, can not of course explain their further increase after the crushing of the various nonconformist organisations. Neither could it explain Lenin's insistence upon the enforcement of totalitarian principles in the extra-Russian organisations of the Communist International.

Trotsky, Apologist for Stalinism

Unable to blame non-bolshevik organisations entirely for Lenin's dictatorship, Trotsky tells "those theoreticians who attempt to prove that the present totalitarian regime of the U.S.S.R. is due . . . to the ugly nature of bolshevism itself," that they forget the years of Civil War, "which laid an indelible impress on the Soviet Government by virtue of the fact that very many of the administrators, a considerable layer of them, had become accustomed to command and demanded unconditional submission to their orders." Stalin, too, he continues, "was moulded by the environment and circumstances of the Civil War, along with the entire group that later helped him to establish his personal dictatorship". The Civil War, however, was initiated by the international bourgeoisie. And thus the ugly sides of Bolshevism under Lenin, as well as under Stalin, find their chief and final cause in capitalism's enmity to Bolshevism which, if it is a monster, is only a reluctant monster, killing and torturing in mere self-defence.

And so, if only in a roundabout way, Trotsky's Bolshevism, despite its saturation with hatred for Stalin, leads in the end merely to a defence of Stalinism as the only possible self-defence for Trotsky. This explains the superficiality of the ideological differences between Stalinism and Trotskyism. The impossibility of attacking Stalin without attacking Lenin helps to explain, furthermore, Trotsky's great difficulties as an oppositionist. Trotsky's own past and theories preclude on his part the initiation of a movement to the *left* of Stalinism and condemned 'Trotskyism' to remain a mere collecting agency for unsuccessful Bolsheviks. As such it could maintain itself outside of Russia because of the ceaseless competitive struggles for power and positions within the so-called 'communist' world-movement. But it could not achieve significance for it had nothing to offer but the replacement of one set of politicians by another. The Trotskyist defence of Russia in the Second World War was consistent with all the previous policies of this, Stalin's most bitter, but also most loyal, opposition.

Trotsky's defence of Stalinism does not exhaust itself with showing how the Civil War transformed the Bolsheviks from servants into masters of the working class. He points to the more important fact that it is the "bureaucracy's law of life and death to guard the nationalisation of the means of production and of the land". This means that "in spite of the most monstrous bureaucratic distortions, the class basis of the U.S.S.R. remains proletarian". For a while – we notice – Stalin had Trotsky worried. In 1921, Lenin had been disturbed by the question as to whether the *New Economic Policy* was merely a 'tactic' or an 'evolution'. Because the *NEP* released private-capitalistic tendencies, Trotsky saw in the growing Stalinist bureaucracy "nothing else than the first stage of bourgeois restoration". But his worries were unfounded; "the struggle against equality and the establishment of very deep social differentiations has so far been unable to eliminate the socialist consciousness of the masses or the nationalisation of the means of production and the land, which were the basic social conquests of the revolution". Stalin, of course, had nothing to do with this, for "the Russian Thermidor would have undoubtedly opened a new era of bourgeois rule, if that rule had not proved obsolete throughout the world".

The Result: State Capitalism

With this last statement of Trotsky's we approach the essence of the matter under discussion. We have said before that the *concrete* results of the revolution of 1917 were neither socialistic nor bourgeois but state-capitalistic. It was Trotsky's belief that Stalin would destroy the state-capitalist nature of the economy in favour of a bourgeois economy. This was to be the Thermidor. The decay of bourgeois economy all over the world prevented Stalin from bringing this about. All he could do was to introduce the ugly features of his personal dictatorship into that society which had been brought into existence by Lenin and Trotsky. In this way, and despite the fact that Stalin still occupies the Kremlin, Trotskyism has triumphed over Stalinism.

It all depends on an equation of state-capitalism with socialism. And although some of Trotsky's disciples have recently found it impossible to continue making the equation, Trotsky was bound to it, for it is the beginning and the end of Leninism and, in a wider sense, of the whole of the social-democratic world-movement of which Leninism was only the more realistic part. Realistic, that is, with regard to Russia. What was, and still is, understood by this movement under 'workers' state' is governmental rule by the party; what is meant by 'socialism' is the nationalisation of the means of production. By adding control over the economy to the political control of the government the totalitarian rule over all of society emerges in full. The government secures its totalitarian rule by way of the party, which maintains the social hierarchy and is itself a hierarchical institution.

This idea of 'socialism' is now in the process of becoming discredited, but only because of the experience of Russia and similar if less extensive experiences in other countries. Prior to 1914, what was meant by the seizure of power, either peacefully or violently, was the seizure of the government machinery, replacing a given set of administrators and law-makers with another set. Economically, the 'anarchy' of the capitalistic market was to be replaced by a planned production under the control of the state. As the socialist state would by definition be a 'just' state, being itself controlled by the masses by way of the democratic processes, there was no reason to expect that its decisions would run counter to socialistic ideals. This theory was sufficient to organise parts of the working class into more or less powerful parties.

The theory of socialism boiled down to the demand for centralised economic planning in the interest of all. The centralisation process, inherent in capital-accumulation itself, was regarded as a *socialistic* tendency. The growing influence of 'labour' within the state-machinery was hailed as a step in the direction of socialism. But actually the centralisation process of capital indicated something else than its self-transformation into social property. It was identical with the destruction of *laissez faire* economy and therewith with the end of the traditional business-cycle as the regulator of the economy. With the beginning of the twentieth century the character of capitalism changed. From that time on it found itself under permanent crisis conditions which could not be resolved by the 'automatic' workings of the market. Monopolistic regulations, state-interferences, national policies shifted the burden of the crisis to the capitalistically under-privileged in the world-economy. All 'economic' policy became imperialistic policy, culminating twice in world-wide conflagrations.

In this situation, to reconstruct a broken-down political and economic system meant to adapt it to these new conditions. The Bolshevik theory of socialisation fitted this need in an admirable way. In order to restore the national power of Russia it was necessary to do in a radical fashion what in the Western nations had been merely an evolutionary process. Even then it would take time to close the gap between the Russian economy and that of the Western powers. Meanwhile the ideology of the socialist movement served well as protection. The socialist origin of Bolshevism made it particularly fitted for the state-capitalist reconstruction of Russia. Its organisational principles, which had turned the party into a well-functioning institution, would re-establish order in the country as well.

The Bolsheviks of course were convinced that what they were building in Russia was, if not socialism, at least the next best thing to socialism, for they were completing the process which in the Western nations was still only the main *trend* of development. They had abolished the market-economy and had expropriated the bourgeoisie; they also had gained complete control over the government. For the Russian workers, however, nothing had changed; they were merely faced by another set of bosses, politicians and indoctrinators. Their position equalled the workers' position in all capitalist countries during times of war. State-capitalism is a war-economy, and all extra-Russian economic systems transformed themselves into war-economies, into state-capitalistic systems fitted to the imperialistic needs of modern capitalism. Other nations did not copy all the innovations of Russian state-capitalism but only those best suited to their specific needs. The Second World War led to the further unfolding of state-capitalism on a world-wide scale. The peculiarities of the various nations and their special situations within the world-power frame provided a great variety of developmental processes towards state-capitalism.

The fact that state-capitalism and fascism did not, and do not grow everywhere in a uniform manner provided Trotsky with the argument of the basic difference between bolshevism, fascism and capitalism plain and simple. This argument necessarily stresses superficialities of social development. In all essential aspects all three of these systems are identical and represent only various stages of the same development – a development which aims at manipulating the mass of the population by dictatorial governments in a more or less authoritarian fashion, in order to secure the government and the privileged social layers which support it and to enable those governments to participate in the international economy of today by preparing for war, waging war, and profiting by war.

Trotsky could not permit himself to recognise in Bolshevism one aspect of the world-wide trend towards a 'fascist' world economy. As late as 1940 he held the view that Bolshevism prevented the rise of Fascism in the Russia of 1917. It should have long since been clear, however, that all that Lenin and Trotsky prevented in Russia was the use of a non-Marxian ideology for the 'fascist' reconstruction of Russia.

Because the Marxian ideology of Bolshevism merely served state-capitalistic ends, it, too, has been discredited. From any view that goes beyond the capitalist system of exploitation, Stalinism and Trotskyism are both relics of the past.

1947

1 *Stalin. An appraisal of the man and his influence. Edited and translated from the Russian by Charles Malamuth.* The first seven chapters and the appendix, that is, the bulk of the book, Trotsky wrote and revised himself. The last four chapters, consisting of notes, excerpts, documents and other raw materials, have been edited.

2 See for instance, L. Trotsky's "Dictatorship vs. Democracy", New York, 1922; particularly from page 135 to page 150.

CHAPTER V

Council Communism

There can be no doubt that those social forces generally known as the 'labour movement' which rose during the last hundred years and, quantitatively, reached their widest expansion shortly before and after the world war, are now definitely on the decline. Though this situation is either happily or reluctantly acknowledged by people concerned with labour questions, realistic explanations of this phenomenon are scarce. Where the labour movement was destroyed by outside forces there remains the problem of how it was eliminated despite the apparent strength that it had acquired in its long period of development. Where it disintegrated of its own accord there remains the question why a new labour movement did not appear, since the social conditions that produce such movements still exist.

I

Most of the explanations offered fail to convince, because they are offered solely with the purpose of serving the specific, immediate interests of the partisans involved in labour problems, not to mention their limitations in theoretical and empirical knowledge. But worse than a false or inadequate position on the question of responsibility for the present impasse of the labour movement is the resulting inability to formulate courses leading to new *independent* working class action. There is no dearth of proposals as to how to revive the labour movement; however, the serious investigator cannot help noticing that all such proposals for a 'new beginning' are in reality but the restatement and rediscovery of ideas and forms of activity developed with much greater clarity and consistency during the beginnings of the modern labour movement. In refuting the idea of successful application of these rediscovered and – in comparison with later developments –

radical principles, it must be considered not only that these principles must be inadequate, since they were necessarily bound to a quite different stage of development of capitalist society, but that they no longer fit, and can no longer be made to fit, a labour movement which has based its philosophy, forms of organisation and activities for too long a time, and with too much success, on aspirations quite contrary to the content of these earlier principles.

A revival of the old labour movement is not to be expected; that workers' movement which may be considered *new* will have to destroy the very features of the old labour movement that were considered its strength. It must avoid its successes, and it cannot aspire merely to a 'better-than-before' organisational expression; it must understand all the implications of the present stage of capitalistic development and organise accordingly; it must base its forms of action not on traditional ideas, but on the given possibilities and necessities. To return to the ideals of the past, under the present general social conditions, would only mean an earlier death for the labour movement. Not merely the cowardice of the masters of labour organisations and the labour bureaucracy attached to them brought about the many defeats suffered in recent conflicts with the ruling classes, and determined the outcome of the 'general' strike in France, but, more so, a clear or instinctive recognition that the present labour movement cannot operate against capitalistic needs, can in one way or another only serve specific and historically determined capitalistic interests.

Disregarding those organisations and officials who from the beginning conceived their function to be no more than their participation in the distribution of the wealth created by the workers, either by open racketeering or by organising the labour market, this much is obvious: today the leaders of labour as well as the workers themselves are more or less conscious of their inability to operate against capitalism, and the cynicism displayed by so many labour leaders in such practical policies as are still possible, i.e. to 'sell out', may be regarded also as the most realistic attitude, derived from a full recognition of a changed situation. The sense of futility predominant in the labour movement of today cannot be dispelled by a more lavish use of radical phraseology, nor by a complete subordination to the ruling classes, as is attempted in many countries where labour leaders clamour for 'national planning'[1] and a solution of the social problem within the present conditions of production. On such a basis of action, the old labour movement cannot help copying from the vague proposals of fascistic movements, and as imitators they will have even less success than the originators. Fascism, and the abolition of the present labour movement connected therewith, cannot be arrested with fascistic methods and the adoption of fascistic goals by the labour movement itself.

II

Though often attempted, it is impossible to explain the present miserable status of the labour movement as the result of the many 'betrayals' at the hands of 'renegades', or to the 'lack of insight' into the real needs of the working class on the part of its leaders. Nor is it possible to blame specific forms of organisations, or certain philosophical trends, for the many defeats that have occurred. Nor is it possible to explain the decline of the movement by attributing it to 'national characteristics' or 'psychological peculiarities'. The decline of the labour movement is a general decline; all organisations, regardless of their specific forms and attitudes, are thereby affected; and no country and no people have been able to escape this downward trend. No country, watching the destruction of the labour movement in other lands, has been able 'to draw lessons from their defeats'; no organisation, seeing others collapse, was able 'to learn to avoid this fate'. The emasculation of all workers' power in Russia in 1920 was easily copied in Turkey, in Italy, in China, in Germany, in Austria, in Czechoslovakia, in Spain, and now in France, and soon in England. It is true that in each country, because of peculiarities of economic and social development, the destruction of labour organisations *capable of functioning as such* varied from case to case; however, none can deny that in all these countries the *independence* of the labour movement was abolished. What still exists there under the name of labour organisation has nothing in common with the labour movement that developed historically, or that, in the more backward countries, was in the process of development, and that was founded to maintain an insuperable opposition to a society divided into powerless workers and exploiters controlling all the economic and the consequent political power. *What still exists there in the form of parties, trade and industrial unions, labour fronts and other organisations is so completely integrated within the existing societal form that it is unable to function other than as an instrument of that society.*

It is, furthermore, not possible to blame the most important theoretical expression thus far developed in the labour movement – Marxism – for the many shortcomings of the labour movement and for its present destruction. That labour movement which is now passing had very little to do with Marxism. Such a criticism of Marxism can arise only from a lack of all knowledge as to its contents. Nor was Marxism misunderstood; it was *rejected* by both the labour movement and its critics, and was never taken for what it is: "an undogmatic guide for scientific research and revolutionary action".[2] In both cases, by those who adopted it as a meaningless phrase and by those who fought even this meaningless phrase, it was utilised rather as an instrument to conceal a practice which, on the one hand, confirmed the scientific soundness of Marxian social science, and, on the other hand, was strongly opposed to the corresponding and disturbing reality.

Although developed under the influence of Marxism this declining labour movement now has completely repudiated its revolutionary beginnings, even where its adherence has been merely nominal, and operates on entirely bourgeois grounds. As soon as this fact is recognised, there is no need to look for the reasons of the decline of the labour movement in some vaguely constructed and actually disregarded philosophy; instead, this decline becomes a quite obvious parallel to the decline of capitalism. Bound to an expanding capitalism, totally integrated into the whole of the social fabric, *the old labour movement can only stagnate with stagnating capitalism and decline with declining capitalism.* It cannot divorce itself from capitalist society, unless it breaks completely with its own past, which is possible only by breaking up the old organisations, as far as they still exist. This possibility, however, is precluded because of the vested interests developed in those organisations. A rebirth of the labour movement is conceivable only as a rebellion of the masses against 'their' organisations. Just as the relations of production, to speak in Marxian terms, prevent the further unfolding of the productive forces of society, and are responsible for the present capitalistic decline, so the labour organisations of today prevent the full unfolding of the new proletarian class forces and their attempts at new actions serving the class interests of the workers. These conflicting tendencies between working class interests and the predominant labour organisations were most clearly revealed in Europe, where the capitalist expansion process was arrested and the economic contraction was felt more severely, resulting in fascist forms of control over the population. But in America as well, where the forces of capitalist economy have been less exhausted than in Europe, the old labour leaders are joined by those of the newer, apparently more progressive, labour organisations in supporting a struggling capitalist class to maintain its system even after its social and historical basis has vanished.

III

It is a paradox only to the superficial observer that the decline of the European labour movement was accompanied by a new spurt in labour organisations in the United States. This situation indicates only the tremendous strength and reserve that capitalism in America still possesses. However, it is also an expression of weakness in American capitalism as compared with that of the more centralised capitalism of European countries. Being both an advantage and a disadvantage, the present American labour situation illustrates merely the attempts to utilise the advantage to help eliminate the disadvantage. The centralisation of all possible economic and political powers in the hands of the State (which, due to the declining economy is impelled to participate in larger internal and external struggles) is still opposed in the United States by powerfully individualistic capitalistic interests rightly fearing they will be victimised by this very process. So arises another paradox, that it is precisely the persisting strength of private capital, capable of counteracting state-capitalist trends and of fighting against the organisation of labour, that is largely responsible for the continued existence of these labour organisations. For the indirect but very forceful support the labour movement has found in those governmental policies which are directed against anarchic, individual, capitalistic procedures in an effort to safeguard the present society, will inevitably serve only the State. The State will then have made profitable use of the labour organisation, not the organisation of the State. The more government fosters the interests of labour, the more labour interests disappear, the more these labour organisations make themselves superfluous.

The rise in the American labour movement experienced recently is but a veiled symptom of its decline. As was indicated in the first CIO convention held recently, the organised workers are completely subordinated to the most efficient and centralised union leadership. From this complete emasculation of workers' initiative within their own organisation to the complete subordination of the whole organisation to the State is only a step. Not only capital, as Marx said, is its own grave digger, but also the labour organisations, where they are not destroyed from without, destroy themselves. They destroy themselves in the very attempt to become powerful forces within the capitalist system. They adopt the methods necessary under capitalistic conditions to grow in importance, and thereby in turn continuously strengthen those forces which will eventually 'take them over'. There is, therefore, no chance to profit from their efforts, for, in the last analysis, the real powers in society decide what shall remain and what shall be eliminated.

Nor is there any hope that, in recognition of the services given to the exploitative society, the labour organisers and their followers will find their proper reward in a completely state-controlled economic system; for all social changes in the present antagonistic society occur by way of struggle. A harmonising of interests between two different kinds of bureaucracies is possible only in exceptional cases, as in the case of war breaking out before the totalitarian system is completed; otherwise the taking over of the old labour movement by the state system leaves the old leaders in the streets, or brings them to the concentration camps, as was so aptly demonstrated in Germany. Nor could the recognition that such a future is probable cause labour leaders to avoid preparing it, as there is given to the present non-revolutionary labour movement no possibility but to pave the way toward it. The only alternative, revolutionary activity, would exclude all those aspects of labour activity which are hailed as the painfully won victories of a long struggle, and would mean the sacrifice of all those values and activities which today make it worth while to work in labour organisations, and which induce workers to enter them.

If the recent development of so-called 'economically' organised labour in America is itself an indication of the general decline of the labour movement of the world, and is tellingly illustrated by John L. Lewis's recent declaration that his organisation stands ready "to support a war of defence against Germany", or, in other words, that he and his organisation are ready to fight for the interests of American capitalism, there is not even the necessity of proving the decline of the old labour movement in the United States' political field. Since specific historical and social factors excluded the growth of a political labour movement of any consequence in America, an American political labour movement cannot decline, since it does not exist. With the exception of a number of spontaneous movements that disappeared as quickly as they arose, what hitherto was experienced in the form of a political labour movement in this country was of no significance. The total absence of class consciousness in the 'economic' movements here is so well recognised that it is superfluous to mention this fact again. With the exception of the Industrial Workers of the World (I.W.W.), the labour organisations in recent history were always considered as complementary to capitalism – as one of its assets. The objective observer must admit that all the organised and unorganised working masses are still under the sway of capitalism, because there developed with expanding capitalism not a labour movement, but a capitalist movement of labourers.

IV

From the negative position developed here it can easily be seen that the future activity of the working class cannot be denoted as a 'new beginning', but merely as a beginning. The century of class fight behind us "developed invaluable theoretical knowledge; it found gallant revolutionary words in defiance of the capitalist claim of being a final social system; it awakened the workers from the hopelessness of misery. But its actual fight was within the confines of capitalism; it was action through the medium of leaders and sought only to place easy masters in the place of hard ones."[3] The previous history of the labour movement must be regarded only as a prelude to future action. Although there can be no doubt that this prelude has already forecast some of the implications of the coming struggle, nevertheless, it remained only an introduction, not a summary, of what is to follow.

The European labour movement disappeared with so little struggle because its organisation had no forward perspective; they knew or felt that there was no room for them in a socialistic system, and their fear that the class society would disappear was no less than that of other privileged groups. Capable of functioning only under capitalistic conditions, they contemplated with disfavour the end of capitalism; a choice between two ways of dying has never enlivened anyone. The fact that such labour organisations can function only in capitalism explains also their rather curious concepts as to what would constitute a socialist society. Their 'socialism' was and is a 'socialism' that resembled capitalism; they are 'progressive' capitalists rather than socialists. All their theories, from that of the 'Marxian' revisionist, Bernstein, to those of a 'market socialism' in vogue today are only methods of achieving acquiescence in capitalism.

Therefore it is not surprising that such a clearly discernible state-capitalist system as exists in Russia is generally accepted by them as a completed socialistic system, or as a transitory stage to socialism. Criticism directed against the Russian system considers only the lack of democracy, or an alleged malice or stupidity of its bureaucracy, and concerns itself little or not at all with the fact that *the relations of production now existing in Russia do not essentially differ from those of other capitalistic countries*, or the fact that the Russian workers have no voice whatever in the productive and social affairs of their country, but are subjected politically and economically to exploitative conditions and individuals like the workers of any other nation. Though the large majority of the Russian workers no longer face individual entrepreneurs in their struggle for existence and better living conditions, their present authorities show that even the old aspiration of the labour movement, the replacement of hard masters with benevolent ones, has not been fulfilled there.

They show also that the disappearance of the individual capitalist alone does not end the capitalist form of exploitation. His transformation into a state official, or his replacement by state officers, still leaves intact the system of exploitation which is peculiar to capitalism. The separation of the workers from the means of production and, with this, class rule, are continued in Russia, with the addition of a highly centralised, single-minded exploitative apparatus that now makes more difficult the struggle of the workers for their objectives, so that Russia reveals itself only as a modified capitalistic development expressed in a new terminology. Attempts at a greater national sufficiency, forced upon Russia, as it has been forced upon all other capitalistic countries, is now celebrated as 'the building up of socialism in one country'. The disruption of world economy, which explains and allows the forced development of state capitalism in Russia, is now described as 'a side-by-side existence of two fundamentally different social systems'. However, the optimism of the labour movement seems to increase with each defeat it suffers. The greater progress class differentiation makes in Russia, the more the new ruling class succeeds in suppressing opposition to an increasing and highly celebrated exploitation, the more Russia participates in the capitalist world economy and becomes an imperialistic power among the others, the more socialism is deemed to be fully realised in that country. Just as the labour movement has been able to see socialism marching in capitalist accumulation, it celebrates now the march toward barbarism as so many steps toward the new society.

However divided the old labour movement may be by disagreements on various topics, on the question of socialism it stands united. Hilferding's abstract 'General-Cartel', Lenin's admiration for the German war socialism and the German postal service, Kautsky's eternalisation of the value-price-money economy (desiring to do consciously what in capitalism is performed by blind market laws), Trotsky's war communism equipped with supply and demand features, and Stalin's institutional economics – all these concepts have at their base the continuation of the existing conditions of production. As a matter of fact, they are mere reflections of what is actually going on in capitalist society. Indeed, such 'socialism' is discussed today by famous bourgeois economists like Pigou, Hayek, Robbins, Keynes, to mention only a few, and has created a considerable literature to which the socialists now turn for their material. Furthermore, bourgeois economists from Marshall to Mitchell, from the neo-classicists to the modern institutionalists, have concerned themselves with the question of how to bring order into the disorderly capitalist system, the trend of their thought paralleling the trend of an ever greater intrusion of the State into competitive society, a process resulting in 'New Deals', 'National-Socialism', and 'Bolshevism', the *various names for the different degrees and variations of the centralisation and concentration process of the capitalist system.*

V

It has recently become almost a fad to describe the inconsistencies of the labour movement as a tragic contradiction between means and ends. However, such an inconsistency does not exist. Socialism has not been the desired 'end' of the old labour movement; it was merely a term employed to hide an entirely different objective, which was political power within a society based on rulers and ruled for a share in the created surplus value. This was the end that determined the means.

The means-and-ends problem is that of ideology and reality based on class relations in society. However, the problem is artificial because it cannot be solved without dissolving the class relations. It is also meaningless, as it exists only in thought; no such contradiction exists in actuality. The actions of classes and groups may be explained at any time on the basis of the productive relations existing in society. When actions do not correspond to proclaimed ends, it is only because *those ends* really are not fought for, these apparent ends, instead, reflect a dissatisfaction unable to turn to action, or a desire to conceal the *real ends.* No class really can act incorrectly, i.e., act in any way at variance with determinant social forces, though it has unlimited possibilities to think incorrectly. Within capitalism's social production each class depends upon the other; their antagonism is their identity of interests; and so long as this society exists, there can be no choice of action. Only by breaking through the confines of this society is it possible to co-ordinate means and ends deliberately, to establish true unity of theory and practice.

In capitalist society there is only an apparent contradiction between means and ends, the disparity being only a weapon to serve an actual practice not at all out of harmony with the desires involved. One need only to discover the actual end behind the ideological end to smooth out the apparent inconsistency. To use a practical example: if one believes that trade unions are interested in strikes as a method of minimising profits and increasing wages, as they contend, he will be surprised to discover that when trade unions were apparently most powerful and when the need to increase wages was the greatest, trade unions were more reluctant than ever to use the strike medium in the interest of their goal. The unions turned to means less appropriate to the end aspired to, such as arbitration and governmental regulations. The fact is that wage increase under all conditions is no longer the end of trade unions; they are no longer what they were at their start; their true end is now the maintenance of the organisational apparatus under all conditions; the new means are those tactics most appropriate to this goal. But to disclose their changed character would be to alienate the workers from the organisation. Thus, the mere ideological end becomes a weapon for securing the real end, becomes only an instrument in a quite realistic and well-integrated activity.

Nevertheless, the ends-and-means problem excited the old labour movement considerably and explains in part why the real character of that movement was recognised so slowly and why illusions flourished as to the possibilities of reforming it. The most important attempt to revolutionise the old labour movement was made when the Russian revolution of 1905 had interrupted the everyday business in which the labour movement was then engaged and the question of an actual social change came to the fore again. But even here, in its apparent opposition, the old labour movement revealed its innate capitalistic character. Lenin's serious attempts to solve the problem of power led him straight back into the camp of the bourgeois revolutionists. This resulted not only from the backward Russian conditions, but also from the theoretical development of Western socialism, which had only further emphasised the bourgeois character it had inherited from earlier revolutions. The capitalist nature of the labour movement also appeared in its economic theory, which, following the trend in bourgeois economics, viewed the problems of society more and more as a question of distribution, as a market problem. Even the revolutionary onslaught of Rosa Luxemburg in her *Akkumulation des Kapitals* against the 'revisionists' was still an argument on the level established by her antagonists. She, too, deduced the limitations of the capitalist society *mainly* from its inability, because of limited markets, to realise the surplus value. Not the sphere of production, but the sphere of circulation seemed of predominant importance, determining the life and death of capitalism.

However, from the pre-war *left* (which included Luxemburg, Liebknecht, Pannekoek and Gorter), coupled with the actual struggles of workers in mass strikes in the East as well as the West, there arose a movement during the war which continued for a few years as a truly anti-capitalistic trend and found its organisational expression in various anti-parliamentarian and anti-trade union groups in a number of countries. In its beginnings and despite all its inconsistencies, this movement was from the outset strictly opposed to the whole of capitalism, as well as to the whole of the labour movement that was a part of the system. Recognising that the assumption of power by a party meant only a change of exploiters, it proclaimed that society must be controlled *directly* by the workers themselves. The old slogans of abolition of the classes, abolition of the wage system, abolition of capital production, ceased to be slogans and became the immediate ends of the new organisations. Not a new ruling group in society, willing to act 'for the workers' and, with this power, able to act against them, was their aim, but the direct control by the workers over the means of production through an organisation of production securing this control. These groups[4] refused to distinguish between the different parties and trade unions, but saw in them remains of a past stage of development restricted to group struggles within the capitalist society. They were no longer interested in bringing new life to the old organisations, but in making known the need for organisations of an entirely different character – *class organisation* capable not only of changing society, but capable also of organising the new society in such manner as to make exploitation impossible.

What remains of this movement, as far as it found permanent organisational expression, exists today under the name of Groups of Council Communists. They consider themselves Marxists and, with that, internationalists. Recognising that all problems of today are international problems, they refuse to think in nationalistic terms, contending that all special national considerations serve only capitalistic competitive needs. In their own interest the workers must develop the forces of production further, a condition which presupposes a consequent internationalism. However, this position does not overlook national peculiarities and therefore does not lead to attempts to pursue identical policies in different countries. Each national group must base its activities on an understanding of its surroundings, without interference from any other group, though an exchange of experiences is expected to lead to co-ordinated activities wherever possible. These groups are Marxist because there has not as yet developed a social science superior to that originated by Marx, and because the Marxian principles of scientific research still are the most realistic and allow incorporation of new experiences growing out of continuing capitalistic development. Marxism is not conceived as a closed system, but as the present state of a growing social science capable of serving as a theory of the practical class struggle of the workers.

So far the main functions of these organisations consisted of critique. However, this critique is no longer directed against the capitalism that existed at the time of Marx. It includes a critique of that transformation of capitalism which appears under the name of 'socialism'. Critique and propaganda are the only practical activities possible today, and their apparent fruitlessness only reflects an apparent non-revolutionary situation. The decline of the old labour movement, involving the difficulty and even impossibility of bringing forth a new one, is a lamentable prospect only for the old labour movement; it is neither hailed nor bewailed by the Groups of Council Communists, but simply recognised as a fact. The latter recognise also that the disappearance of the organised labour movement changes nothing of the social class structure; that the class struggle must continue, and will be forced to operate on the basis of given possibilities. "A class in which the revolutionary interests of society are concentrated, so soon as it has risen up, finds directly in its own situation the content and the material of its revolutionary activity: foes to be laid low; measures (dictated by the needs of the struggle) to be taken; the consequences of its own deeds to drive it on. It makes no theoretical inquiries into its own task."[5] Even a fascist society cannot end class struggles – the fascist workers will be forced to change the relations of production. However, there is actually no such thing as a fascist society just as there is no such thing as a democratic society. Both are only different stages of the same society, neither higher nor lower, but simply different, as a result of shifts of class forces within the capitalist society which have their basis in a number of economic contradictions.

The Groups of Council Communists recognise also that no real social change is possible under present conditions unless the anti-capitalistic forces grow stronger than the pro-capitalist forces, and that it is impossible to *organise* anti-capitalistic forces of such a strength within capitalistic relations. From the analysis of present-day society and from a study of previous class struggles it concludes that spontaneous actions of dissatisfied masses will, in the process of their rebellion, create their own organisations, and that these organisations, arising out of the social conditions, alone can end the present social arrangement. The question of organisation as discussed today is regarded as a superfluous question, as the enterprises, public works, relief stations, armies in the coming war, are sufficient organisations to allow for mass action-organisations which cannot be eliminated regardless of what character capitalist society may assume. As an organisational frame for the new society is proposed a *council organisation* based on industry and the productive process, and the adoption of the *social average labour time* as a measurement for production, reproduction and distribution in so far as measurements are necessary to secure economic equality despite the existing division of labour. This society, it is believed, will be able to plan its production according to the needs and the enjoyment desired by the people.

The Groups further realise, as already stated, that *such a society can function only with the direct participation of the workers in all decisions necessary;* its concept of socialism is unrealisable on the basis of a separation between workers and organisers. The Groups do not claim to be acting *for the workers*, but consider themselves as those members of the working class who have, for one reason or another, recognised evolutionary trends towards capitalism's downfall, and who attempt to co-ordinate the present activities of the workers to that end. They know that they are no more than propaganda groups, able only to suggest necessary courses of action, but unable to perform them in the 'interest of the class'. This the class has to do itself. The present functions of the Groups, though related to the perspectives of the future, attempt to base themselves entirely on the present needs of the workers. On all occasions, they try to foster self-initiative and self-action of the workers. The Groups participate wherever possible in any action of the working population, not proposing a separate programme, but adopting the programme of those workers and endeavouring to increase the direct participation of those workers in all decisions. They demonstrate in word and deed that the labour movement must foster its own interests exclusively; that society as a whole cannot truly exist until classes are abolished; that the workers, considering nothing but their specific, most immediate interests, must and do attack all the other classes and interests of the exploitative society; that they can do no wrong as long as they do what helps them economically and socially; that this is possible only as long as they do this themselves; that they must begin to solve their affairs today and so prepare themselves to solve the even more urgent problems of the morrow.

1939

1 See *Economic Planning and Labour Plans* (Paris: International Federation of Trade Unions, 1936).

2 See *Karl Marx* by Karl Korsch. A re-statement of the most important principles and contents of Marx's social science. (New York: John Wiley, 1938.)
3 J. Harper, "General Remarks on the Question of Organisation", *Living Marxism*, November, 1938, p 153.
4 'Left', or *workers'* communist organisations, trace their earliest beginnings to the left opposition developing in the Socialist and Communist parties before, during and shortly after the war. Their concepts of direct workers' control assumed real significance with the coming of 'soviets' in the Russian Revolution, the shop stewards in England during the war, and the workers' factory delegates in Germany during the war, and the workers' and soldiers' councils after the war. These groups were expelled from the Communist International in 1920. Lenin's pamphlet, *Left Wing Communism: An Infantile Disorder* (1920), was written to destroy the influence of these groups in western Europe. These groups considered the Bolshevik policies counter-revolutionary as regards the class interests of the international working class, and it was defeated by this counter-revolution which combined with the reformist movement and the capitalist class proper to destroy the first beginnings of a radical movement directed against all forms of capitalism. What still remains of this movement today are small groups in America, Germany, Holland, France and Belgium unable to do more than propaganda work influencing extremely small groups of workers.
5 Karl Marx, *The Class Struggles in France*, 1848-50.

CHAPTER VI

Otto Rühle and the German Labour Movement

Otto Rühle's activity in the German Labour Movement was related to the work of small and restricted minorities within and outside of the official labour organisations. The groups which he directly adhered to were at no time of real significance. And even within these groups he held a peculiar position; he could never completely identify himself with any organisation. He never lost sight of the general interests of the working class, no matter what specific political strategy he was advocating at any particular time. He could not regard organisations as an end in themselves, but merely as mediums for the establishment of real social relations and for the fuller development of the individual. Because of his broad view of life he was at times suspected of apostasy, yet he died as he lived – a Socialist in the true sense of the word.

Today every programme and designation has lost its meaning: socialists speak in capitalistic terms, capitalists in socialistic terms and everybody believes anything and nothing. This situation is merely the climax of a long development which has been initiated by the labour movement itself. It is now quite clear that only those in the traditional labour movement who opposed its undemocratic organisations and their tactics can properly be called socialists. The labour leaders of yesterday and today did not and do not represent a workers' movement but only a capitalistic movement of workers. Only by standing outside the labour movement has it been possible to work towards decisive social changes. The fact that even within the dominant labour organisations Rühle remained an outsider attests to his sincerity and integrity. His whole thinking was, however, determined by the movement which he opposed and it is necessary to analyse its characteristics in order to understand the man himself.

The official labour movement functioned neither in accordance with its original ideology nor with its real immediate interests. For a time it served as a control instrument of the ruling clases. First losing its independence, it was soon to lose its very existence. Vested interests under capitalism can be maintained only by the accumulation of power. The process of the concentration of capital and political power forces any socially important movement to attempt either to destroy capitalism or to serve it consistently. The old labour movement could not do the latter and was neither willing nor able to do the former. Content to be one monopoly among others it was swept aside by the capitalistic development toward the monopolistic control of monopolies.

Essentially the history of the old labour movement is the history of the capitalist market approached from a 'proletarian' point of view. The so-called market laws were to be utilised in favour of the commodity, labour power. Collective actions should lead to the highest possible wages. 'Economic power' gained in this manner was to be secured by way of social reform. To get the highest profits possible, the capitalists increased the organised control over the market. But this opposition between capital and labour also expressed an identity of interests. Both sides fostered the monopolistic re-organisation of capitalist society, though, to be sure, behind their consciously-directed activities there was finally nothing but the expansive need of capital itself. Their policies and aspirations, however much based on real considerations of facts and special needs, were still determined by the fetishistic character of their system of production.

Aside from commodity-fetishism, whatever meaning the market laws may have with regard to special fortunes and losses, and however they may be manipulated by one or another interest group, under no circumstances can they be used in favour of the working class as a whole. It is not the market which controls the people and determines the prevailing social relations but rather the fact that a separate group in society either owns or controls both the means of production and the instruments of suppression. Market situations, whatever they may be, always favour capital. And if they do not do so they will be altered, set aside or supplemented with more direct, more forceful and more basic powers inherent in the ownership or control of the means of production.

To overcome capitalism, actions outside the labour-capital-market relations are necessary, actions that do away with both the market and with class relations. Restricted to actions within the framework of capitalism, the old labour movement fought from the very beginning on unequal terms. It was bound to destroy itself or to be destroyed from without. It was destined either to be broken up internally by its own revolutionary opposition, which would give rise to new organisations, or doomed to be destroyed by the capitalistic change from a market to a controlled-market economy and the accompanying political alterations. Actually, the latter happened, for the revolutionary opposition within the labour movement failed to grow. It had a voice but no power and no immediate future, as the working class had just spent half a century entrenching its capitalistic enemy and building a huge prison for itself in the form of the labour movement. It is, therefore, still necessary to single out men like Otto Rühle in order to describe the modern revolutionary opposition, although such singling out is quite contrary to his own point of view and to the needs of the workers who must learn to think in terms of classes rather than in terms of revolutionary personalities.

II

The first world war and the positive reaction of the labour movement to the slaughter surprised only those who did not understand capitalist society and the successful labour movement within its confines. But only a few actually understood. Just as the pre-war opposition within the labour movement can be brought into focus by mentioning the literary and scientific products of a few individuals among whom Rühle must be counted, so the 'workers' opposition' to the war may also be expressed in names like Liebknecht, Luxemburg, Mehring, Rühle and others. It is quite revealing that the anti-war attitude, in order to be effective at all, had first to find parliamentary permission. It had to be dramatised on the stage of a bourgeois institution, thus indicating its limitations from the very beginning. In fact, it served only as a forerunner of the bourgeois-liberal peace movement that finally succeeded in ending the war without disturbing the capitalistic *status quo*. If, in the beginning, most of the workers were behind the war-majority, they were no less behind the anti-war activity of their bourgeoisie which ended in the Weimar Republic. The anti-war slogans, although raised by revolutionists, merely served a particular brand of bourgeois politics and ended up where they started – in the bourgeois democratic parliament.

The real opposition to war and imperialism came to the fore in desertions from army and factory and in the slowly growing recognition on the part of many workers that their struggle against war and exploitation must include the fight against the old labour movement and all its concepts. It speaks in Rühle's favour that his own name disappeared quickly from the honour roll of the war opposition. It is clear, of course, that Liebknecht and Luxemburg were celebrated up to the beginning of the second world war only because they died long before the warring world had been restored to 'normalcy' and was again in need of dead labour heroes to support the living labour leaders who carried out a 'realistic' policy of reforms or served the foreign policy of bolshevik Russia.

The first world war revealed more than anything else that the labour movement was part and parcel of bourgeois society. The various organisations in every nation proved that they had neither the intention nor the means to fight capitalism, that they were interested only in securing their own existence within the capitalistic structure. In Germany this was especially obvious because within the international movement the German organisations were the largest and most unified. To hold on to what had been built up since Bismarck's anti-socialist laws, the minority opposition within the socialist party displayed a self-restraint to an extent unknown in other countries. But, then, the exiled Russian opposition had less to lose; it had, furthermore, split away from the reformists and class-collaborationists a decade before the outbreak of the war. And it is quite difficult to see in the meek pacifist arguments of the Independent Labour Party any real opposition to the social patriotism that had saturated the British labour movement. But more had been expected of the German left-wing than of any other group within the International, and its behaviour at the outbreak of the war was therefore particularly disappointing. Apart from the psychological conditions of individuals, this behaviour was the product of the organisation-fetishism prevailing in the movement.

This fetishism demanded discipline and strict adherence to democratic formulae – the minority must submit to the will of the majority. And although it is clear that under capitalistic conditions these democratic formulae merely hide facts to the contrary, the opposition failed to perceive that democracy within the labour movement did not differ from bourgeois democracy in general. A minority owned and controlled the organisations just as the capitalist minority owns and controls the means of production and the state apparatus. In both cases, the minorities by virtue of this control determine the behaviour of the majorities. But by force of traditional procedures, in the name of discipline and unity, uneasy and against its better knowledge, the anti-war minority supported social-democratic chauvinism. There was just one man in the German Reichstag of August 1914 – Fritz Kunert – who was not able to vote for war credits but who was also not able to vote against them and thus, to satisfy his conscience, abstained from voting altogether. In the spring of 1915

Liebknecht and Rühle were the first to vote against the granting of war credits to the government. They remained alone for quite some time and found new companions only to the degree that the chances of a victorious peace disappeared in the military stalemate. After 1916 the radical anti-war attitude was supported and soon swallowed up by a bourgeois movement in search of a negotiated peace, a movement which, finally, was to inherit the bankrupt stock of German imperialism.

As violators of discipline Liebknecht and Rühle were expelled from the social-democratic Reichstag faction. Together with Rosa Luxemburg, Franz Mehring and others, more or less forgotten by now, they organised the group, *Internationale*, publishing a magazine of the same title in order to uphold the idea of internationalism in the warring world. In 1916 they organised the *Spartakusbund* which cooperated with other left-wing formations such as the *Internationale Sozialist* with Julian Borchardt as their spokesman, and the group around Johann Knief and the radical Bremen paper, *Arbeiterpolitik.* In retrospect it seems that the last-named group was the most advanced, that is, advanced away from social-democratic traditions and toward a new approach to the proletarian class struggle. How much the *Spartakusbund* still adhered to the organisation and unity fetish that ruled the German labour movement came to light in their vacillating attitude toward the first attempts at re-orienting the international socialist movement in Zimmerwald and Kienthal. The Spartacists were not in favour of a clean break with the old labour movement in the direction of the earlier bolshevik example. They still hoped to win the party over to their own position and carefully avoided irreconcilable policies. In April 1917 the *Spartakusbund* merged with the Independent Socialists (Unabhängige Sozialdemokratische Partei Deutschlands) which formed the centre in the old labour movement but was no longer willing to cover up the chauvinism of the conservative majority-wing of the social-democratic party. Relatively independent, yet still within the Independent Socialist Party, the *Spartakusbund* left this organisation only at the end of the year 1918.

III

Within the *Spartakusbund* Otto Rühle shared Liebknecht's and Rosa Luxemburg's position which had been attacked by the Bolsheviks as inconsistent. And inconsistent it was but for pertinent reasons. At first glance, the main reason seemed to be based on the illusion that the social-democratic party could be reformed. With changing circumstances, it was hoped, the masses would cease to follow their conservative leaders and support the left-wing of the party. And although such illusions did exist, first with regard to the old party and later with regard to the Independent Socialists, they do not altogether explain the hesitancy on the part of the Spartacist leaders to adopt the ways of Bolshevism. Actually, the Spartacists faced a dilemma no matter in what direction they looked. By not trying – at the right time – to break resolutely with social-democracy, they forfeited their chance to form a strong organisation capable of playing a decisive role in the expected social upheavals. Yet, in view of the real situation in Germany, in view of the history of the German labour movement, it was quite difficult to believe in the possibility of quickly forming a counter-party to the dominant labour organisations. Of course, it might have been possible to form a party in the Leninist manner, a party of professional revolutionists, willing to usurp power, if necessary, against the will of the majority of the working class. But this was precisely what the people around Rosa Luxemburg did not aspire to. Throughout the years of their opposition to reformism and revisionism, they had never narrowed their distance from the Russian 'left', from Lenin's concept of organisation and revolution. In sharp controversies, Rosa Luxemburg had pointed out that Lenin's concepts were of a Jacobin nature and inapplicable in Western Europe where not a bourgeois but a proletarian revolution was the order of the day. Although she, too, spoke of the dictatorship of the proletariat, it meant for her, in distinction to Lenin, "the manner in which democracy is employed, not in its abolition – it was to be the work of the class, and not of a small minority in the name of the class".

Enthusiastically as Liebknecht, Luxemburg and Rühle greeted the overthrow of Czarism, they did not lose their critical capacities, nor did they forget the character of the bolshevik party, nor the historical limitations of the Russian Revolution. But regardless of the immediate realities and the final outcome of this revolution, it had to be supported as a first break in the imperialistic phalanx and as the forerunner of the expected German revolution. Of the latter many signs had appeared in strikes, hunger riots, mutinies and all kinds of passive resistances. But the growing opposition to the war and to Ludendorff's dictatorship did not find organisational expression to any significant extent. Instead of going to the left, the masses followed their old organisations, which lined up with the liberal bourgeoisie. The upheavals in the German Navy and finally the November rebellion were carried on in the spirit of social-democracy, that is, in the spirit of the defeated German bourgeoisie.

The German revolution appeared to be more significant than it really was. The spontaneous enthusiasm of the workers was more for ending the war than for changing existing social relations. Their demands, expressed through workers' and soldiers' councils, did not transcend the possibilities of bourgeois society. Even the revolutionary minority, and here particularly the *Spartakusbund*, failed to develop a consistent revolutionary programme. Its political and economic demands were of a twofold nature; they were constructed to serve as demands to be agreed upon by the bourgeoisie and its social-democratic allies, and as slogans of a revolution which was to do away with bourgeois society and its supporters.

Of course, within the ocean of mediocrity that was the German revolution there were revolutionary streams which warmed the hearts of the radicals and induced them to undertake actions historically quite out of place. Partial successes, due to the temporary stunning of the ruling classes and the general passivity of the broad masses – exhausted as they were by four years of hunger and war – nourished the hope that the revolution might end in a socialist society. Only no one really knew what the socialist society would be like, what steps ought to be taken to usher it into existence. 'All power to the workers' and soldiers' councils,' however attractive as a slogan, still left all essential questions open. The revolutionary struggles that followed November 1918 were thus not determined by the consciously concocted plans of the revolutionary minority but were thrust upon it by the slowly developing counter-revolution which was backed by the majority of the people. The fact was that the broad German masses inside and outside the labour movement did not look forward to the establishment of a new society, but backwards to the restoration of liberal capitalism without its bad aspects, its political inequalities, its militarism and imperialism. They merely desired the completion of the reforms started before the war which were designed to lead into a benevolent capitalistic system.

The ambiguity which characterised the policy of the *Spartakusbund* was largely the result of the conservatism of the masses. The Spartacist leaders were ready, on the one hand, to follow the clear revolutionary course desired by the so-called 'ultra-left' and on the other hand they felt sure that such a policy could not be successful in view of the prevailing mass attitude and the international situation.

The effect of the Russian Revolution upon Germany had hardly been noticeable. Nor was there any reason to expect that a radical turn in Germany would have any greater repercussions in France, England and America. If it had been difficult for the Allies to interfere decisively in Russia, they would face lesser difficulties in crushing a German communist uprising. Emerging from the war victories, the capitalism of these nations had been enormously strengthened; there was no real indication that their patriotic masses would refuse to fight against a weaker revolutionary Germany. At any rate, aside from such considerations, there was little reason to believe that the German masses, engaged in getting rid of their arms, would resume the war against foreign capitalism in order to get rid of their own. The policy which was apparently the most 'realistic' for dealing with the international situation and which was soon to be proposed by Wolfheim and Lauffenberg under the name of National-Bolshevism was still unrealistic in view of the real power relations after the war. The plan to resume the war with Russia's help against Allied capitalism failed to consider that the bolsheviks were neither ready nor able to participate in such a venture. Of course, the bolsheviks were not averse to Germany or any other nation making difficulties for the victorious imperialists, yet they did not encourage the idea of a new large-scale war to carry on the 'world-revolution'. They desired support for their own regime, whose permanency was still questioned by the bolsheviks themselves, but they were not interested in supporting revolutions in other countries by military means. Both to follow a nationalistic course, independent of the question of alliances, and to unite Germany once more for a war of 'liberation' from foreign oppression was out of the question for the reason that these social layers which the 'national revolutionists' would have to win over to their cause were precisely the people who ended the war before the complete defeat of the German armies in order to prevent a further spreading of 'bolshevism'. Unable to become the masters of international capitalism, they had preferred to maintain themselves as its best servants. Yet, there was no way of dealing with internal German questions which did not involve a definite foreign policy. The radical German revolution was thus defeated even before it could arise both by its own and by world capitalism.

The need to consider seriously international relations never arose, however, for the German Left. Perhaps this was the clearest indication of its insignificance. Neither was the question as to what to do with political power, once it was captured, raised concretely. No one seemed to believe that these questions would have to be answered. Liebknecht and Luxemburg felt sure that a long period of class struggles was facing the German proletariat with no sign of an early victory. They wanted to make the best of it, suggesting a return to parliament and to trade-union work. However, in their previous activities they had already overstepped the boundaries of bourgeois politics; they could no longer return to the prisons of tradition. They had rallied around themselves the most radical element of the German proletariat which was now determined to consider any fight the final struggle against capitalism. These workers interpreted the Russian revolution in accordance with their own needs and their own mentality; they cared less about difficulties lurking in the future than about destroying as much as possible of the forces of the past. There were only two ways open for the revolutionists: either to go down with the forces whose cause was lost in advance, or to return to the fold of bourgeois democracy and perform social work for the ruling classes. For the real revolutionist there was, of course, only one way: to go down with the fighting workers. This is why Eugen Levine spoke of the revolutionist as "a dead person on furlough", and why Rosa Luxemburg and Karl Liebknecht went to their death almost somnambulistically. It was a mere accident that Otto Rühle and many others of the determined Left remained alive.

IV

The fact that the international bourgeoisie could conclude its war with no more than the temporary loss of Russian business determined the whole post-war history down to the second world war. In retrospect, the struggles of the German proletariat from 1919 to 1923 appear as minor frictions that accompanied the capitalistic re-organisation process which followed the war crisis. But there has always been a tendency to consider the by-products of violent changes in the capitalist structure as expressions of the revolutionary will of the proletariat. The radical optimists, however, were merely whistling in the dark. The darkness is real, to be sure, and the noise is encouraging, yet at this late hour there is no need to take it too seriously. As impressive as Otto Rühle's record as a practical revolutionist may be, as exciting as it is to recall the days of proletarian actions in Dresden, in Saxonia, in Germany – the mass meetings, demonstrations, strikes, street-fights, the heated discussions, the hopes, fears and disappointments, the bitterness of defeat and the pain of prison and death – yet no lessons but negative ones can be drawn from all these undertakings. All the energy and all the enthusiasm were not enough to bring about a social change or to alter the contemporary mind. The lesson learned was how not to proceed. How to realise the revolutionary needs of the proletariat was not discovered.

The emotional upheavals provided a never-ending incentive for research. Revolution, which for so long had been a mere theory and a vague hope, had appeared for a moment as a practical possibility. The chance had been missed, no doubt, but it would return to be better utilised next time. If not the people, at least the 'times' were revolutionary and the prevailing crisis conditions would sooner or later revolutionise the minds of the workers. If actions had been brought to an end by the firing-squads of the social-democratic police, if the workers' initiative was once more destroyed through the emasculation of their councils by way of legalisation, if their leaders were again acting not with the class but 'on behalf of the class' in the various capitalistic institutions – nevertheless the war had revealed that the fundamental capitalistic contradictions could not be solved and that crisis conditions were now the 'normal' conditions of capitalism. New revolutionary actions were probable and would find the revolutionists better prepared.

Although the revolutions in Germany, Austria and Hungary had failed, there was still the Russian Revolution to remind the world of the reality of the proletarian claims. All discussions circled around this revolution, and rightly so, for this revolution was to determine the future course of the German Left. In December 1919 the Communist Party of Germany was formed. After the murder of Liebknecht and Luxemburg it was led by Paul Levi and Karl Radek. This new leadership was at once attacked by a left opposition within the party to which Rühle belonged because of its tendency to advocate a return to parliamentary activities. At the foundation of the party its radical elements had succeeded in giving it an anti-parliamentarian character and a wide democratic control in distinction to the Leninist type of organisation. An anti-trade union policy had also been adopted. Liebknecht and Luxemburg subordinated their own divergent views to those of the radical majority. Not so Levi and Radek. Already in the summer of 1919 they made it clear that they would split the party in order to participate in parliamentary elections. Simultaneously they began to propagandise for a return to trade-union work despite the fact that the party was already engaged in the formation of new organisations no longer based on trades or even industries, but on factories. These factory organisations were combined into one class organisation, the General Labour Union (Allgemeine Arbeiter Union Deutschlands). At the Heidelberg convention in October 1919 all the delegates who disagreed with the new central committee and maintained the position taken at the founding of the Communist Party were expelled. The following February the central committee decided to get rid of all districts controlled by the left opposition. The opposition had the Amsterdam bureau of the Communist International on its side which led to the dissolution of that bureau by the International in order to support the Levi-Radek combination. And finally in April 1920 the left wing founded the Communist Workers' Party (Kommunistische Arbeiter Partei Deutschlands). Throughout this period Otto Rühle was on the side of the left opposition.

The Communist Workers' Party did not as yet realise that its struggle against the groups around Levi and Radek was the resumption of the old fight of the German Left against bolshevism, and in a larger sense against the new structure of world capitalism which was slowly taking shape. It was decided to enter the Communist International. It seemed to be more bolshevik than the bolsheviks. Of all the revolutionary groups, for example, it was the most insistent upon direct help for the bolsheviks during the Russian-Polish war. But the Communist International did not need to decide anew against the 'ultra-left'; its leaders had made their decision twenty years before. Nevertheless, the executive committee of the Communist International still tried to keep in contact with the Communist Workers' Party not only because it still contained the majority of the old Communist Party, but also because both Levi and Radek, although doing the work of the bolsheviks in Germany, had been the closest disciples not of Lenin but of Rosa Luxemburg. At the second world congress of the Third International in 1920 the Russian bolsheviks were already in a position to dictate the policy of the International. Otto Rühle, attending the congress, recognised the impossibility of altering this situation and the immediate need of fighting the bolshevik International in the interest of the proletarian revolution.

The Communist Workers' Party sent a new delegation to Moscow only to return with the same results. These were summed up in Herman Gorter's *Open Letter to Lenin*, which answered Lenin's *Left Wing Communism – An Infantile Disorder*. The actions of the International against the 'ultra-left' were the first open attempts to interfere with and control all the various national sections. The pressure upon the Communist Workers' Party to return to parliamentarianism and trade-unionism was constantly increased, but the Communist Workers' Party withdrew from the International after its third congress.

V

At the second world congress the bolshevik leaders, in order to secure control over the International proposed twenty-one conditions of admission to the Communist International. Since they controlled the congress they had no difficulty in getting these conditions adopted. Thereupon the struggle on questions of organisation which, twenty years previously, had caused the controversies between Luxemburg and

Lenin were openly resumed. Behind the debated organisational questions were, of course, the fundamental differences between the bolshevik revolution and the needs of the Western proletariat.

For Otto Rühle these twenty-one conditions were enough to destroy his last illusions about the bolshevik regime. These conditions endowed the executive of the International, that is, the leaders of the Russian party, with complete control and authority over all national sections. In Lenin's opinion, it was not possible to realise dictatorship on an international scale "without a strictly centralised, disciplined party, capable of leading and managing every branch, every sphere, every variety of political and cultural work". To Rühle it seemed at first that behind Lenin's autocratic attitude there was merely the arrogance of the victor trying to thrust upon the world the methods of struggle and the type of organisation that had brought power to the bolsheviks. This attitude – which insisted on applying the Russian experience to Western Europe where entirely different conditions prevailed – appeared as an error, a political mistake, a lack of understanding of the peculiarities of Western capitalism and the result of Lenin's fanatical pre-occupation with Russian problems. Lenin's policy seemed to be determined by the backwardness of the Russian capitalistic development, and though it had to be fought in Western Europe since it tended to support the capitalist restoration, it could not be called an out-right counter-revolutionary force. This benevolent view towards the bolshevik revolution was soon to be destroyed by the further activities of the bolsheviks themselves.

The bolsheviks went from small 'mistakes' to always greater 'mistakes'. Although the German communist party which was affiliated with the Third International grew steadily, particularly after its unification with the Independent Socialists, the proletarian class, already on the defensive, lost one position after another to the forces of capitalist reaction. Competing with the social-democratic party, which represented parts of the middle-class and the so-called trade-unionist labour aristocracy, the Communist Party could not help growing as these social layers became pauperised in the permanent depression in which German capitalism found itself. With the steady growth of unemployment, dissatisfaction with the *status quo* and its staunchest supporters, the German social-democrats, also increased.

Only the heroic side of the Russian Revolution was popularised, the real every day character of the bolshevik regime was hidden by both its friends and foes. For, at this time, the state capitalism that was unfolding in Russia was still as foreign to the bourgeoisie, indoctrinated with *laissez faire* ideology, as was socialism proper. And socialism was conceived by most socialists as a kind of state control of industry and natural resources. The Russian Revolution became a powerful and skilfully fostered myth, accepted by the impoverished sections of the German proletariat to compensate for their increasing misery. The myth was bolstered by the reactionaries to increase their followers' hatred for the German workers and for all revolutionary tendencies generally.

Against the myth, against the powerful propaganda apparatus of the Communist International that built up the myth, which was accompanied and supported by a general onslaught of capital against labour all over the world – against all this, reason could not prevail. All radical groups to the left of the Communist Party went from stagnation to disintegration. It did not help that these groups had the 'right' policy and the Communist Party the 'wrong' policy, for no questions of revolutionary strategy were here involved. What was taking place was that world capitalism was going through a stabilisation process and ridding itself of the disturbing proletarian elements which under the crisis conditions of war and military collapse had tried to assert themselves politically.

Russia, which of all nations was most in need of stabilisation, was the first country to destroy its labour movement by way of the bolshevik party dictatorship. Under conditions of imperialism, however, internal stabilisation is possible only by external power politics. The character of Russia's foreign policy under the bolsheviks was determined by the peculiarities of the European post-war situation. Modern imperialism is no longer content with merely asserting itself by means of military pressure and actual warfare. The 'fifth column' is the recognised weapon of all nations. Yet the imperialist virtue of today was still a sheer necessity for the bolsheviks who were trying to hold their own in a world of imperialist competition. There was nothing contradictory in the bolshevik policy of taking all power from the Russian workers and, at the same time, attempting to build up strong labour organisations in other nations. Just as these organisations had to be flexible in order to move in accordance with Russia's changing political needs, so their control from above had to be rigid.

Of course, the bolsheviks did not regard the various sections of their International as mere foreign legions in the service of the 'workers' fatherland'; they believed that what helped Russia was also serving progress elsewhere. They believed, and rightly so, that the Russian Revolution had initiated a general and world-wide movement from monopoly-capitalism to state-capitalism, and they held that this new state of affairs was a step in the direction of socialism. In other words, if not in their tactics, then in their theory they were still social-democrats and from their point of view the social-democratic leaders were really traitors to their own cause when they helped preserve the *laissez faire* capitalism of yesterday. Against social-democracy they felt themselves to be true revolutionists; against the 'ultra-left' they felt they were realists, the true representatives of scientific socialism.

But what they thought of themselves and what they really were are different things. In so far as they continued to misunderstand their historical mission, they were continuously defeating their own cause; in so far as they were forced to live up to the objective needs of their revolution, they became the greatest counter-revolutionary force of modern capitalism. By fighting as true social-democrats for predominance in the socialist world movement, by identifying the narrow nationalistic interests of state-capitalistic Russia with the interests of the world proletariat, and by attempting to maintain at all cost the power position they had won in 1917, they were merely preparing their own downfall, which was dramatised in numerous factional struggles, reached its climax in the Moscow trials, and ended in the Stalinist Russia of today – one imperialist nation among others.

In view of this development, what was more important than Otto Rühle's relentless criticism of the actual policies of the bolsheviks in Germany and the world at large was his early recognition of the real historical importance of the bolshevik movement, that is, of militant social-democracy. What a conservative social-democratic movement was capable of doing and not doing, the parties in Germany, France and England had revealed only too clearly. The bolsheviks showed what they would have done had they still been a subversive movement. They would have attempted to organise unorganised capitalism and to replace individual entrepreneurs by bureaucrats. They had no other plans and even these were only extensions of the process of cartellisation, trustification and centralisation which was going on all over the capitalist world. In Western Europe, however, the socialist parties could no longer act bolshevistically, for their bourgeoisie was already instituting this kind of 'socialisation' of their own accord. All that the socialists could do was to lend them a hand, that is, to grow slowly into the emerging 'socialist society'.

The meaning of bolshevism was completely revealed only with the emergence of fascism. To fight the latter, it was necessary, in Otto Rühle's words, to recognise that "the struggle against fascism begins with the struggle against bolshevism". In the light of the present, the 'ultra-left' groups in Germany and Holland must be considered the first anti-fascist organisations, anticipating in their struggle against the communist parties the future need of the working class to fight the fascist form of capitalism. The first theorists of anti-fascism are to be found among the spokesmen of the radical sects: Gorter and Pannekoek in Holland; Rühle, Pfempfert, Broh and Fraenkel in Germany; and they can be considered as such by reason of their struggle against the concept of party-rule and state-control, by their attempts to actualise the concepts of the council movement towards the direct determination of its destiny, and by their upholding the struggle of the German Left against both social-democracy and its Leninistic branch.

Not long before his death, Rühle, in summing up his findings with regard to bolshevism, did not hesitate to place Russia first among the totalitarian states. "It has served as the model for other capitalistic dictatorships. Ideological divergences do not really differentiate socio-economic systems. The abolition of private property in the means of production (combined with) the control of workers over the products of their labour and the end of the wages system." Both these conditions, however, are unfulfilled in Russia as well as in the fascist states.

To make clear the fascist character of the Russian system, Rühle turned once more to Lenin's *Left Wing Communism – An Infantile Disorder*, for "of all programmatic declarations of bolshevism it was the most revealing of its real character". When in 1933 Hitler suppressed all socialist literature in Germany, Rühle related, Lenin's pamphlet was allowed publication and distribution. In this work Lenin insists that the party must be a sort of war academy of professional revolutionists. Its chief requirements were unconditional leader authority, rigid centralism, iron discipline, conformity, militancy, and the sacrifice of personality for party interests. And Lenin actually developed an elite of intellectuals, a centre which, when thrown into the revolution, was to capture leadership and assume power. "There is no use trying," Rühle said, "to determine logically and abstractly if this kind of preparation for revolution is wrong or right . . . Other questions must be raised first; what kind of revolution was in preparation? And what was the goal of the revolution?" He answered by showing that Lenin's party worked within the belated bourgeois revolution in Russia to overthrow the feudal regime of Czarism. What may be regarded as a solution for revolutionary problems in a bourgeois revolution cannot, however, at the same time be regarded as a solution for the proletarian revolution. The decisive structural differences between capitalist and socialist society exclude such an attitude. According to Lenin's revolutionary method, the leaders appear as the head of the masses. "This distinction between head and body," Rühle pointed out, "between intellectuals and workers, officers and privates, corresponds to the duality of class society. One class is educated to rule; the other to be ruled. Lenin's organisation is only a replica of bourgeois society. His revolution is objectively determined by the forces that create a social order incorporating these class relations, regardless of the subjective goals accompanying this process."

To be sure, whoever wants to have a bourgeois order will find in the divorce of leader and masses, the advance guard and the working class, the right strategical preparation for revolution. In aspiring to lead the bourgeois revolution in Russia, Lenin's party was highly appropriate. When, however, the Russian Revolution showed its proletarian features, Lenin's tactical and strategical methods ceased to be of value. His success was due not to his advance guard, but to the soviet movement which had not at all been incorporated in his revolutionary plans. And when Lenin, after the successful revolution had been made by the soviets, dispensed with this movement, all that had been proletarian in the revolution was also dispensed with. The bourgeois character of the revolution came to the fore again and eventually found its 'natural' completion in Stalinism.

Lenin, Rühle has said, thought in rigid, mechanical rules, despite all his pre-occupation with Marxian dialectics. There was only one party for him – his own; only one revolution – the Russian; only one method – the bolshevik. "The monotonous application of a once-discovered formula moved in an egocentric circle undisturbed by time and circumstances, developmental degrees, cultural standards, ideas and men. In Lenin there came to light with great clarity the rule of the machine age in politics; he was the 'technician', the 'inventor' of the revolution. All the fundamental characteristics of fascism were in his doctrine, his strategy, his 'social planning' and his art of dealing with men . . . He never learned to know the prerequisites for the freeing of the workers; he was not bothered by the false consciousness of the masses and their human self-alienation. The whole problem to him was nothing more or less than a problem of power."

Bolshevism as representing a militant power policy, does not differ from traditional bourgeois forms of rule. The rule serves as the great example of organisation. Bolshevism is a dictatorship, a nationalistic doctrine, an authoritarian system with a capitalistic social structure. Its 'planning' concerns technical-organisational not socio-economic questions. It is revolutionary only within the framework of capitalistic development, establishing not socialism but state-capitalism. It represents the present stage of capitalism and not a first step towards a new society.

VI

The Russian soviets and the German workers' and soldiers' councils represented the proletarian element in both the Russian and the German revolution. In both nations these movements were soon suppressed by military and judicial means. What remained of the Russian soviets after the firm entrenchment of the bolshevik party dictatorship was merely the Russian version of the later Nazi labour-front. The legalised German council movement turned into an appendage of trade-unionism and soon into a capitalistic instrument of control. Even the spontaneously formed councils of 1918 were – the majority of them – far from being revolutionary. Their form of organisation, based on class needs and not on the various special interests resulting from the capitalistic division of labour was all that was radical about them. But whatever their shortcomings, it must be said that there was nothing else on which to base revolutionary hopes. Although they frequently turned against the *Left*, still it was expected that the objective needs of this movement would bring it inevitably into conflict with the traditional powers. This form of organisation was to be preserved in its original character and built up in preparation for coming struggles.

Thinking in terms of a continued German revolution, the 'ultra-left' was committed to a fight to the finish against trade-unions and against the existing parliamentary parties; in brief, against all forms of opportunism and compromise. Thinking in terms of the probability of a side-by-side existence with the old capitalist powers, the Russian bolsheviks could not conceive a policy without compromises. Lenin's arguments in defence of the bolshevik position in relation to trade-unions, parliamentarianism and opportunism in general elevated the particular needs of bolshevism into false revolutionary principles. Yet it would not do to show the illogical character of the bolshevik arguments, for as illogical as the arguments were from a revolutionary point of view, they emanated logically from the peculiar role of the bolsheviks within the Russian capitalistic emancipation and from the bolshevik international policy which supported Russia's national interests.

That Lenin's principles were false from a proletarian point of view in both Russia and in Western Europe, Otto Rühle demonstrated in various pamphlets and in numerous articles in the press of the General Labour Union and in Franz Pfempfert's left-wing magazine, *Die Aktion*.

He exposed the expedient trickery involved in giving these principles a logical appearance, trickery which consisted in citing a specific experience at a given period under particular circumstances in order to draw from it conclusions of immediate and general application. Because trade unions had once been of some value, because parliament had once served revolutionary propaganda needs, because occasionally opportunism had resulted in certain gains for workers, they remained for Lenin the most important mediums of proletarian policy for all times and under all circumstances. And as if all this would not convince the adversary, Lenin was fond of pointing out that whether or not these policies and organisations were the right ones, it was still a fact that the workers adhered to them and that the revolutionist must always be where the masses are.

This strategy flowed from Lenin's capitalistic approach to politics. It never seemed to enter his mind that the masses were also in factories and that revolutionary factory organisations could not lose contact with the masses even if they tried. It never seemed to occur to him that with the same logic that was to hold the revolutionists in the reactionary organisations, he could demand their presence in the church, in fascist organisations, or wherever masses could be found. The latter, to be sure, would have occurred to him had the need arisen to unite openly with the forces of reaction as happened at a later day under the Stalinist regime.

It was clear to Lenin that for the purposes of bolshevism, council organisations were the least suitable. Not only is there small room in factory organisations for professional revolutionists, but the Russian experience had shown how difficult it was to 'manage' a soviet movement. At any rate, the bolsheviks did not intend to wait for chances of revolutionary interference in political processes; they were actively engaged in everyday politics and concerned with immediate results in their favour. In order to influence the Western labour movement with a view to eventually controlling it, it was far easier for them to enter into, and to deal with, existing organisations. In the competitive struggles waged between and within these organisations, they saw a chance to gain a foothold quickly. To build up entirely new organisations opposed to all the existing ones would be to attempt what could have only belated results – if any at all. Being in power in Russia, the bolsheviks could no longer indulge in long-view politics; in order to maintain their power they had to march up all the avenues of politics, not only the revolutionary ones. It must be said, however, that aside from their being forced to do so, the bolsheviks were more than willing to participate in the many political games that accompany the capitalistic exploitation process. To be able to participate they needed trade unions and parliaments and parties and also capitalistic supporters, which made opportunism both a necessity and a pleasure.

There is no longer any need to point to the many 'misdeeds' of bolshevism in Germany and in the world at large. In theory and in practice the Stalinist regime declares itself a capitalistic, imperialistic power, opposing not only the proletarian revolution, but even the fascist reforms of capitalism. And it actually does favour the maintenance of bourgeois democracy in order to utilise more fully its own fascistic structure. Just as Germany was very little interested in spreading fascism over her borders and the borders of her allies since she had no intention of strengthening her imperialistic competitors, so Russia concerns herself with safeguarding democracy everywhere save within her own territory. Her friendship with bourgeois-democracy is a true friendship; fascism is no article for export, for it ceases to be an advantage as soon as it is generalised. Despite the Stalin-Hitler pact, there are no greater 'anti-fascists' than the bolsheviks on behalf of their own native fascism. Only so far as their imperialistic expansion, if any, will reach, will they be guilty of consciously supporting the general fascistic trend.

This general fascistic trend does not stem from bolshevism but incorporates it. It stems from the peculiar developmental laws of capitalist economy. If Russia finally becomes a 'decent' member of the capitalist family of nations, the 'indecencies' of her fascistic youth will in some quarters still be mistaken for a revolutionary past. The opposition to Stalinism, however, unless it includes opposition to Leninism and to the bolshevism of 1917, is no opposition but just a quarrel among political competitors. In so far as the myth of bolshevism is still defended against the Stalinist reality, Otto Rühle's work in showing that the Stalinism of today is merely the Leninism of yesterday, is still of contemporary importance, the more so as attempts might be made to recapture the bolshevik past in the social upheavals of the future.

The whole history of bolshevism could be anticipated by Rühle and the 'ultra-left' movement because of their early recognition of the real content of the bolshevik revolution and the real character of the old social-democratic movement. After 1920 all activities of bolshevism could be only harmful to the workers of the world. No common actions with its various organisations were any longer possible and none were attempted.

VII

Together with 'ultra-left' groups in Dresden, Frankfurt am Main and other places, Otto Rühle went one step beyond the anti-bolshevism of the Communist Workers' Party and its adherents in the General Labour Union. He thought that the history of the social-democratic parties and the practices of the bolshevik parties proved sufficiently that it was futile to attempt to replace reactionary parties with revolutionary parties for the reason that the party-form of organisation itself had become useless and even dangerous. As early as 1920 he proclaimed that 'the revolution is not a party affair' but demands the destruction of all parties in favour of the council movement. Working chiefly within the General Labour Union, he agitated against the need of a special political party until this organisation was split in two. One section (Allgemeine Arbeiter Union – Einheitsorganisation) shared Rühle's views, the other remained as the 'economic organisation' of the Communist Party. The organisation represented by Rühle leaned toward the syndicalist and anarchist movements without, however, giving up its Marxian *Weltanschauung*. The other considered itself the heir to all that had been revolutionary in the Marxian movement of the past. It attempted to bring about a Fourth International but succeeded only in effecting a closer cooperation with similar groups in a few European countries.

In Rühle's opinion a proletarian revolution was possible only with the conscious and active participation of the broad proletarian masses. This again presupposed a form of organisation that could not be controlled from above, but was determined by the will of its members. The factory organisation and the structure of the General Labour Union would, he thought, prevent a divorce between organisational and class interests; it would prevent the emergence of a powerful bureaucracy served by the organisation instead of serving it. It would, finally, prepare the workers to take over the industries and manage them according to their own needs and thus prevent the arising of new states of exploitation.

The Communist Workers' Party shared these general ideas and its own factory organisations were hardly distinguishable from those that agreed with Rühle. But the party maintained that at this stage of development factory organisation alone could not guarantee a clear-cut revolutionary policy. All kinds of people would enter these organisations, there would be no method of proper selection, and politically undeveloped workers might determine the character of the organisations, which thus might not be able to live up to revolutionary requirements of the day. This point was well demonstrated by the relatively backward character of the council movement of 1918. The Communist Workers' Party held that class-consciousness, Marxian-trained revolutionists, although belonging to factory organisations should, at the same time, be combined in a separate party in order to safeguard and develop revolutionary theory and, so to speak, watch over the factory organisations to prevent them from going astray.

The Communist Workers' Party saw in Rühle's position a kind of disappointment seeking refuge in a new form of utopianism. It maintained that Rühle merely generalised the experiences of the old parties and it insisted that the revolutionary character of its organisation was the result of its own party form. It rejected the centralistic principles of Leninism but insisted upon keeping the party small so that it should be free of all opportunism. There were other arguments supporting the party idea. Some referred to international problems, some were concerned with the questions of illegality, but all arguments failed to convince Rühle and his followers. They saw in the party the perpetuation of the leader-mass principle, the contradiction between party and class, and feared a repetition of bolshevism in the German *Left*.

Neither of the two groups could prove its theory. History by-passed them both; they were arguing in a vacuum. Neither the Communist Workers' Party nor the two General Labour Unions overcame their status of being 'ultra-left' sects. Their internal problems became quite artificial, for there was actually no difference between the Communist Workers' Party and the General Labour Union. Despite their theories, Rühle's followers did not function in the factories either. Both unions indulged in the same activities. Hence all theoretical divergencies had no practical meaning.

These organisations – remnants of the proletarian attempt to play a role in the upheavals of 1918 – attempted to apply their experiences within a development which was consistently moving in the opposite direction from that in which these experiences originated. The Communist Party alone, by virtue of Russian control, could really grow within this trend towards fascism. But by representing Russian, not German fascism, it, too, had to succumb to the emerging Nazi-movement which, recognising and accepting prevailing capitalist tendencies, finally inherited the old German labour movement in its entirety.

After 1923 the German 'ultra-left' movement ceased to be a serious political factor in the German labour movement. Its last attempt to force the trend of development in its direction was dissipated in the short-lived activity in March 1921 under the popular leadership of Max Hoelz. Its most militant members, being forced into illegality, introduced methods of conspiracy and expropriation into the movement, thereby hastening its disintegration. Although organisationally the 'ultra-left' groups continued to exist up to the beginning of Hitler's dictatorship, their functions were restricted to that of discussion clubs trying to understand their own failures and that of the German revolution.

VIII

The decline of the 'ultra-left' movement, the changes in Russia and in the composition of the bolshevik parties, the rise of fascism in Italy and Germany restored the old relationship between economics and politics that had been disturbed during and shortly after the first world war. All over the world capitalism was now sufficiently stabilised to determine the main political trend. Fascism and bolshevism, products of crisis conditions were – like the crisis itself – also mediums for a new prosperity, a new expansion of capital and the resumption of the imperialistic competitive struggles. But just as any major crisis appears as the final crisis to those who suffer most, so the accompanying political changes appeared as expressions of the breakdown of capitalism. But the wide gap between appearance and reality sooner or later changes an exaggerated optimism into an exaggerated pessimism with regard to revolutionary possibilities. Two ways, then, remain open for the revolutionist: he can capitulate to the dominant political processes, or he can retire into a life of contemplation and wait for the turn of events.

Until the final collapse of the German labour movement, the retreat of the 'ultra-left' appeared to be a return to theoretical work. The organisations existed in the form of weekly and monthly publications, pamphlets and books. The publications secured the organisations, the organisations the publications. While mass-organisations served small capitalistic minorities, the mass of the workers were represented by individuals. The contradiction between the theories of the 'ultra-left' and the prevailing conditions became unbearable. The more one thought in collective terms the more isolated one became. Capitalism, in its fascistic form, appeared as the only real collectivism, anti-fascism as a return to an early bourgeois individualism. The mediocrity of capitalist man, and therefore the revolutionist under capitalist conditions, became painfully obvious within the small stagnating organisations. More and more people, starting from the premise that the 'objective conditions' were ripe for revolution, explained its absence with such 'subjective factors' as lack of class consciousness and lack of understanding and character on the part of the workers. These lacks themselves, however, had again to be explained by 'objective conditions', for the shortcomings of the proletariat undoubtedly resulted from their special position within the social relations of capitalism. The necessity of restricting activity to educational work became a virtue: developing the class-consciousness of the workers was regarded as the most essential of all revolutionary tasks. But the old social-democratic belief that 'knowledge is power' was no longer convincing for there is no direct connection between knowledge and its application.

The breakdown of *laissez faire* capitalism and the increasing centralist control over always greater masses through capitalistic production and war increased intellectual interest in the previously neglected fields of psychology and sociology. These branches of bourgeois 'science' served to explain the bewilderment of that part of the bourgeoisie which had been displayed by more powerful competitors and of that part of the petty-bourgeoisie reduced to proletarian levels of existence during the depression. In its early stages the capitalistic concentration process of wealth and power had been accompanied by the absolute growth of the bourgeois lays of society. After the war the situation changed; the European depression hit both bourgeoisie and proletariat and generally destroyed confidence in the system and in the individuals themselves. Psychology and sociology, however, were not only expressions of bourgeois bewilderment and insecurity but, simultaneously, served the need for a more direct determination of mass behaviour and ideological control than has been necessary under less centralistic conditions. Those who lost power in the political struggles which accompanied the concentration of capital as well as those who gained power offered psychological and sociological explanations for their full failures or successes. What to one was the 'rape of the masses' to the other was a newly-won insight – to be systematised and incorporated in the science of exploitation and control – into the social processes.

Under the capitalistic division of labour the maintenance and extension of prevailing ideologies is the job of the intellectual layers of the bourgeoisie and petty-bourgeoisie. This division of labour is, of course, determined more by existing class conditions than by the productive needs of the complex society. What we know we know by way of a capitalist production of knowledge. But as there is no other, the proletarian approach to all that is brought forth by bourgeois science and pseudo-science must always be a critical one. To make this knowledge serve other than capitalistic purposes means to cleanse it of all the elements entering it which are related to the capitalistic class structure. It would be as false as it would be impossible to reject wholesale all that is produced by bourgeois science. Yet it can only be approached sceptically. The proletarian critique – again on account of the capitalistic division of labour – is quite limited. It is of real importance only where bourgeois knowledge deals with social relationships. Here its theories can be tested as to their validity and their meaning for the various classes and for society as a whole. There arose, then, with the vogue of psychology and sociology, the need to examine the new findings in these fields from the critical point of view of the suppressed classes.

It was unavoidable that the vogue for psychology should penetrate the labour movement. But the whole decay of this movement was once more revealed by its attempt to use the new theories of bourgeois psychology and sociology for a critical investigation of its own theories instead of using the Marxian theory to criticise the new bourgeois pseudo-science. Behind this attitude was the growing distrust of Marxism due to the failures of the German and Russian revolutions. Behind it also was the inability to go beyond Marx in a Marxian sense, an inability clearly brought to light by the fact that all that appeared new in bourgeois sociology had been taken from Marx in the first place. Unfortunately, from our point of view, Otto Rühle was one of the first to clothe the more popular ideas of Marx in the new language of bourgeois sociology and psychology. In his hands the materialistic conception of history now became 'sociology' in so far as it dealt with society; in so far as it dealt with the individual, it was now 'psychology'. The principles of this theory were to serve both the analysis of society and the analysis of the psychological complexities of its individuals. In his biography of Marx, Rühle applied his new psycho-sociological concept of Marxism which could only help to support the tendency toward incorporating an emasculated Marxism into capitalistic ideology. This kind of 'historical materialism', which searched for reasons of 'inferiority and superiority complexes' in the endless domains of biology, anthropology, sociology, economics and so forth in order to discover a kind of 'balance-of-power of complexes by way of compensations' which could be considered the proper adjustment between individual and society, this kind of Marxism was not able to serve any of the practical needs of the workers, nor could it help in their education. This part of Rühle's activity, whether one evaluates it positively or negatively, has little, if anything, to do with the problems that beset the German proletariat. It is, therefore, unnecessary to deal here with Rühle's psychological work. We mention it, nevertheless, for the double reason that it may serve as an additional illustration of the general despair of the revolutionist in the period of counter-revolution and as a further manifestation of the sincerity of the revolutionist, Rühle, within the conditions of despair. For in this phase of his literary activity, as in every other that dealt with pedagogical-psychological, historical-cultural, or economic-political questions, he also speaks out against the inhuman conditions of capitalism, against possible new forms of physical and mental slavery, and for a society befitting a free humanity.

IX

The triumph of German fascism ended the long period of revolutionary discouragement, disillusionment and despair. Everything became once more extremely clear; the immediate future was outlined in all its brutality. The labour movement proved for the last time that the criticism directed against it by the revolutionists was more than justified. The fight of the 'ultra-left' against the official labour movement proved to have been the only consistent struggle against capitalism that had thus far been waged.

The triumph of German fascism, which was not an isolated phenomenon but was closely connected with the previous development of the whole of the capitalist world, did not cause but merely helped to initiate the new world conflict of the imperialist powers. The days of 1914 had returned. But not for Germany. The German labour leaders were deprived of the 'moving experience' of declaring themselves once more the truest sons of the fatherland. To organise for war meant to institute totalitarianism, and that meant that many special interests had to be eliminated. Under the conditions of the Weimar Republic and within the framework of world imperialism, this was possible only by way of internal struggles. The 'resistance' of the German labour movement to fascism, half-hearted in the first place, must not, however, be mistaken for a resistance to war. In the case of social-democracy and the trade unions it was not a resistance but merely an abdication accompanied by verbal protests to save face. And even this came only in the wake of Hitler's refusal to incorporate these institutions, in their traditional form and with their 'experienced' leaders, into the fascist scheme of things. Neither was the 'resistance' on the part of the Communist Party a resistance to war and fascism as such but only in so far as they were directed against Russia. If the official labour organisations in Germany were prevented from siding with their bourgeoisie, in all other nations they did so without deliberation and without struggle.

A second time in his life, the exiled Otto Rühle had to decide which side to take in the new world-wide struggle. This time it seemed somewhat more difficult because Hitler's consistent totalitarianism was designed to prevent a repetition of the vacillating days of liberalism during the last world war. This situation allowed the second world war to masquerade as a struggle between democracy and fascism and provided the social chauvinists with better excuses. The exiled labour leaders, in step with the labour organisations in their adopted countries, could still point to the political differences between the two forms of the capitalistic system although they were unable to deny the capitalistic nature of their new fatherlands. The theory of the lesser evil served to make plausible the reason why the democracies should be defended against the further spreading of fascism. Rühle, however, maintained his old position of 1914. For him the 'enemy was still at home', in the democracies as well as in the fascist states. The proletariat could not, or rather should not, side with any of them but oppose both with equal vehemence. Rühle pointed out that all the political, ideological, racial and psychological arguments offered in defence of a pro-war position could not really cover up the capitalistic reason for war: the struggle for profits among the imperialist competitors. In letters and articles he reiterated all the implications of the laws of capitalist development as established by Marx in order to combat the nonsense of popular 'anti-fascism' which could only hasten the fascisation process of world capitalism.

For Rühle fascism and state-capitalism were not the inventions of vicious politicians but the outcome of the capitalist process of concentration and centralisation in which the accumulation of capital manifests itself. The class relationship in capitalist production is beset by many insoluble contradictions. The main contradiction, Rühle saw, lies in the fact that capital accumulation means also a tendency toward a falling rate of profit. This tendency can be combatted only by a more rapid capital accumulation – which implies an increase of exploitation. But in spite of the fact that exploitation is increased in relation to the rate of accumulation necessary to avoid crises and depressions, profits continue to show a tendency to fall. During depressions capital is re-organised to allow for a new period of capital expansion. If nationally a crisis implies the destruction of weaker capital and capital concentration by ordinary business means, internationally re-organisation finally demands war. This means the destruction of the weaker capitalist nations in favour of the victorious imperialisms in order to bring about a new capital expansion and its further concentration and centralisation. Every capitalist crisis – at this stage of capital accumulation – involves the world; likewise every war is at once a world-wide war. Not particular nations but the whole of the world capitalism is responsible for war and crisis. This, Rühle saw, is the enemy and he is everywhere.

To be sure Rühle had no doubt that totalitarianism was worse for the workers than bourgeois democracy. He had fought against Russian totalitarianism since its inception. He was fighting German fascism, but he could not fight in the name of bourgeois democracy because he knew that the peculiar developmental laws of capitalist production would change bourgeois democracy sooner or later into fascism and state-capitalism. To fight totalitarianism meant to oppose capitalism in all its forms. "Private Capitalism," he wrote, "and with it democracy, which is trying to save it, are obsolete and going the way of all mortal things. State-Capitalism – and with it fascism, which paves the way for it – are growing and seizing power. The old is gone forever and no exorcism works against the new. No matter how hard we may try to revive democracy, all efforts will be futile. All hopes for a victory of democracy over fascism are the crassest illusions, all belief in the return of democracy as a form of capitalist government has only the value of cunning betrayal and cowardly self-delusion . . . It is the misfortune of the proletariat that its obsolete organisations based upon an opportunistic tactic make it defenceless against the onslaught of fascism. It has thus lost its own political position in the body politic at the present time. It has ceased to be a history-making factor at the present epoch. It has been swept upon the dungheap of history and will rot on the side of democracy as well as on the side of fascism, for the democracy of today will be the fascism of tomorrow."

X

Although Otto Rühle faced the second world war as uncompromisingly as he had faced the first, his attitude with regard to the labour movement was different from that of 1914. This time he could not help being certain that "no hope could spring from the miserable remnants of the old movement in the still-democratic nations for the final uprising of the proletariat and its historical deliverance. Still less could hope spring from the shabby fragments of those party traditions that were scattered and spilled in the emigration of the world, nor from the stereotyped notions of past revolutions, regardless of whether one believes in the blessings of violence or in peaceful transition." Yet he did not look hopelessly into the future. He felt sure that new urges and new impulses will animate the masses and force them to make their own history.

The reasons for this confidence were the same as those that convinced Rühle of the inevitability of the capitalist development toward fascism and state-capitalism. They were based on the insoluble contradictions inherent in the capitalist system of production. Just as the re-organisation of capital during the crisis is simultaneously a preparation for greater crises, so war can breed only bigger and more devastating wars. Capitalistic anarchy can become only more chaotic, no matter how much its supporters try to bring order into it. Always greater parts of the capitalist world will be destroyed so that the stronger capitalistic groups can keep on accumulating. The miseries of the masses of the world will mount until a breaking point is reached and new social upsurges will destroy the murderous system of capitalist production.

Rühle was as little able as anybody else at this time to state by what specific means fascism would be overcome. But he felt certain that the mechanics and dynamics of revolution will undergo fundamental changes. In the self-expropriation and proletarianisation of the bourgeoisie by the second world war, in the surmounting of nationalism by the abolition of small states, in the state-capitalistic world politic based on state federations he saw not only the immediately negative side but also the positive aspects of providing new starting-points for anti-capitalist actions. To the day of his death he was certain that the class concept was bound to spread until it would foster a majority interest in socialism. He looked for the class struggle to be transformed from an abstract-ideological category into a practical-positive-economic category. And he envisioned the rise of factory councils within the unfolding of labour democracy as a reaction to bureaucratic terror. For him the labour movement was not dead but was still to be born in the social struggles of the future.

If Rühle, finally, had nothing more to offer than the 'hope' that the future will solve the problems which the old labour movement failed to solve, this hope did not spring from faith but from knowledge, knowledge which consisted in recognising actual social trends. It did not contain a clue as to *how* to achieve the necessary social transformation. It demanded, however, dissociation from futile activities and hopeless organisations. It demanded recognition of the reasons that led to the disintegration of the old labour movement and a search for the elements that point to the limitations of the prevailing totalitarian systems. It demanded a sharper distinction between ideology and reality in order to discover in the latter the factors that escape the control of the totalitarian organisers.

How little or how much is needed to transform society is always discovered only after that fact. But the balance-scale of society is delicate, and is particularly sensitive at the present time. The most powerful controls over men are really weak when compared with the tremendous contradictions that rend the world today. Otto Rühle was right in pointing out that the activities which will finally tip the scale of society in favour of socialism will not be discovered by means and methods related to previous activities and traditional organisations. They must be discovered within the changing social relationships which are still determined by the contradiction between the capitalist relations of production and the direction in which the productive forces of society are moving. To discover those relationships, that is, to recognise the coming revolution in the realities of today, will be the job of those who carry on in the spirit of Otto Rühle.

CHAPTER VII

Spontaneity and Organisation

The question of organisation and spontaneity was approached in the labour movement as a problem of class consciousness, involving the relations of the revolutionary minority to the mass of the capitalistically-indoctrinated proletariat. It was considered unlikely that more than a minority would accept, and, by organising itself, maintain and apply a revolutionary consciousness. The mass of the workers would act as revolutionaries only by force of circumstances. Lenin accepted this situation optimistically. Others, like Rosa Luxemburg, thought differently about it. In order to realise a party dictatorship, Lenin concerned himself first of all with questions of organisation. In order to escape the danger of a new dictatorship *over* the workers, Rosa Luxemburg stressed spontaneity. Both, however, held that just as under certain conditions the bourgeoisie determined the ideas and activities of the labouring masses, so under different conditions a revolutionary minority could do likewise. At the same time that Lenin saw this as a chance to usher in the socialist society, Rosa Luxemburg feared that any minority, placed in the position of a ruling class, might soon think and act just like the bourgeoisie of old.

Behind these attitudes there was the conviction that the economic development of capitalism would force its proletarian masses into anti-capitalistic activities. Although Lenin counted on, he simultaneously feared, spontaneous movements. He justified the need for conscious interferences in spontaneously-arising revolutions by citing the backwardness of the masses and saw in spontaneity an important destructive but not constructive element. In Lenin's view, the more forceful the spontaneous movement, the greater would be the need to supplement and direct it with organised, planned party-activity. The workers had to be guarded against themselves, so to speak, or they might defeat their own cause through ignorance, and, by dissipating their powers, open the way for counter-revolution.

Rosa Luxemburg thought differently because she saw the counter-revolution not only lurking in the traditional powers and organisations but capable of developing within the revolutionary movement itself. She hoped that spontaneous movements would delimit the influence of those organisations that aspired to centralise power in their own hands. Although both Luxemburg and Lenin saw the accumulation of capital as a process that spawned crises, Luxemburg conceived the crisis as more catastrophic than did Lenin. The more devastating a crisis, the more embracing would be the expected spontaneous actions, the less the need for conscious direction and centralistic control, and the greater the chance for the proletariat to learn to think and act in ways appropriate to its own needs. Organisations, in Luxemburg's view, should merely help release the creative forces inherent in mass actions and should integrate themselves in the independent proletarian attempts to organise a new society. This approach presupposed not a clear, comprehending revolutionary consciousness but a highly-developed working class, capable of discovering by its own efforts ways and means of utilising the productive apparatus and its own capacities for a socialist society.

There was still another approach to the question of organisation and spontaneity. Georges Sorel and the syndicalists were not only convinced that the proletariat could emancipate itself without the guidance of the intelligentsia, but that it has to emancipate itself from the middle-class elements that control political organisations. In Sorel's view, a government of socialists would in no sense alter the social position of the workers. In order to be free, the workers themselves would have to resort to actions and weapons exclusively their own. Capitalism, he thought, had already organised the whole proletariat in its industries. All that was left to do was to suppress the state and property. To accomplish this, the proletariat was not so much in need of a so-called scientific insight into necessary social trends as of a kind of intuitive conviction that revolution and socialism were the inevitable outcome of their own continuous struggles. The strike was seen as the workers' revolutionary apprenticeship. The growing number of strikes, the extension of strikes, and their increasing duration pointed towards a possible *general strike,* that is, to the impending social revolution. Each particular strike was a reduced facsimile of the general strike and a preparation for this final upheaval. The growing *revolutionary will* could not be gauged by the successes of political parties, but by the frequency of strikes and the *elan* therein displayed. Organisation was preparation for direct action and the latter, in turn, formed the character of the organisation. The spontaneously-occurring strikes were the organisational forms of revolt and were also part of the social organisation of the future in which the producers themselves control their production. The revolution proceeded from action to action in a continuous merging of spontaneous and organisational aspects of the proletarian fight for emancipation.

II

By stressing spontaneity, labour organisations admitted their own weakness. Since they did not know *how* to change society, they indulged in the hope that the future would solve the problem. This hope, to be sure, was based on the recognition of some actual trends such as the further development of technology, the continuation of the concentration and centralisation processes accompanying capitalistic development, the increase of social frictions, etc. It was nevertheless a mere hope which compensated for the lack of organisational power and the inability to act effectively. Spontaneity had to lend 'reality' to their apparently hopeless tasks, to excuse an enforced inactivity and justify consistency.

Strong organisations, on the other hand, were inclined to disregard spontaneity. Their optimism was based on their own successes not on the probability of spontaneous movements coming to their aid at some later date. They advocated either that organised force must be defeated by organised force, or held to the view that the school of practical every-day activity as carried on by party and trade union would lead more and more workers to recognise the inescapable necessity of changing existing social relations. In the steady growth of their own organisations, they saw the development of proletarian class consciousness and at times they dreamed that these organisations would comprise the whole of the working class.

All organisations, however, fit into the general social structure. They have no absolute 'independence'; in one way or another all are determined by society and help determine society in turn. None of the organisations in capitalism can consistently be anti-capitalistic. 'Consistency' refers merely to a limited ideological activity and is the privilege of sects and individuals. To attain social importance, organisations must be opportunistic in order to affect the social processes and to serve their own ends simultaneously.

Apparently opportunism and 'realism' are the same thing. The former cannot be defeated by a radical ideology which opposes the whole of the existing social relations. It is not possible to slowly assemble revolutionary forces into powerful organisations ready to act at favourable moments. All attempts in this respect have failed. Only those organisations that did not disturb the prevailing basic social relationships grew to any importance. If they started out with a revolutionary ideology, their growth implied a subsequent discrepancy between their ideology and their functions. Opposed to capitalism, but also organised within it, they could not help supporting their opponents. Those organisations not destroyed by competitive adversaries finally succumbed to the forces of capitalism by virtue of their own successful activity.

In the matter of organisation this, then is the dilemma of the radical: in order to do something of social significance, actions must be organised. Organised actions, however, turn into capitalistic channels. It seems that in order to do something *now*, one can do only the wrong thing and in order to avoid false steps, one should undertake none at all. The political mind of the radical is destined to be miserable; it is aware of its utopianism and it experiences nothing but failures. In mere self-defence, the radical stresses spontaneity always, unless he is a mystic, with the secretly-held thought that he is talking nonsense. But his persistence seems to prove that he never ceases to see some sense in the nonsense.

Taking refuge in the idea of spontaneity is indicative of an actual or imagined inability to form effective organisations and a refusal to fight existing organisations in a 'realistic' manner. For to fight them *successfully* would necessitate the formation of counter-organisations, which, by themselves, would defeat the reason for their existence. 'Spontaneity' is thus a negative approach to the problem of social change and only in a purely ideological sense may it also be considered positive as it involves a mental divorce from those activities that favour the prevailing society. It sharpens critical faculty and leads to dis-association from futile activities and hopeless organisations. It looks for indications of social disintegration and for the limitations of class control. It results in a sharper distinction between appearance and reality and is, in brief, the trade mark of a revolutionary attitude. Since it is clear that some social forces, relations and organisations tend to disappear and others tend to take hold, those interested in the future, in the new forces in the making, will emphasise spontaneity; those more intimately connected with the old ones will stress the need for organisation.

III

Even a superficial study of organised activity reveals that all important organisations, no matter what their ideology, support the *status quo*, or, at best, foster a limited development within the general conditions characteristic of a particular society in a particular historical period. The term *status quo* is helpful in clarifying the concept of rest within the concept of change. It must be regarded as is any theory or practical tool, and it has its uses quite apart from all its philosophical implications. It is clear, of course, that pre-capitalistic conditions, however transformed, are incorporated in capitalistic conditions and that, likewise, post-capitalistic conditions, in one form or another, are appearing within capitalistic conditions. But this refers to general development and though the specific cannot really be divorced from the general, it is continuously separated by the practical activities of men.

Status quo, as here applied to capitalism, means a period of social history in which the workers, within the conditions of a complex social interdependence, are divorced from the means of production and are thereby controlled by a ruling class. The particulars of political control are based on the particulars of economic control. So long as the capital-labour relationship determines social life, so long shall we find society basically 'unchanged', no matter how much it may appear to have changed otherwise. *Laissez-faire*, monopoly or state-capitalism are developmental stages within the *status quo*. While not denying differences between these stages, we must stress their basic identity and by opposing what they have in common oppose not only one or another but all of them simultaneously.

Development or merely change within the *status quo* may be 'good' or 'bad' from the time-conditioned point of view of the controlled. An example of the first would be the workers' successful fight for better living conditions and greater political freedom; of the second, the loss of both with the ascendancy of fascism – quite apart from the question of whether or not the first is a partial cause of the second. Participation in organisations that foster development within the *status quo* is often an inescapable necessity. It is therefore of no avail to oppose such organisations with a maximum programme realisable only outside the *status quo*. Nevertheless, before entering or remaining in 'realistic' organisations, it is necessary to inquire in what direction changes within the *status quo* may go and how they may affect the working population.

For a long time now trade unions and political labour parties have ceased to act in accordance with their original radical intentions. 'Problems of the day' transformed these movements and led to a situation in which there are no 'real' labour organisations despite the numerous pseudo-organisations still at large. Even the socialist wing of the movement conceives of reform not as a transition to socialism but as the means to a better, more agreeable capitalism, despite the fact that its literature often continues to employ socialistic terms.

The fight for better living conditions within the market economy, because it was a fight over the price of labour power, transformed the labour movement into a capitalistic movement of labourers. The greater the proletarian pressure, the greater became the capitalistic need to increase the productivity of labour by technological and organisational procedures and by the national and international extension of business activities. Like competition in general, the proletarian struggle, too, served as an instrument for increasing the pace of capital accumulation, for pushing society from one production level to another. Not only the leaders of labour but the rank and file, too, lost their early revolutionary aspirations as the rising productivity of labour accelerated capital expansion and allowed for both higher profits and better wages. Although wages diminished in relation to production, they increased in absolute terms and raised the living standards of great masses of industrial workers in the leading capitalist countries. Profits were augmented and capital formation was further hastened by foreign trade and colonial exploitation. This helped to stabilise the conditions of a rising so-called labour aristocracy. Periodically the process was interrupted by crises and depressions which acted, although blindly, as co-ordinating factors in the capitalistic re-organisation process. In the long run, however, the double-barrelled support of capital expansion by both working class and capitalistic competition led to a complete fusion of interests between labour organisations and the controllers of capital.

There were, of course, organisations that fought against the integration of the labour movement into the capitalistic structure. They interpreted reform as a step towards revolution and tried to engage in capitalistic activities and at the same time maintain a revolutionary goal. They saw the fusion of capital and labour as a temporary affair, to be suffered or utilised while it lasted. Their half-heartedness in matters of collaboration prevented their attaining organisational significance; and this, in turn, led them to emphasise spontaneity. Left wing socialists and revolutionary syndicalists belong in this category.

Some countries have higher living standards than others, the high wages of some labouring groups imply low wages for others. Equalising tendencies operating in competitive capitalism with regard to productivity, profit-rates and wage levels, tend to eliminate special interests and particular privileges. Just as the capitalists try to escape this levelling process through monopolisation, so organised labour groups try to secure their special positions despite the class-needs of the proletariat as a whole. These special interests are bound to become 'national' interests. By defending their political and economic organisations in order to retain the socio-economic privileges secured through them, the workers defend not only that particular stage of capitalistic development which guarantees their special position but also their nations' imperialistic policies.

IV

In order to maintain the *status quo*, basic social relations are more 'efficiently' organised and re-organised. Present-day re-organisation within the social class structure is totalitarian in character. Ideology, too, becomes totalitarian both as a precondition and as a result of this re-organisation. Non-totalitarian organisations turn totalitarian in an attempt to preserve themselves. In totalitarian nations the so-called labour organisations act exclusively on behalf of the ruling classes. They do so in 'democratic' countries too, although in a less obvious manner and with a partly different ideology. Apparently there is no way to replace these organisations with new ones of a revolutionary character – a hopeless situation for those who want to *organise* the new society within the shell of the old and for those still bent upon 'improvements' within the *status quo*, since all reforms would now require totalitarian means. Bourgeois democracy within the conditions of *laissez faire* – that is, the social situation in which labour organisations of the traditional type could form and develop – either no longer exists or is on the way out. The whole discussion around the question of organisation and spontaneity which agitated the old labour movement has now lost its meaning. Both types of organisations, those depending on spontaneity and those trying to master it, are disappearing. Propaganda for new organisations amounts to no more than the hope that they will spontaneously arise. Like the believers in spontaneity, the advocates of organisation, too, are now 'utopians' in face of the emerging totalitarian reality.

To some, however, the existence of bolshevik Russia seems to contradict both the statement that the old labour movement has disappeared and the contention that discussion about organisation and spontaneity has become meaningless because of altered social conditions. After all, those who stressed organisation had their way in Russia and continue to exert their power in the name of socialism. They may regard their success as a verification of their theory and so may also those reformist organisations that became government parties as, for instance, the British Labour Party. They may regard their present position not as a transformation into totalitarian capitalism but as a step towards the socialisation of society.

The Labour Government and its supporting organisations merely demonstrate, however, that the old labour movement has been brought to an end by its organisational success. It is quite obvious that the Labourites' sole concern is in maintaining the *status quo*. They are, of course, still engaged in re-organising the political and governmental structure, but the defence of capitalism has become the defence of their own existence. And to defend capitalism means to continue and to accelerate the concentration and centralisation of economic and political power camouflaged as the 'nationalisation' of key industries. It involves social changes which both increase and secure the manipulative and controlling powers of capital and government and which integrate the labour movement into a developing network of totalitarian organisations that serve none but the ruling classes.

If organisations such as those that dominate the British labour movement gain political influence and do not use it for revolutionary ends, it is not because their 'democratic ideology' forbids them to come to real, as distinct from governmental, power by means other than majority consent. Their own organisations, 'democratic' only in terminology, are determined by a bureaucracy and closely resemble the capitalistic democratic structure which presupposes the absolute rule of the owners and controllers of capital. Neither do they fear what strength remains in their capitalistic adversaries; their conservatism stems directly from their own organisational interests which are bound up with the pre-totalitarian stage of capitalistic development.

The totalitarian evolution of these organisations is a small-scale repetition of the transformation of the liberal into the authoritarian society. It is a slow and contradictory process and implies an inter-organisational struggle as well as a fight against competing political movements. It takes place at a time when the international extension of the capitalistic concentration process turns monopolistic into nationalistic interests; when the world economy is the monopoly of a few nations or power blocs and the direct control over production and marketing that exists in each advanced nation is being realised on a world-wide scale. Under these conditions, the labour movement is no longer able to support capital expansion solely by fighting for its special group interests. It must become a *national* movement and must partake in the re-organisation of the world economy in accordance with changing power-relationships. However, the labour movement, hampered by tradition and having vested interests of its own finds it difficult to turn from a mere supporter of nationalism into a driving force of imperialism. New political movements spring up to exploit this inflexibility and, where it persists, to replace the labour movement by a *national-socialist* movement.

To be sure, the national-socialist movement is 'national' only in order to be imperialistic. Bourgeois 'internationalism' that is, the free world market, was a fiction. It was 'free' only because it was free from competition against the leading industrial nations and the international trusts. Capital expansion while delimiting competition on the one hand spread competition on the other; old monopolistic positions were destroyed in favour of new monopolistic constellations. If monopolistic interferences in the 'free' world market hindered capitalistic expansion, at the same time they forced newly-developing nations, and arising private interests within them, to establish their own competitive monopolistic restrictions in order to secure for themselves a place within the world economy.

The fight to enter the 'free' world market, as well as the struggle to keep all newcomers out, hastened general capitalistic development at the price of a growing disproportionality of the economy as a whole. The discrepancy between the total social forces of production thereby released and the privately- and nationally-determined organisation of world-production and trade became the wider the more capitalistic progress was made. Unable to arrest the growth of the productive forces because of the competitive situation, re-organisations of the world economy in accordance with the changing distribution of economic power proceeded by way of crises and wars. This led, in turn, to a renewed emphasis on nationalism although all political and economic issues are determined by the capitalistic nature of the world economy. Nationalism is merely the instrument for large-scale competition; it is the 'internationalism' of capitalist society.

Proletarian internationalism was based on an acceptance of the fictitious 'free-trade' principle of the bourgeoisie. It conceived of international development as a mere quantitative extension of the familiar national development. Just as capitalist enterprise broke through national boundaries, so the labour movement gained an international base without changing its form or activities. The only qualitative change that could be expected in the wake of the quantitative changes was the proletarian revolution, and this because of the idea of the polarisation of society: which means that an always smaller number of rulers would face an always growing mass of the ruled. Logically, this process could lead either into absurdity or to the social expropriation of individual expropriators.

If the fight over the price of labour power was regarded as resulting in the steady growth of proletarian class consciousness and the creation of an objective base for socialism, the whole of the capitalist concentration process was also welcomed as a necessary developmental step in the direction of the new society. Large-scale business, cartellisation, trustification, financial control, state-interferences, nationalism, and even imperialism were held to be signposts of the 'ripening' of capitalist society toward social revolution. If it encouraged the reformists to envision the legally-won control of government as a sufficient requirement for social change, it also made it possible for revolutionaries to hope that even under less 'ripe' conditions socialism could be instituted through the capture of governmental powers. The quarrels between socialists and bolsheviks were over tactical issues and did not affect their basic agreement that capitalism's 'last stage' could be transformed to socialism by governmental actions. If the socialists seemed to wait for 'progress' to run its course and hand the government over to them, the bolsheviks were out to make progress and make it faster.

The Russian defeat in the first world war and the widely-supported need to 'modernise' Russia in order to secure her national independence led to the collapse of Czarism and to a revolution that brought the 'progressive elements' to power. The more aggressive wing of the socialist movement soon concentrated power into its own hands. To hasten the socialisation process, the bolsheviks forced the population to act in strict accordance with their political programme. From their point of view it did not matter whether their decisions were still of a capitalistic character so long as they were in line with the general capitalistic development towards state-capitalism and so long as they increased production and maintained the bolshevik government which was seen as a guarantee that in the end, despite all inconsistencies, compromises and concessions to capitalistic principles and capitalist powers, a state of socialism could be decreed from above. The point was to keep the government revolutionary, that is, in bolshevik hands and to preserve its revolutionary character through rigid indoctrination of its members with a basically unchanging ideology. By fostering a fanaticism able to oppose all deviations the bolsheviks attempted to keep the organisational machine more powerful than all its enemies. Government dictatorship, supported by a dictatorially-directed party and a hierarchical system of privileges, was regarded as the inescapable first step in the actualisation of socialism.

Beyond the growth of monopolistic organisation, state interferences in the economy and the organisational requirements of modern imperialism a tendency towards totalitarian control operated in all countries, particularly in those suffering under more or less 'permanent' crisis conditions. If the capitalist crisis, like its economy, is international, it does not hit all countries equally hard nor in identical ways. There are 'richer' and 'poorer' countries with regard to material, human and capitalistic resources. Crises and wars lead to a re-shuffling of power positions and to new trends in economic and political development. They may be expressions of power relocations already actualised or of instruments for bringing them about. In either case the capitalistic world finds itself decisively changed and differently organised. New organisational innovations become general, though not necessarily similar, by way of the competitive struggles. In some countries new forms of social control, ushered in by a high capital concentration, may be predominantly of an economic character, in others they will take on political appearance. Actually there may be more advanced centralistic control in the former than in the latter. But if this is the case, it only forces the less centralistically-determined nations to increase their political control capacities. A fascistic regime results from the social struggles that accompany internal difficulties and from the need to compensate, by way of organisation, for weaknesses not shared by capitalistically stronger nations. The political authoritarian regime is a substitute for the lack of a 'freely-'developed centralistic system of decision making.

If totalitarianism is a result of changes within the world economy, it is also responsible for the now world-wide tendency to supplement economic force by political-organisational means. In other words, the development of totalitarianism can be understood only in terms of the capitalist world situation. Bolshevism, Fascism and Nazism are not independent national products but national reactions to changed forms of world competition, just as the trend towards totalitarianism in 'democratic' nations is in part a reaction to the pressures for and against imperialistic activities. Of course, only the larger capitalistic countries are independent competitors for world control; numerous smaller nations, already out of the race, merely adapt themselves to the social structure of the dominating powers. Still, modern society's totalitarian structure developed first not where it was commonly to be expected – where there was high economic power concentration – but in the weaker capitalist nations. The western-trained bolsheviks saw in state-capitalism, the last stage of capitalist development, an entrance to socialism. To reach the entrance by political means necessitated their dictatorship, and to make it effective meant to be totalitarian. The fascist regimes of Germany, Italy and Japan represented attempts through organisation to make up for what was lacking in terms of traditional capitalistic strength, to find a short-cut to large-scale competition, since the general economic development prevented them either from increasing or keeping their shares in world exploitation.

Approached from this point of view, the whole capitalist development has been moving toward totalitarianism. The trend became apparent with the beginning of the present century. The media for its realisation are crises, wars and revolutions. It restricts itself not to special classes and particular nations, but involves the population of the world. From this point of view, it may also be said that a 'fully-developed' capitalism would be a world-capitalism, centralistically controlled in totalitarian fashion. If realisable, it would correspond to the socialist and bolshevik goal of world-government, planning the whole of social life. It would correspond also to the limited 'internationalism' of capitalists, fascists, socialists and bolsheviks who envision such partial organisations as Pan-Europe, Pan-Slavism, Latin-Bloc, numbered Internationals, Commonwealth, Monroe-Doctrine, Atlantic Charter, United Nations and so forth, as necessary steps towards world government.

In the light of today, nineteenth century capitalism appears to have been an 'undeveloped' capitalism, not fully emancipated from its feudalistic past. Capitalism, challenging not exploitation but only the monopolistic position of a particular form of exploitation, could truly unfold itself 'within the shell' of the old society. Its revolutionary actions were aimed at governmental control merely in order to break through feudalism's restrictive borders and to secure capitalistic liberties. The capitalists were thoroughly occupied with and satisfied by their extension of world trade, their creation of the proletariat and industry and their accumulation of capital. 'Economic freedom' was their chief concern and as long as the state supported their exploitative social position, the state's composition and separateness were none of their concern.

The relative independence of the state was not a main characteristic of capitalism, however, but merely an expression of capitalistic growth within incomplete capitalistic conditions. The further development of capitalism implied the capitalisation of the state. What the state lost in 'independence' it gained in power; what the capitalists lost to the state they regained in increased social control. In time the interests of state and capital became identical, which indicated that the capitalist mode of production and its competitive practice were now generally accepted. State-wide, nationally-organised capitalism made it apparent once more that it had subdued all opposition, that the whole of society, including the labour movement – and no longer merely the capitalist entrepreneurs – had become capitalistic. That the capitalisation of the labour movement was an accomplished fact was manifest in its increasing interest in the state as the instrument of emancipation. To be 'revolutionary' meant escaping the narrow 'trade union consciousness' of the period of Manchester-capitalism, fighting for the control of the state and increasing the latter's importance by extending its powers over ever wider areas of social activity. The merging of state and capital was simultaneously the merging of both with the organised labour movement.

In Russian bolshevism we have the first system in which the merger of capital, labour and the state was accomplished through the political initiative of the radical wing of the old labour movement. In Lenin's view, the bourgeoisie itself was no longer able to revolutionise society. The time for a capitalist revolution in the traditional sense had passed. In order to escape colonial status, the imperialistic stage of capitalism forced backward nations to adopt as their developmental starting point what, under *laissez-faire* conditions, had been considered the possible end of the competitive processes. Backward nations could liberate themselves not by traditional means of capital development but by political struggles in the bolshevik pattern. Challenging not the capitalist system of exploitation but only its restriction to particular groups of entrepreneurs and financiers, the bolshevik party usurped control over the means of production through control of the state. There was no need to submit to the historical scheme of money-making and capital-amassing in order to reach social control positions. Exploitation did not depend on *laissez-faire* conditions but on the control of the means of production. It should be even more profitable and secure with a unified and centralised control system than it had been in the past under the indirect control of the market and with sporadic interventions of the state.

If in Russia the totalitarian initiative came from the radical labour movement, it was because of its close proximity to Western Europe, where similar processes were under way, although they were dealt with in reformist, non-revolutionary fashion. In Japan the initiative was taken by the state and the process took on a different character with the old ruling classes being made the executors of state policies. In Western Europe the capitalisation of the old labour movement and its influence on the state had reached such a point, particularly during the war years, that this movement was drained of initiative with regard to social change. It could not overcome social stagnation (caused partly by its own existence and accentuated by the depressive results of the war), without first radically transforming itself. Attempts at bolshevisation failed, however. Unlike the Russian, the Western bourgeoisie possessed a greater flexibility within the 'progressive' democratic institutions and operated upon a wider and more integrated social base. It was in Germany, capitalistically the strongest country of all the nations which were defeated in the first world war and neglected by the division of its spoils, in which fascism developed last.

But bolshevism had pointed the way to power through party-activity. Totalitarian control by way of the party – the possibility of party-capitalism – was demonstrated in Russia. New political parties, partly bourgeois, partly proletarian, operating with nationalistic-imperialistic ideologies and with more or less consistent state-capitalistic programmes came into being to face the old organisations as new 'revolutionary' forces. With a mass-base of their own, fed by the insoluble crisis, with less respect for legality and traditional procedures and with the support of all the elements that were driving for an imperialistic solution of the crisis conditions, they were able first in Italy and later in Germany to defeat the old organisations. Even in America, the strongest capitalist nation, attempts were made during the Great Depression to secure the state's newly-won increased authority by the creation of mass-support for government-directed class collaboration policies.

The collapse of the fascist nations in the second world war did not alter the totalitarian trend. Although the independence of the defeated nations is at an end, their authoritarian structure remains. Only those aspects of their totalitarianism that were directly concerned with independent war-making have been destroyed or subordinated to the needs of the victorious powers. Although the seats of control have shifted and new methods have been invoked, there is more authoritarianism in the world today than there was prior to and even during the war. Moreover, 'victorious' nations like England and France find themselves in the same position today as the defeated nations after the first world war. It appears that the whole development of Central Europe between the two wars will be repeated in England and France.

Totalitarianism, however, is no longer restricted to the political ambitions of new organisations but is fostered by all active political forces. In order to compete internally against fascist and bolshevik tendencies, the prevailing organisations must, themselves, adapt totalitarian methods. Because all internal struggles reflect imperialistic rivalries, war-preparations push society still further towards totalitarianism. Because the state controls more and more of the social and economic activities, the defence of private and monopolistic interests requires the strengthening of their own centralistic inclinations. In brief, the social forces that were released in two world wars and that are attempting to find solutions within the *status quo*, all tend to support and to develop a totalitarian capitalism.

Under these conditions, a revival of the labour movement as it has been known in the past and as it still exists in emasculated form in some countries is clearly out of the question. All successful movements, under whatever name, will try to adhere to authoritarian principles. Whether social control is exercised in the form of state-monopolistic alliances, fascism or party-capitalism the degree of power in the hands of the controllers signifies the end of *laissez-faire* and the extension of totalitarian capitalism. Of course, it is improbable that capitalism will ever reach an absolute totalitarian form; it had never been a *laissez-faire* system in the full sense of the term. All that these 'labels' designate are the dominant practices within a variety of social practices and differentiations in organisation in accordance with the ruling practice. It is clear, however, that the new powers of the state, highly-concentrated capitalism, modern technology, the control of the world economy, the period of imperialistic wars and so forth make necessary for the maintenance of the capitalistic *status quo* a social organisation without opposition, a comprehensive centralistic control of the socially-effective activities of men.

V

If the end of the old labour movement made the question of organisation and spontaneity meaningless, as seen by this movement and dealt with in its controversies, the question may still be meaningful in a wider sense quite apart from the specific problems of working class organisations of the past. Like revolutionary outbursts, crises and wars also have to be considered as spontaneous occurrences. More information exists and greater experience has been accumulated with regard to crises and wars, however, than with regard to revolution.

In capitalism, the ordering of society's fundamental requirements regarding production and the proportioning of social labour towards the satisfaction of social needs is largely left to the automatism of the market. Monopolistic practices disrupt the mechanism, but even without such interferences this form of socio-economic practice can serve only the peculiar 'social' needs of capitalism. The kind of indirect relation between supply and demand established by the market automatism refers to, and is determined by, the profitability of capital and its accumulation. The conscious 'ordering' aspects of the monopolies, concerned as they are with their own special interests only, increase the irrationality of the system as a whole. Even state-capitalistic planning first of all serves the particular needs and the security of its ruling and privileged groups, not the real needs of society. Because the actions of capitalists are determined by profit requirements and by special, not social interests, the actual results of their decisions may differ from their expectations; the social result of various decisions, individualistically-determined, may disturb social stability and defeat the intentions behind such decisions. Only some, not all, social consequences of individualistic actions are known in advance. Private interests forbid a social organisation which could provide a reasonable certainty about the main consequences of its actions. This implies a social development of growing frictions, disproportionalities, postponed re-organisations leading to violent clashes between old and new interests, to crises and depressions which seem to be spontaneous occurrences because of the lack of organisation to deal with society from a social, non-class point of view.

There is no possibility within the *status quo* of organising social activities in the interests of society as a whole. New organisations are only expressions of shifting class positions and leave the basic class relationship unaffected. Old ruling minorities are replaced by new ruling minorities, the proletarian class is broken up into various status groups, layers of the middle-class disappear, others rise to greater influence. Since all social practical, concrete activity, if it is social at all, is social only in effect and not by design – by 'accident' so to speak – there exists no force in society whose own continuous growth delimits the social 'anarchy' and develops a more complete awareness of social necessities and opportunities, which could lead to social self-determination and to a truly social society. In a way, then, it is the number and variety of organisations in capitalism which prevent the organising of society. This means that not only must all unco-ordinated and contradictory activities result in expected or unexpected crises, but also that the activities of all people, organised as well as unorganised, are more or less 'responsible' for spontaneous outbursts in the form of crisis or war.

There is no way, however, to retrace in all its important details the process that led to crisis or war, and thus explain, after the fact, what particular activities and their arrangements within the developmental processes determined the catastrophe. It is easier, and for capitalistic purposes sufficient, arbitrarily to select a starting point, such as that the war led to crisis and the crisis to war, or less sophisticatedly, to point to Hitler's idiosyncrasies or to Roosevelt's hunger for immortality. Wars appear both as spontaneous outbursts and as organised enterprises. The blame for their outbreak is laid at the doorsteps of particular nations, governments, pressure groups, monopolies, cartels and trusts. Yet, to put the entire blame on specific organisations and particular policies for crises and wars means to overlook the real problem here involved and indicates an inability to meet it effectively. To point to the organisational elements involved without stressing their limitations within the 'anarchic' total social setting promulgates the illusion that possibly 'other organisations' and 'other policies' could have prevented such social catastrophes even within the *status quo*. The *status quo*, however, is only another term for crises and wars.

There was, to be sure, some kind of 'order' observable in capitalism and a definite developmental trend based on this 'order'. It was provided for by the growing productivity of labour. Increased productivity, starting in one or more spheres of production, led to a general modification of the productive level of society and to consequent alterations in all socio-economic relationships. The changes were reflected in altered political relations and led into a changed relationship, less or more contradictory, between the class structure and the productive forces of society.

What are the forces of production? Obviously, labour, technology, and organisation; less obviously, class frictions and therefore ideologies. In other words, productive forces are human actions, not something separate that determines human actions. Therefore, a previous line of development need not necessarily be followed. Social situations may be arrested or conditions may be created that destroy what has previously been built. But if the 'social goal' were the extension and continuation of a previous developmental tendency, history might indeed be the story of 'social progress' through the unfolding of its productive capacities.

That capitalism came into being presupposed a certain growth of the social productive forces, an increase in surplus labour and the capacity to support a growing non-producing class. To speak in terms of 'growing productive forces' as the determinant of the total social development was particularly apt under the commodity-fetishism of *laissez-faire* capitalism, for under its economic individualism it seemed as if 'productive forces' developed independently of capitalistic wishes and necessities. The insatiability for accumulation developed with productive forces rapidly and their enhancement allowed for continuous re-organisation of the socio-economic structure, and, in turn, the re-organisations acted as new incentives for a further raising of social productivity. It was said that capitalism, historically speaking, had justified itself because of its 'blind' but progressive development of the productive forces of society, among which the modern industrial proletariat was considered the greatest.

If it should appear that a full release of society's productive capacities would make possible the formation and maintenance of a classless society, it is perfectly clear that the immediately privileged classes will not give up their present-day control just because of the probability of a future socialist society. At any rate, on such an issue the owners and controllers of production cannot act as a 'class'; a 'revolution by consent' is nonsense. Accumulation for the sake of accumulation continues and leads to further capital and power concentration, that is, to capital destruction, to crises, depressions and wars. For capitalism simultaneously develops and retards the productive forces and widens the gap between actual and potential production. The contradiction between class structure and productive forces excludes the 'freezing' of the prevailing level of production as well as its expansion toward a real abundance.

If for no other reason than force of custom it appears probable that the immediate future, like the immediate past, will be characterised by further growth of the productive forces. This implies the sharpening of competition, despite all attempts at partial or complete control of production. Although larger capitalistic units have absorbed numerous smaller enterprises and secured temporary monopolistic conditions for the whole industries and combinations of industries, this process has merely intensified international competition and the struggle between the remaining non-monopolistic enterprises. In state-capitalism competition takes on a different but most all-inclusive form, because of the complete atomisation by the terroristic state machine of the mass of the population and in the bureaucracy itself because of the hierarchical structure of its organisation.

The application of new technological and organisational forces of production necessitates additional social controls. The disorganisation of the proletariat marks the beginning of the process that leads to the total atomisation of the whole population and to the state monopoly of organisation. At one pole we find all organised force concentrated; at the other pole, an amorphous mass of people unable to combine for a fight in their own interests. In so far as they are organised, the masses are organised by their controllers; in so far as they are able to raise their voices, they speak with their masters' words. In all organisations, the atomised mass of people face always the same enemy, the totalitarian state.

The atomisation of society requires an all-encompassing state organisation. The socialists and bolsheviks considered capitalist society inefficiently organised with regard to production and exchange and in other, extra-economic respects. The emphasis on organisation was emphasis on social control. Socialism was to be first of all the rational organisation of the whole of society. And an efficiently organised society excludes, of course, unforeseen activities capable of issuing into spontaneous occurrences. The spontaneous element in society was to disappear with the planning of production and the centralistically-determined distribution of goods. Not only the bolsheviks, but the fascists, too, spoke of spontaneity only so long as their power was not absolute. When all existing social layers submitted to their authority, they became society's most thorough organisers. And it was precisely this organising activity that they designated with the term *socialism.*

The contradiction between class structure and productive forces remains, however, and therewith the inescapability of crisis and war. Although the inactivated masses can no longer resist totalitarianism in traditional organised fashion, and although they have not evolved new weapons and forms of action adequate to the new tasks, the contradictions of the social class structure remain unresolved. While giving temporary security, the terroristic authoritarian system also reflects the increasing insecurity of totalitarian capitalism. The defence of the *status quo* violates the *status quo* by releasing new, uncontrolled, or uncontrollable activities. The most powerful controls over men are really weak when compared with the tremendous contradictions that rend the world today. Though all contradictions now oppose one organisation, capitalist society was never so badly organised as it is now – when it is completely organised.

If there is no guarantee that socialism must necessarily evolve in the course of further social development, neither is there any reason to assume that the world will come to an end in totalitarian barbarism. The organisation of the *status quo* cannot prevent its disintegration. As there is no absolute totalitarianism, openings for attack remain within its structure. The real social significance of its noticeable weaknesses is still obscure. Some points of disintegration, although theoretically conceivable, are still unobservable and can be described only in very general terms. Just as the modern class-struggle theory required for its formulation not only the capitalistic development but also the actual proletarian struggles within the capitalist system, so it is probably necessary first to observe actual attempts at revolt under totalitarianism in order to be able to formulate specific plans of action, to point to effective forms of resistance, and to find and exploit the weaknesses of the totalitarian system.

The apparent hopelessness and insignificance characteristic of all beginnings is no reason for despair. Neither pessimism nor optimism touch the real problem of social actions. Both attitudes do not decisively affect the individual's actions and reactions, determined as they are by social forces beyond his control. The interdependence of all social activity, while being a medium of control, also sets limits to all controlling activities. The labour process, in both its organisational and technological aspects, depending as it does simultaneously upon anonymous forces and direct decisions, possesses enough relative independence through its changeability to make centralistic manipulations difficult. The totalitarian manipulators cannot free themselves of specific forms of the division of labour which often delimit the powers of centralistic control. They cannot defy definite degrees of industrialisation without endangering their own rule. Resistance will thus be exercised in manifold forms, some meaningless, some self-defeating, and others effective. While some present-day forms of action may be disregarded, older forms may be revived because of certain outward similarities in the totalitarian structure with former authoritarian regimes. If trade union policy no longer implies action 'on the point of production' but manipulations between governmental bodies, effective new ways of sabotage and struggle may be found in industry and in production generally. If political parties express the trend towards totalitarianism, a variety of organisational forms is still conceivable for assembling anti-capitalistic forces for concerted actions. If such actions are to be adapted to totalitarian reality as attempts to overcome that reality, stress must be laid upon self-determination, agreement, freedom and solidarity.

The search for ways and means to end totalitarian capitalism, to bring self determination to the hitherto powerless, to end competitive struggles, exploitation and wars, to develop a rationality which does not set individuals against society but recognises their actual entity in social production and distribution and allows for human progress without social struggles, will go on in the empirical, scientific manner dictated by seriousness. It seems clear, however, that for some time to come the results of all types of resistance and struggle will be described as spontaneous occurrences, though they are nothing but the planned actions or accepted inactivities of men. Spontaneity is a manner of speech, attesting to our inability to treat the social phenomena of capitalism in a scientific, empirical way. Social changes appear as climactic outbursts of periods of capital formation, disorganisation, competitive frictions and long-accumulated social grievances that finally find their organisational expression. Their spontaneity merely demonstrates the unsociality of capitalism's social organisation. The contrast between organisation and spontaneity will exist as long as there exists a class society and attempts to end it.

1949

CHAPTER VIII

Karl Korsch: His Contribution to Revolutionary Marxism

Karl Korsch was born in 1886 in Tostedt in the Luneburger Heath and died in Cambridge, Massachusetts, in 1961. The son of a middle-class family, he attended the *Gymnasium* in Meiningen and studied law, economics, sociology and philosophy in Jena, Munich, Berlin and Geneva. Becoming a Doctor Juris of the University of Jena in 1911, he spent the years from 1912 to 1914 in Great Britain in the study and practice of English and International Law. The First World War brought him back to Germany and into the German Army for the next four years. Twice wounded, demoted and promoted according to the shifting political scene, he expressed his own anti-war attitude by entering the Independent Socialist Party of Germany.

While studying law, Karl Korsch recognised the need to proceed to its underlying material base, to the study of society. A socialist before the war, he became a revolutionary socialist during the debacle. With the merger of the Independent Socialists with the Communist Party in 1921, Korsch became a communist representative in the Thuringian Diet, a Minister of Justice in the short-lived Labour Government of the State of Thuringia and, finally, from 1924 to 1928, a member of the German Reichstag. During this period he wrote extensively on the current political and theoretical issues that agitated the radical post-war labour movement. He became the editor of the theoretical organ of the Communist Party, *Die Internationale*, and soon thereafter edited and wrote for the oppositional paper, *Kommunistische Politik*.

Dissatisfaction with the increasingly opportunistic course of the Communist International after 1921, and an acquaintance with, and understanding of Marxian theory superior to that of most of the prominent party theoreticians brought Korsch into early conflict with the official bolshevik party-ideology and led to a parting of ways in 1926. He now became the spokesman of the radical left-wing of the

Communist Party (*Entschiedene Linke*) which was still within the party but, because of the character of this organisation, was already regarded as an enemy of the Third International. After 1928 Korsch continued his political activity outside any definite organisational frame. He went on to write for publications accessible to him, prepared a new edition of the first volume of Marx's *Capital*, travelled and lectured in various countries, and wrote a study of Karl Marx for a British publisher's series dealing with modern sociologists.[1]

With Hitler's coming to power in 1933, Korsch was forced to leave Germany. He went to England, for a short period to Denmark and then emigrated, in 1936, to the United States. Aside from a teaching engagement in New Orleans, he spent his American years in the pursuit of Marxian theory. As in Germany, so in America, his main influence was that of the educator, of the *Lehrer*, as he was respectfully considered by his friends. An encyclopaedic knowledge and keenness of mind destined him for this particular role even though he would have preferred to be in the 'midst of things', in the actual struggles for the welfare and emancipation of the working class, with which he identified himself. The quality of his mind and his moral integrity set him apart, and excluded him from the opportunistic hustle for positions and prominence characteristic of both the academic world and the official labour movement. That his death remained almost unnoticed may be regarded as a final validation of his conviction that revolutionary Marxism can only exist in conjunction with a revolutionary movement of the working population.

A Critic of Kautsky

The impact of the First World War, and even more, the Russian Revolution brought the long-existing crisis of Marxism and the Western labour movements into violent eruption. Although split on theoretical lines into a so-called 'revisionist' wing, headed by Eduard Bernstein, and an 'orthodox' wing, represented by Karl Kautsky, the war revealed that both these social-democratic tendencies covered an identical reformistic, class-collaborationist and social-patriotic activity. The marginal left-wing elements of the international socialist movement and their most vocal representatives, Lenin in Russia and Rosa Luxemburg in Germany, ceased to operate within the shadow of Marxian 'orthodoxy' by demanding a renewal of the long-lost unity of socialist theory and practice.

Whereas 'revisionism', because of its total rejection of Marxism, was no problem for the radical socialist, Kautsky's 'orthodoxy' required a two-fold struggle against social-democracy and its apparent justification in Marxist terms. 'Back to Marx' became the slogan of this struggle in order to utilise socialism's radical tradition for the new endeavours of a revitalised labour movement. But 'What is Marxism' was also pertinent since both the disciples and the enemies of Kautsky's 'orthodoxy' appealed to the work of Marx. And how far, and in what respect, was the Marxism of Marx's time relevant under the changed conditions of the new century? The revolutionary conditions in the wake of the war brought with them a new interest in Marxian theory.

From 1922 to 1925, Korsch wrote a series of essays[2] against Kautsky's 'orthodoxy' and urged restoration of Marxism's revolutionary content. Korsch returned to a systematic, critical analysis[3] of 'doctrinaire Marxism' on the publication of Kautsky's *The Materialistic Conception of History* in which the author himself abandoned his earlier 'orthodox' point of view. Although Kautsky's terminology remained largely unchanged, his interpretation of the Marxian text now openly aided the revisionist emasculation of the socialist movement. His ideas with regard to development, society, the state, the class struggle and revolution, as Korsch pointed out, served the bourgeoisie rather than the working class. This found its definite theoretical expression in Kautsky's attempt to represent the materialist conception of history as an independent 'science' which was not necessarily associated with the proletarian class struggle. For Korsch this implied the transformation of Marxism into a mere ideology which, by not recognising its own pre-conditions, imagines itself as a 'pure science'.

It was in this ideological form that the dialectical materialism of Marx came to dominate the socialist movement, and it was in this form that it lost its revolutionary meaning. Notwithstanding the designation 'scientific socialism' as against the utopian socialists, Marxism, according to Korsch, is not a 'science' and cannot become a 'science' in the bourgeois sense of the term. Marx's *Capital*, for instance, is not political economy but the 'critique of political economy' from the standpoint of the proletariat. Likewise, with regard to all other aspects of the Marxian system, it is concerned not with supplanting bourgeois philosophy, history or sociology with a new philosophy, history or sociology, but with the criticism of the whole of bourgeois theory and practice. It has no intention of becoming a 'pure science' but uncovers the 'impure' ideological and class-conditioned character of bourgeois science and philosophy.

In his youth Marx accepted a philosophical standpoint which he himself, in a later-developed terminology, characterised as an ideological position from which he had to free himself. From ideological criticism he proceeded to the 'criticism of ideology' and from there to the 'critique' of political economy. The materialistic conception of history, i.e. Marx's proposition that "the economic structure of society constitutes a real foundation on which rise legal and political superstructures and to which correspond definite forms of social consciousness", was gained not from a scientific or philosophical attempt to discover 'general laws of social change' but from the materialistic criticism of bourgeois society and its ideology.

Marxism, in Korsch's view, constitutes neither a positive materialistic philosophy nor a positive science; and all its propositions are specific, historical and concrete, including those that are apparently universal. Even the dialectical philosophy of Hegel, the criticism of which formed the starting point of Marx's own development, cannot properly be understood except in connection with social revolution and not then as a philosophy of revolution in general, but only as the conceptual expression of the bourgeois revolution. As such it does not reflect the entire process of this revolution, but only its closing phase, as indicated by its reconciliation with the immediately-given reality.

With the revolutionary process a thing of the past, the dialectical relationship between the real development and the development of ideas lost its meaning for the bourgeoisie; not so, however, for the proletarian class subjected to their rule and exploitation. Just as bourgeois theory cannot transcend the social practice of bourgeois society, except in idealist-ideological fashion, so it could not go beyond, but only away from Hegel's philosophy. It could not discover the rational kernel within its mystifying hull, nor subject it to a materialistic critique which would lay bare, with prevailing class relations, the historical limitations of bourgeois society.

This was possible only from the standpoint of the proletariat, from its actual opposition to bourgeois class society. The dialectical point of view, then, involved the whole historical process which started with the bourgeois revolution and culminated in the idealistic philosophy of Hegel, only to bring forth the revolutionary movement of the working class and its theoretical expression in Marxism. This was not the theory of a proletarian movement that had developed on its own basis, but a theory that had just emerged from the bourgeois revolution and which, therefore, in content and form, still carried the birthmarks of bourgeois-revolutionary theory.

Neither Marx nor Engels denied the historical connection between their materialistic theories and bourgeois philosophy, which also connects the bourgeois with the proletarian revolution. But this connection does not imply, so Korsch relates in *Marxism and*

Philosophy, that socialist theory in its further independent development retains its philosophical character, nor that the *Jacobinism* of bourgeois-revolutionary theory remains an aspect of the proletarian revolution. In fact, Marx and Engels ceased to consider their materialistic position as a philosophical one and spoke of the end of all philosophy. But what they meant thereby, according to Korsch, was not a mere preference for the various positive sciences to philosophy. Rather, their own materialistic position was the theoretical expression of an actually-occurring revolutionary process which would abolish bourgeois science and philosophy by abolishing the material conditions and social relations which found their ideological expression in bourgeois science and philosophy.

Although one of Marx's *Theses on Feuerbach* states that "the philosophers have only interpreted the world in various ways; the point, however, is to change it", this change itself is both theoretical and practical. In Korsch's interpretation it is thus impossible to ignore philosophy and equally impossible to remove the philosophical elements of Marxism. The struggle against bourgeois society is also a philosophical struggle, even if the revolutionary philosophy has no other function than that of partaking in the changing of the existing world. Korsch held that Marx's materialism, in contradistinction to Feuerbach's abstract natural materialism was and has always remained a historical, dialectical materialism, i.e. a materialism incorporating, comprehending and altering the totality of the historically-given social conditions. The relative neglect of philosophy on the part of the mature Marx does not affect his recognition that ideology and philosophy are real social forces which must be overcome both on their own grounds and by a change in the conditions that they relate to.

The Russian Revolution and its Aftermath

Karl Korsch's fresh concern with the relation between Marxism and philosophy sprang not from a specific interest in philosophy but rather from the need and desire to free the prevailing Marxism from its ideological and dogmatic encumbrances. It was a theoretical consequence of the new revolutionary trend released by war and revolution; for Marxism, which illuminates the dialectical relationship between social consciousness and its material base, is applicable to Marxism itself and to the labour movement. There was nothing surprising in the fact that the Marxism of 1848 and the *Communist Manifesto* was something other than the Marxist movement which developed – together with an expanding capitalism – in a non-revolutionary period of long duration which came to its temporary end only with the revolutionary upheavals of the First World War. Marxist 'revisionism' was merely the theory of a non-revolutionary practice and Marxist 'orthodoxy' was a theory divorced from all practice, which thus served as an indirect, ideological support of bourgeois reformism.

The new revolutionary movement initiated by the Russian Revolution saw itself restoring original Marxism. In Korsch's view, this could only be an apparent and ideological restoration which would not eliminate the need for a further development of Marxist theory and practice in accordance with the specific historical situation in which the revolutionary movement found itself. Yet as a first attempt to combat the non-revolutionary and therefore counter-revolutionary practice of the reformist movement, the Marxism of Marx was an advance by raising anew the questions of revolution and the dictatorship of the proletariat.

The revolutionary movement fought under the slogan, 'All Power to the Workers' Councils' . However vague the ideas behind the slogan, it expressed the revolutionary will of the class-conscious proletariat to end capitalist society. Even if, with regard to Russia, there existed from the very beginning a wide and apparently unbridgeable gap between the soviet idea and the possibility of its realisation, this was no reason not to attempt a revolutionary solution in nations more fortunate in this respect. If the proletarian revolution in the West should succeed it would, perhaps, provide the very conditions for a socialist development in industrially less-advanced nations. Like all revolutionaries of the time, Korsch sided with the Bolshevik Revolution by siding with the revolutionary workers in Germany and elsewhere.

By 1921, however, the post-war revolutionary wave began to subside and with it the hope for world revolution. Counter-revolution in the West was bound to affect the character of the Russian Revolution whose national restrictions, whatever its early international aspirations, limited its revolutionary potentialities and turned it, finally, into one particular aspect of the international counter-revolution. The bolshevik regime in Russia could maintain itself only by doing concretely what it was ideologically obliged to deny, namely, to expand and extend the capitalist mode of production. Since this had not been the original goal of bolshevism, the goal itself now stood revealed as a mere ideological one, unrelated to the country's economic structure and to the class forces within it, and as such it continued to exist. Marxism as ideology served the non-Marxian practice of transforming Russia into a modern capitalist state.

Under these circumstances it was no surprise that Korsch's *Marxism and Philosophy* should disturb not only Kautsky and his disciples but the bolshevik ideologists as well. To apply the materialist conception of history to Marxism itself was to unmask the differences between the theory and practice of the whole of the existing socialist movement. The quickly-established common front against Korsch's work revealed that the Leninist movement was still part and parcel of Kautsky's 'orthodoxy'. And just as Kautsky's ideological adherence to the 'final aims' of socialism only served Bernstein's 'aimless' reformism, so Lenin's dogmatism could only function as the false consciousness of a counter-revolutionary practice.

Ideologists of the Third International declared *Marxism and Philosophy* a 'revisionist heresy'. Since they accepted Lenin's and Kautsky's 'orthodoxy' as Marxism they were of course right. The debate[4] around Korsch's work, which was apparently strictly theoretical, soon took on a more political character. Communist strategy in the post-war world, which embraced participation in socialist governments where possible and revolutionary uprisings when opportune, suffered a decisive defeat in the German political occurrences of 1923. This led to new internal crises in the communist movement. There were right and ultra-right, left and ultra-left tendencies, all vying for control of the various national organisations and of the Third International. Deviations from the official, even though shifting, party-line by one or another group, were attacked not only as tactical differences but as digressions from Marxism itself. Korsch's criticism of communist policies after the 1923 events was considered a consequence of the 'heretical' position displayed in *Marxism and Philosophy*. But not before 1926 were Korsch and his group actually expelled.

From the vantage point of 1926 the revolutionary upheavals of the First World War appeared as feeble as they actually had been. But capitalism was far from being stabilised and a new revolutionary wave remained a possibility. To prepare for it required, in Korsch's view[5], a sharpening not a softening of the class struggle and a greater determination to win political power. But while the possibility of a new rising was not excluded, the counter-revolution gained strength. All the anti-communist forces from the reactionary *Right* to the reformist *Left* combined against a revolutionary solution of the existing crisis conditions. They found in the bolshevik need to maintain and consolidate the party's power in Russia and in the world at large an undesired but effective ally. The international communist movement became a political instrument of the Russian state and thus ceased being a revolutionary force in the Marxian sense. To subordinate international communism to Russia's national needs, so it appeared to Korsch, was to repeat the performance of the Second International on the eve of the First World War - sacrificing proletarian internationalism to national imperialism.

It now no longer made sense to criticise bolshevik policy in detail, for what determined this policy was not a mistaken reading of the real situation with respect to proletarian aspirations, or the absence of such aspirations; nor was it determined by a wrong theory which could be corrected by way of discussion. Rather, it found its direct source in the specific and concrete needs of the Russian state, its economy, its national interests, and in those of its new ruling class, the bolshevik decision-makers and their large bureaucratic retinue. Proletarian communism had to dissociate itself from Russia and the Third International as, previously, it had to break away from social-reformism and the Second International. With this, of course, and for the time being, proletarian communism itself was doomed. The combined ideological and actual powers of traditional capitalism, its social-reformist supporters, and Russia's state-capitalism in Marxian disguise were more than enough to destroy a revolutionary minority not yet able to acknowledge defeat.

No attempt was made by Korsch or his new friends in the so-called 'ultra-left' communist groupings[6] to advocate the capture or the reform of the organisations of the Third International, or to line up with one or the other of the bolshevik factions fighting for control of the Russian state-apparatus in support of one or another tactical move to safeguard the bolshevik regime. What was important to Korsch, however, was an emerging proletarian opposition to the new bolshevik state-capitalist, or state-socialist, form of capital production. As regards Russia, it was the *workers opposition*, known under the name of one of its founders, Sapronov, with which Korsch established contact because it stressed the class character of the proletarian struggle against the Russian Communist Party. This group realised that its fight had to be waged outside the party, among the workers generally. But along with all other oppositional groups, the *workers opposition*, too, fell victim to the rising Stalinist terror.

Proletarian Self-determination

What the Second International failed to complete, namely, transforming the labour movement into organisations controlling the workers, was now completed by the Third International. Proletarian self-determination would have to assert itself against all existing labour organisations whether of an economic or a political character. The traditional political party of bourgeois democracy, as well as trade-unionism in its craft or industrial form, were now manipulative instruments in the hands of huge labour bureaucracies that identified their special interests with the social *status quo*, or were becoming government institutions of control and dependence. It was obvious that the organisational forms in which Marx and Engels, under entirely different conditions, had set their hopes for the development of proletarian class consciousness, could no longer be regarded as emancipatory forces. Rather, they had become new and additional forms of proletarian enslavement. However reluctantly – due to the absence of new and more adequate organisational forms of proletarian class struggle – Korsch now came to recognise that the ending of capitalism presupposes and involves ending traditional labour organisations. In so far as these organisations still enjoyed approbation by workers, this itself indicated to what extent proletarian class consciousness was lacking.

Manifestations of proletarian independence through direct actions for working class objectives, however fleeting and localised at first, Korsch now perceived as so many signs pointing to a revival of proletarian class consciousness within the totalitarian expansion of authoritarian controls over always larger spheres of the social life. Where independent working class actions were still to be found, revolutionary Marxism was not dead. Not ideological adherence to Marxist doctine but actions by the working class on its own behalf was the decisive point for the rebirth of a revolutionary movement. This type of action was to some extent still the practice in the anarcho-syndicalist movement. Korsch turned to the anarchists without giving up his Marxist conceptions; not to the petty-bourgeois anarchists of *laissez faire* ideology, but to the anarchist workers and poor peasants of Spain who had not yet succumbed to the international counter-revolution which now counted among its symbols the name of Marx as well.

Anarchism found its place in Marxist doctrine, if only, as is sometimes claimed, to pacify the anarchist elements who shared in the formation of the First International. The anarchist emphasis on freedom and spontaneity, on self-determination, and, therefore, decentralisation, on action rather than ideology, on solidarity more than on economic interest were precisely the qualities that had been lost to the socialist movement in its rise to political influence and power in the expanding capitalist nations. It did not matter to Korsch whether his anarchistically-biased interpretation of revolutionary

Marxism was true to Marx or not. What mattered, under the conditions of twentieth-century capitalism, was to recapture these anarchist attitudes in order to have a labour movement at all. There was the closest connection, Korsch pointed out, between Russian totalitarianism and Lenin's conviction that working class spontaneity had to be feared, not fostered – that it was the function of non-proletarian layers of society – the intelligentsia – to carry revolutionary awareness into the masses, which were unable to become class conscious on their own accord. But Lenin only spelled out, and adapted to Russian conditions, what had since been long, if silently, accepted in the socialist movement, i.e. the rule of the organisation over the organised and the control of the organisation by its leading hierarchy.

The Bourgeois and the Proletarian Revolutions

The ideas of the bourgeois revolution – freedom and independence, reason and democracy -- could not be realised in bourgeois class society. Marx's critique of political economy was thus at once a programme of proletarian revolution towards the abolition of social class relations. It did not matter that the larger part of the world had still to experience, or found itself, in the throes of bourgeois revolutions. Where such revolutions had been successful they also created their own negation in the aspirations of the industrial proletariat. The bourgeois revolution was not the end but the beginning of a social revolution 'in permanence', that is, until it ceased to be an instrument of social development in the classless society. How long this process would take was not predictable. This depended on the growth of class awareness and the intensity of the actual struggles of the proletariat. Yet the existence of such awareness, and proletarian struggles for working class objectives even within the confines of the bourgeois revolution, justified the prediction of a proletarian revolution as the final product of capitalist development.

Meanwhile, however, the world belonged to the bourgeoisie and the revolutionary functions of the proletariat, with respect to both theory and practice, were strictly and exclusively critical – critical even of the shortcomings of the bourgeois revolution, for capitalism was considered the pre-condition of socialism. But the development of capitalism was hastened and its life-span shortened by the simultaneous growth of working class initiative and proletarian class actions. Whenever it was necessary to support bourgeois revolutions, it was only to gain a starting point for the proletarian revolution. And to do so without merely serving the bourgeoisie required a persistent and clear class consciousness which did not lose sight of the socialist goal. That Marx himself aided and abetted bourgeois movements of a national and democratic nature did not contradict his theory of proletarian revolution but merely indicated the still-existing gap between the bourgeois and the proletarian revolution, between the creation and the emancipation of the working class.

The failure of the revolutions of 1848 and the consequent capital development under counter-revolutionary auspices did not prevent the rise of the labour movement. This movement, which originated within the bourgeois revolution, adapted itself to the non-revolutionary conditions resulting from a compromise of the emerging capitalist class with the still semi-feudal state. But even in countries where the government was only the executive of the ruling capitalist class, the developing labour movement did not display a revolutionary character in accordance with Marx's expectations. The political programme of the Marx of 1848 had no real bearing upon capital-labour relations in an advanced bourgeois society. It made room for a social-reformist programme embellished with Marxian ideology wherever the traditions of 1848 were honoured.

Marx's support of bourgeois revolutions was not a tactical move to gain control of these revolutions and to transform them into proletarian revolutions and socialism, but was a real support of an upcoming class which, by its emergence, gave rise also to its counterpart, the proletarian class, and thus assured a new revolution by virtue of its own success. This support was bound to the conditions of continental Europe in 1848 and had no meaning outside these conditions. The Marx of *Capital* and of the First International no longer saw the working class as the spearhead of the bourgeois revolution but saw it as exclusively concerned with its own working class aims in its struggle against the bourgeoisie, which was no longer in opposition, but in control, of the feudal residue.

This was apparently not true for Russia. Here the social conditions seemed analogous to those prevailing in Western Europe in 1848. Both the bourgeoisie and the proletariat faced not only the semi-feudal conditions of Czarism but also the non-socialistic aspirations of the peasant masses. A social revolution was nonetheless at hand. But it was neither a proletarian revolution in the Marxian sense, nor a bourgeois revolution in the tradition of the French Revolution. Although it contained elements of both, it was, first of all, a peasant revolution in a nation capitalistically-backward but already under the control of the capitalist world market and thus embroiled in and partaking of all the capitalistic and imperialistic, as well as the socialistic activities and upheavals that constitute national and international politics.

Although Lenin conceived of the expected Russian Revolution as bourgeois-democratic, the actual revolution of 1917 was termed 'proletarian' because the bolsheviks succeeded in gaining control over the state; and the bolsheviks were a Marxist party. The slowly-established totalitarian rule of the party over the whole of society was presented as the 'dictatorship of the proletariat' even though the proletariat as a dominant class had first to be created by the forced transformation of backward Russia into a modern industrial state. The interval between the outbreak of revolution and the taking of power by the bolsheviks was viewed as the transition from the bourgeois-democratic to the proletarian revolution or, rather, as the compression of bourgeois and proletarian into one revolution, that is, as the elimination of a whole social developmental stage by political means, the creation of the proletariat and of the pre-conditions of socialism not through capitalist class relations but by way of Marxist ideology and the direct power of the state. This was an entirely non-Marxian position which, however, could be justified by conceiving the Russian Revolution not as a national affair but as part of a world-revolutionary process which, if successful, would embrace the less-developed regions of the world together with the socialist countries, just as previously, capitalism had brought all nations, despite all their variations, into a capitalistically-determined world economy.

So long, then, as there existed the possibility of its westward extension, the Leninist attempt to drive the Russian Revolution beyond its objective limitations was in conformity with the requirements of a Western proletarian revolution. Without this revolution, however, this was no longer true. But movements of the scope of the bolshevik revolution may be destroyed but they cannot be re-called. Once in power, this power has to be secured at all costs, for the alternative is not retreat but death. And staying in power was to accept the Marxist truth that social productive forces determine social production relations and therewith political superstructures, not *vice versa*. What in other nations had been accomplished by the bourgeoisie had now to be done by the Russian Marxists, i.e. the creation of capital by way of 'primitive accumulation' and the exploitation of the proletariat. That this was done without giving up the Marxist ideology is nothing to be wondered at, for in capitalism, too, the ruling ideology does not reflect actually-existing conditions. It is the function of ideologies to cover up and to justify an unpalatable social practice.

The purpose of this digression is to condense Korsch's ideas and attitudes laid down in a number of articles on the relationship between the Russian, the bourgeois, and the proletarian revolution. Just as Marx had to adjust himself to the reality of the bourgeois revolution and its aftermath, even though he saw capitalism as only an intermediary stage in a revolutionary process which would find its solution in socialism, so Korsch, and everyone else, had to take a stand on the questions posed by the bolshevik revolution and by its peculiarly non-Marxian character. So long as conditions made it possible to hope for a revolution in the West – a period coinciding with the so-called 'heroic' period of the Russian Revolution, with war-communism and civil-war – the stand to take was obvious. To oppose the bolshevik regime under then-existing circumstances was to join the counter-revolution not only in Russia but everywhere. Whatever the mental reservations, the support of the Russian Revolution was a necessity for the German revolutionists. Only when the bolsheviks themselves turned against their own and the revolutionists of the West – and indirectly but effectively sued for peace with the capitalist world – was it possible to turn against the bolshevik regime without simultaneously aiding international counter-revolution.

Although Marxism could elucidate conditions such as existed in pre-bolshevik Russia and other capitalistically backward countries, it could not provide a programme of social reconstruction for their revolutionary movements. Its relevance was restricted to the proletarian revolution in capitalistically-advanced nations and here the revolution did not stir; where it did, it failed. But where a social revolution succeeded, though it was not of a proletarian character, it took its ideology from Marxism, for the idea of revolution was irretrievably associated with Marxian socialism. It thus became necessary to dissociate these revolutions from proletarian socialism and to that end circumscribe the true and limited meaning of Marxian doctrine.

Marxist Political Economy

All Marxist propositions, Korsch pointed out, "represent only an historical outline of the rise and development of capitalism in Western Europe and have universal validity beyond that only in the same way in which every thorough empirical knowledge of natural and historical form applies to more than the individual case considered".[7] Marxism operates thus on "two levels of generality; as a general law of historical development in the form of so-called historical materialism, and as a particular law of development of the present-day capitalist mode of production and of the bourgeois society originating from it".[8] And here it is not concerned with the "existing capitalist society in its affirmative state, but with the declining capitalist society as revealed in the demonstrably operative tendencies of its breaking-up and decay".[9]

By being an effective critique of political economy, Marx's *Capital* was, of course, also a contribution to economic science. But in the light of historical materialism, political economy is not only a theoretical system of propositions, either false or true, but embodies a piece of historical reality, i.e. the totality and history of bourgeois society. Because this totality forms the subject matter of *Capital*, it is as much an historical and sociological as an economic theory.

Being subordinated to the competitive market mechanism and the exploitative capital-labour relations, the science of bourgeois economy has only descriptive and ideological functions. No matter how hard it may strive for practical applicability, its very structure as an 'independent' science deprives it of success. Despite its socio-economic character Marxist theory does not intend to enrich economic science but wants to destroy it through the destruction of the social relations which this science tries to justify and defend. Marxism wants to understand capitalist economy only in so far as such understanding aids in the destruction of capitalism; it is never 'operational' in the bourgeois sense of the term. Neither can this economic science "which the proletarian class inherited from the bourgeoisie, by a mere elimination of its inherent bourgeois bias and a consistent working out of its premises, be transformed into a theoretical weapon for the proletarian revolution".[10] To end the exploitation of labour "one must not apply a different interpretation of bourgeois economics but rather, through a real change in society, bring about a practical situation in which its economic laws will cease to hold good and thus the science of economics will become void of content and ultimately vanish altogether".[11]

According to Korsch, Marx's economic analysis applies solely to bourgeois conditions. Capital production is not a relation between men and nature, "but a relation between men and men based on a relation between men and nature". Marx's economic and social research, which ultimately transcended all phases and forms of bourgeois economy, proved "the most general ideas and principles of Political Economy to be mere fetishes disguising actual social relations, prevailing between individuals and classes within a definite historical epoch of the socio-economic formation".[12] There was no way to reach the classless society short of overcoming the fetishistic social relation of capitalist production and a truly socialist society could not be based on the 'law of value'. Korsch's precise delineation of Marx's social and economic theories opposes attempts to look upon Marxism as a mere phase in an unbroken continuity of economic theory, as well as endeavours to utilise 'Marxian economics' for socialism.

Marxian 'Philosophy'

The principle of specification applies equally well to Marxian 'philosophy'. Notwithstanding Marx's unquestioned acceptance of the genetic priority of external nature to all historical and human events, Marxism, according to Korsch, is primarily interested only in the phenomena and inter-relation of historical and social life – where it can enter as a practical, influential force. The inflation of dialectical materialism into an eternal law of cosmic development, which Friedrich Engels initiated and Lenin completed, is entirely foreign to Marxism. But the fact that it was introduced by Engels indicates the early transformation of the theory of proletarian revolution into a *Weltanschauung* independent of the proletarian class struggle. In this ideological form it could be used for other than strictly proletarian purposes and was so used by Lenin and the 'intelligentsia' in their struggle to modernise Russian society.

Moreover, because Marx's main interest at the time of his own revolutionary activity was centred on the creation of a political-revolutionary party, Lenin's emphasis on the party as against the proletariat appeared to be harmonious with revolutionary Marxism. And though Marx spoke of the ultimate destruction of fetishistic capital production by a fully conscious and direct social organisation of labour, his pronouncements in this respect remained opaque. They could be understood in various ways, particularly because Marx recognised the transformation from capitalism to socialism not as one revolutionary act but as a revolutionary process which, for some time, would still exhibit many characteristics of bourgeois society. The planned economy controlled from above, the new state-apparatus which realised party dictatorship – all this, when seen as transitory stages towards a stateless and self-determined socialist society, could well appear to conform to Marxian theory. For at this point Marx's scientific materialism changed into utopian expectations.

The fact that Lenin's 'orthodoxy' and its revolutionary application could be of service to a historically-modified but nevertheless capitalist revolution indicated that the Marxism evolved by Marx and Engels and the early labour movement had not been able to rid itself of its bourgeois inheritance. What in Marxian theory and practice often appeared as anti-bourgeois proved to be assimilable by the capitalist mode of production. What seemed to be a road to socialism led to a new type of capitalism. What in Marxian perspective seemed to transcend capitalism turned out to be a new way of perpetuating the capitalist system of exploitation. Korsch's criticism of Marxian 'orthodoxy', and of Leninism in particular, thus became a criticism of Marxism itself and therewith, of course, a self-criticism.

Generally, the reaction on the part of academic Marxists to the failure of Marxism was to cease being Marxists. Some comforted themselves by seeing in the disappearance of Marxism as a separate school of thought and the incorporation of its assimilable parts into the various bourgeois social sciences a great triumph of Marx's genius. Others merely declared Marxism *passé*, along with the *laissez faire* capitalism and all other aspects of the Victorian age. What they overlooked, of course, as Korsch pointed out, was that the Marxian analysis of the workings of the capitalist mode of production and of its historical development is as pertinent as ever, and that none of the social problems that beset Marx's world have ceased besetting the world of today and are visibly driving it towards its own destruction. They merely notice that at this juncture there is no evidence of a revolutionary proletariat in the Marxian sense and that, therefore, there will not be such a proletariat tomorrow.

But the proletariat not only exists but increases all over the globe with the capitalistic industrialisation of hitherto-under-developed nations. It grows with the further class polarisation in the advanced countries in the wake of the relentless and politically-enforced concentration and centralisation of capital. Even if, in some countries, and for the time being, the social consequences of this process may still be alleviated by an extraordinary increase of productivity, making for social stability, this increase of productivity is itself limited by prevailing class relations. In brief, all capitalistic contradictions remain intact and require other than capitalistic solutions. All that the present period of counter-revolution proves as far as Korsch was concerned is that the evolution of capitalist society had not reached its utter historical limits when liberal capitalism and reformist socialism reached the limits of their evolutionary possibilities.

For Korsch, all the imperfections of Marx's revolutionary theory which, in retrospect, are explainable by the circumstances out of which it arose, do not alter the fact that Marxism remains superior to all other social theories even today, despite its apparent failure as a social movement. It is this failure which demands not the rejection of Marxism but a Marxian critique of Marxism, that is, the further proletarisation of the concept of social revolution. There was no doubt in Korsch's mind, that the period of counter-revolution is historically limited like everything else – that the new social productive forces embodied in a socialist revolution would re-assert themselves and find a revolutionary theory adequate to their practical tasks.

1962

1 Chapman & Hall, 1938
2 Collected under the title *Marxismus und Philosophie*, Leipzig, 1930. (*Marxism and Philosophy*, separately, was published first in 1923.)
3 *Die Materialistische Geschichtsauffassung*, Eine Auseinandersetzung mit Karl Kautsky, Leipzig, 1929.
4 The debate included George Lukacs' *History and Class Consciousness*, 1923, which, like Korsch's work, was considered an idealist deviation from Marxism.
5 K. Korsch, *Der Weg der Komintern*, Berlin, 1926.
6 Kommunistische Arbeiter Partei, Allgemeine Arbeiter Union, and the political groups associated with F. Pfempfert, O. Rühle, and the journal *Die Aktion*.
7 Introduction to *Das Kapital*, Berlin, 1933, p.33.
8 *Ibid.*
9 K. Korsch, *Why I am a Marxist*, Modern Monthly, New York, Vol.IX, No.2, p.88.
10 K. Korsch, *Karl Marx*, London, 1938, p.90.
11 *Ibid.*, p.91.
12 *Ibid.*, p.114.

CHAPTER IX

Humanism and Socialism

Like science, industry, nationalism and the modern state, humanism is a product of capitalist development. It crowns the ideology of the bourgeoisie, which arose within the social relations of feudalism, whose main ideological support was religion. Humanism is a product of history, i.e. the product of men engaged in changing one social formation into another. Because it evolved with the rise and development of capitalism, it is necessary to consider the humanism of bourgeois society before dealing with its relationship to socialism, or with 'socialist humanism'.

Pre-capitalist social relations developed so slowly that changes were almost imperceptible. Absolute stagnation does not exist, however, and the rise of capitalism after the Middle Ages, which saw the end of one epoch of social development and the beginnings of another, was the result of many isolated, drawn-out but cumulative changes in production processes and property relations. The accumulation of great wealth and its concentration in urban centres, as well as the limitations on the amassing of wealth imposed by persistent feudal conditions, led to an intellectual movement opposed to the other-wordly medieval Christian discipline which had sustained the feudal social structure and the power of the Church. But like commercial wealth itself, the newly-developing irreligious attitude, which made Western man once again 'the measure of all things', remained for some time the privilege of the rich and their retainers. Humanism seemed to exhaust itself after freeing the mind of theology's dogmatisms and after its return to, and fresh appreciation of, the Greek classics.

Being itself an expression of a general developmental trend, humanism could not help affecting this trend, in turn, through its critical attitude toward the medieval Church. In this way it helped support the Reformation, even though the reformed Church could not adapt itself to humanism. Until the eighteenth century it remained an intellectual pastime, but ensuing revolutionary events brought it to full flower as part of the general ideology of the middle classes, which aspired to add political power to their growing economic importance within the decaying feudal regimes.

The revolutionary middle class identified its own specific class interests with the needs and desires of the large majority of society suffering under the tyrannical rule of an aristocratic minority. Its own political emancipation it saw as the emancipation of humanity from all forms of oppression and superstition. This was both a necessity and a conviction, even though the rich middle class had no real intention of altering the lot of the lower classes. Otherwise, however, there was to be liberty, fraternity and equality. The men of the *Enlightenment* felt themselves to be true humanists, opposing the supernatural and emphasising the truly human, to which alone belonged the right to fashion society in accordance with human nature and reasoning.

With the bourgeoisie securely established, humanism degenerated into humanitarianism for the alleviation of the social misery that accompanied the capital formation process. Although the capitalist mode of production was adjudged unalterable – it was thought to conform best to both natural law and the nature of man – social reformers, imbued with the humanist tradition, thought it nonetheless possible to combine the system of private capital production with a more egalitarian system of distribution. The harsh rules of natural economic laws were to be tempered by human compassion and charity.

The cockier the bourgeoisie became through its success, and the more the enormous increase of wealth overshadowed the plight of the working classes, the less did bourgeois ideology refer to the humanist past. Instead, Malthusian doctrine and social Darwinism questioned the rationality of humanitarian attitudes and policies which were found to contradict the natural law of the 'survival of the fittest'. Humanism was superseded by *economic man* as the 'final' and 'scientifically established' recognition of the true nature of man and the laws of nature.

The 'survival of the fittest' involves both force and ideology. The force brought to bear upon the 'unfit', i.e. the working classes, resides in the capitalist class possessing the means of production and its control over the political means of coercion. The ideology which supports this condition and, thus, the exploitation of labour by capital, maintains that capital production and the social relations at its base are natural relations independent of the influence of time. To make this doubly sure, old superstitions were revived and added to the new. Once more men were turned into passive victims of superhuman forces beyond their control. The humanisation process which had accompanied the rise of capitalism turned into a new and more powerful dehumanisation process through the subordination of all human endeavour to the new fetish of capital production.

The history of capitalism, as distinct from that of its early protagonists, is the history of the increasing dehumanisation of the social relations of production and of social life in general. In all previous social systems, wealth confronted labour concretely in the directly discernible social relations of master and slave, lord and serf, oppressor and oppressed. Slavery and serfdom were sanctioned by the gods, or by God, and could not be questioned. To make slavery convenient, slaves were relegated to the animal world, but their masters knew what they were doing when they put them to work. The landlord and the serf both knew their stations in society, even though the serf might, at times, have wondered at the wisdom of these arrangements. But, then, the ways of the Lord were inscrutable. Nonetheless, slavery and forced labour were human activities, to be suffered by one class, enjoyed by another, and understood by both for what they were.

The fetish of religion which helped secure these conditions did not becloud the real social relations at their base; it merely made them acceptable. In any case, the early humanists were not bothered by class relations, as their great affection for pre-Christian slave society testifies. Neither did it bother the middle class engaged, as it was, in replacing the feudal with the capitalist system of exploitation. Its concern was with the nature, or essence, of individual man, with human nature in general, and with society only in so far as it encroached upon the realisation of man's assumed potentialities as a species-being.

This was a philosophy of man appropriate for the still-embattled emerging capitalist society of individual entrepreneurs, who justified individual self-interest with the assumption that it was the very instrument for achieving the freedom of the individual and the welfare of society. Just as the revolutionary middle class identified its own specific class interests with the needs of society as a whole, so it identified the particularities of 'human nature' under capitalistic conditions with human nature in general.

In reality, of course, the abstract concept of individual man and of his nature was confronted by real men holding opposite positions in the social production process. The world of men was the world of buyers and sellers of labour power; their relations to one another appeared as market relations. Production for exchange was the production and accumulation of exchange-value – expressible in terms of money. But only the buyers of labour power enriched themselves. The sellers merely reproduced their wretched conditions as wage workers. The selling and buying of labour power could not, and obviously was not, an equal exchange, for part of the labour was not exchanged at all but simply appropriated as surplus-value, a process hidden by the market, or price, form of commodity production. However, the exploitation of labour by capital was recognised at an early stage of capital formation. Lamented by the exploited it was taken for granted by the exploiters.

This by itself, however, did not imply an *increasing* dehumanisation of society. Humanistic attitudes had evolved under conditions of class exploitation prior to the specific capitalist relations of production and could, perhaps, slowly ameliorate, and finally overcome, the class determination of the economy. This was indeed the hope of the well-meaning among the bourgeoisie, and of the early utopian socialists, who stressed the common humanity of man and appealed to their innate sense of justice to set things right.

II

If only for a short time, this hope was shared by the young Marx during his phase of *philosophical communism* and – in an extremely tortured philosophical form – found its expression in the *Economic and Philosophical Manuscripts of 1844*. According to Marx, and in context with his criticism of Hegelian idealism, man had gone astray by alienating himself from his true essence, in consequence of which he experienced the products of his labour as alien objects exercising power over him, and the external world as an alien world antagonistically opposed to him. Alienation was seen under the aspect of Feuerbach's materialism and was dealt with in a criticism of bourgeois economy. This economy was itself, however, conceived as a specific form of human self-estrangement. Marx deemed it necessary to make man aware of his essential nature and of the nature of his alienation. This was to be the function of philosophy, of a positive humanism. It was expected to end all forms of alienation – of man from his true nature, of man from his work, of man from his fellow-man and, by doing so, end the various manifestations of alienation such as religion and private property. Humanism, in Marx's view, equated with communism and communism with the end of man's alienation.

What was the essence of man? It was, according to the young Marx, what differentiated man from the animal. Whereas the animal is immediately identical with his life-activity, man "makes his life-activity itself the object of his will . . . In creating an *objective world* by his practical activity, man proves himself a conscious species being, that is, a being that treats the species as its own essential being, or that treats itself as a species being. Production is his active species life. Through and because of this production, nature appears as his work and his reality. The object of labour is, therefore, the *objectification* of man's species life; for he duplicates himself not only, as in consciousness, intellectually, but also actively, in reality, and therefore he contemplates himself in a world that he has created."[1]

But why did Marx bother with the nature of man in a work that dealt *mainly* with problems of political economy? After all, as he said, his real concern was with the "*actual* economic fact" of the alienation of the labourer from his product, which then confronts the labourer as an alien and independent power. The product of labour, Marx wrote, "is labour which has been congealed in an object, which has become material: it is the *objectification* of labour. Labour's realisation is its objectification. In the conditions dealt with by political economy this realisation of labour appears as a *loss of reality* for the worker; *objectification* as a *loss of the object* and of object-bondage; appropriation as estrangement, as *alienation*. So much so does labour's realisation appear as a loss of reality that the worker loses reality to the point of starving to death . . . Indeed, labour itself becomes an object which he can get hold of only with the greatest effort and with the most irregular interruptions. So much so does the appropriation of the object appear as estrangement that the more objects the worker produces the fewer can he possess, and the more he falls under the domination of his product, capital."[2]

The fetishism of commodity and capital production of Marx's *Capital* is here fully anticipated, but relates itself not only to the specific social relations of bourgeois society but also to the nature of man as a species-being consciously producing the conditions of his life. Now the nature of man, as conceived by the young Marx, is the same for capitalist and worker – for those who find it difficult to realise their labour and for those who find it easy to appropriate the objects of other men's labour. What Marx said was that capitalism not only exploits labour but also violates human nature. The bourgeois assertion that its system of capital production was a natural system corresponding to human nature Marx countered with the assertion that it distorts the nature of man.

It did not take Marx long to notice that as a Young Hegelian he had been spouting the same 'rubbish' in his criticism of bourgeois society as the bourgeoisie had produced in its own defence. Within less than two years after his philosophical concern with the essence of man, he ridiculed this very concern in *The German Ideology*. He still held that production is man's "active species life", but he was no longer interested in man in general but only in "real, historical men". And what these men were, at any particular time, depended on *what* and *how* they produced. Their nature "depended on the material conditions determining their production. This production only makes its appearance with the increase of population. In its turn this presupposes the intercourse of individuals with one another. The form of this intercourse is again determined by production."[3] By developing their material production and their material intercourse, men "alter, along with this, their real existence, their thinking and the products of their thinking".[4]

Human nature, Marx now held, cannot be abstracted from the isolated individual because it derives from an "ensemble of social relations". Man can be no more than what men actually do in their concrete historical and social environment. By changing their environment, they change themselves; history may thus be regarded as the continuous transformation of human nature. This is not to say that there are no fixed drives which are characteristic of man and which changing social circumstances may only be able to modify in their form and direction. But these do not affect the mutability of human nature in the course of social and historical development.

In any case, society means relations between individuals, not the individual. One cannot say, for instance, that "from the standpoint of society neither slave nor master exist for both are human beings. That, however, they are only *outside* society; slave and master being social determinations."[5] Humanism can thus neither be related to, nor derived from, the essence of man. It refers to social conditions and relations which determine the behaviour of men. It must be produced by men, and – to come back to our starting-point – was the product of particular social and historical circumstances. Developed within class society, it was necessarily of a more ideological nature, i.e., it represented the false consciousness of a class aspiring to rule society and for that reason identified its own interests with those of humanity.

As an emancipatory value humanism was discarded by the bourgeoisie as soon as it gained full control of society. Humanism was revived by the working class to achieve its own emancipation – but with a difference. It was now recognised that humanism was incompatible with exploitation and class relations, and could become a practical reality only through the establishment of a non-exploitative, classless society. Humanism was still equated with communism. It was no longer seen as an ideal, however, to which reality should adjust itself, but as the real social movement which stood in opposition to the capitalist system. Socialist humanism was nothing less nor more than the proletarian class struggle to end capitalism and thus create the objective conditions for a humanist society, or a socialised humanity.

The struggle for a humanist society incorporates humanism as an 'ideal' because it is not as yet a reality. Socialism, by looking at things as they are, cannot help contemplating what they ought to be. But it does so only with regard to practically achievable ends as determined by existing conditions. What ought to be relates not to abstract ethical goals but to concrete social conditions that can be changed for the better, that is, to what men, at any given time, consider to be better. This excludes, of course, all those who are satisfied with existing conditions which, generally, means the ruling and privileged classes. Only those intent on improving their lot by way of social change will adhere to the practical ethics of social change that find their expression in the requirements of the social struggle itself. Individualism gives way here to class consciousness and economic self-interest to proletarian solidarity, as preconditions for establishing a society which, in its existence and further development, will no longer be determined by class relations and will thus be enabled to realise the humanist 'ideals'.

Humanism as a practical reality presupposes socialism. Until then neither man, nor men, but only a particular social class of men will attempt to change its ideological state into a weapon for its concrete realisation. This attempt is at once a practical struggle against existing oppression and misery, a taking of sides against all forms of inhumanity perpetrated in defence of the *status quo*. The socialist movement is thus an ethical movement in so far as morals involve actual human behaviour and not 'eternal truths' associated with the nature, or God-given nature, of man. It will attempt within its own ranks, and within society at large, to realise those historically-evolved rules, norms, and standards of behaviour which assure and improve the well-being of all members of society, and will oppose those that serve only special interests. To do so means to lay bare the inconsistency of bourgeois morals within bourgeois practice, and to prepare for social conditions within which moral rules can actually be applied.

The fetishistic ethics of bourgeois society found opposition in the historical materialist ethics of the proletarian class. Bourgeois humanism was supplanted by proletarian humanism, expressed in the class struggle, and providing the means to humanist ends. These means, however, are not only determined by the ends they intend to serve; they are co-determined by bourgeois resistance to social change. The actual forms the class struggle takes on derive as much from the socialist goal as from the reality of existing power relations within capitalism. It is thus not possible to find 'unadulterated' humanistic means to achieve humanist ends. This could be possible only *outside* the class struggle, that is, through the realisation of humanism by the bourgeoisie itself, which is both an empty hope and an objective impossibility.

III

According to Marx, capitalism represents the present stage of a long developmental process of changing modes and relations of social production. This process was based on the social division of labour, which was, from the outset, a division of the conditions of labour, that is, of tools and materials, or, in modern parlance, of the splitting up of accumulated capital among different owners, and thus also, the division between labour and capital, and the different forms of property. With the growth of social production went the extension of exchange and the increasing use of money. Considered at first a mere medium of exchange to further social production, money, and the exchange it facilitated, soon took on an apparently independent character. The fortunes of the individual producers became dependent upon market relations, for it was only by way of exchange that social realities could assert themselves and thus control the producers instead of being controlled by them.

Bourgeois economic theory rationalised the discrepancy between private production and market exchange with the concept of the market equilibrium. It was assumed that the competitive price and market mechanism would lead to the most economical allocation of the social labour and assure to each and all the equivalent of their particular contributions to the production process. It was precisely by maximising private self-interest within the market relations that the latter, like an 'invisible hand', would bring forth the optimum of social well-being. All this is contradicted by the reality of crises and depressions and was theoretically disproven by Marxian theory. But what interests us here is merely the proudly-acknowledged fact that capitalist production and distribution are not determined consciously and directly by men, but only indirectly – by the vicissitudes of uncontrollable market occurrences.

This is only half the story, however, even though it is the whole of it for bourgeois economy which refuses to acknowledge the exploitation of labour by capital. Capitalistic production is the production of unpaid labour as capital – expressible in money terms. The exchange between labour and capital leaves surplus-labour, materialised in commodities, in the hands of the capitalists. This surplus-labour has to be realised outside the capital-labour exchange, and is so realised through the consumption of the non-producing population and the formation of capital. The increasing productivity of labour devalues the existing capital and reduces the amount of surplus-labour extractable through the medium of a *given capital*, which compels the capitalists constantly to increase their capital. This is not the place to enter into the extremely complex subject of capitalist dynamics. It is enough merely to assert what everyone may recognise for himself, namely, that capital competition implies the constant enlargement of capital. The control of the producers by the market is simultaneously the control of the producers *and the market* by the compulsion of capital accumulation.

Behaviour in capitalism is subordinated to the capital expansion process. This process is the direct result of the development of the social forces of production under private property relations, which, in turn, are determined by the class structure of society and its exploitation mechanism. The expansion of production is thus practically the 'self-expansion' of capital, for no capitalist can abstain from single-mindedly devoting himself to the expansion of his capital. Moreover, only as long as capital expands as capital can material production be carried on; the satisfaction of human needs depends on the formation of capital. Instead of using the means of production to satisfy these needs, these means, as capital, determine the conditions of social existence for both labour and capital.

The various manifestations of the 'alienation' of modern men, with which current social criticism concerns itself, follow from the fundamental fact of fetishistic capital production, which appears on the market as commodity fetishism. Because capital production must be realised through the circulation process, the drive for a larger capital in terms of money values and with complete disregard for the real social requirements in terms of human values, turns all social relationships into economic relationships, that is, human relationships can only be consummated by way of economic relationships and actually have, or assume, a commodity character. Everything is for sale and all can be bought. The social compulsion to accumulate capital compels individuals to put their trust in money rather than in men. And as only the possession of money allows for social intercourse, social intercourse itself it only a means of making money. Every man is a means to another man to secure and improve his own economic position, no matter what his interests may be in extra-economic terms. Although a social being, he is such only outside society. He may find his social behaviour both enjoyable and defensible, but actually he has no control over it and remains a helpless victim of circumstances.

Excluded by the objectively given conditions of capital production, humanism, as attitude and behaviour, restricts itself to the socially rather meaningless accidental subjective dispositions of individuals, and may, or may not, have beneficial effects. In so far as it exists, it is a private affair with no effect whatever on the cannibalistic nature of capitalism. Adolf Eichmann is, perhaps, the best exemplification of the degree of 'humanism' left to the individuals of this society. Feeling himself incapable of killing a single human being, he was quite ready to help arrange for the killing of millions of people by other men. Yet his case is only a more dramatic instance of a prevailing attitude. The individual sees only himself as real; other men he regards as expendable or manipulative abstractions. The various inventors, designers, producers and users of modern weapons of war may all be sharing Eichmann's 'weakness' but do exactly, either actually or potentially, what Eichmann was doing. And so do the capitalists, financiers, merchants, statesmen, politicians, scientists, educators, ideologists, poets, labour leaders and the workers themselves in the name of one, or another, of the fetishes that help maintain and perpetuate existing conditions.

This is not a new characteristic of capitalism but in its enormity corresponds to its present stage of development. To refer to the increasing dehumanisation is merely to note the expansion and extension of capitalism, and the simultaneous loss of the only humanising force operating within it, that is, the destruction of the socialist movement. Marx certainly overstated the workers' capacity to develop a socialist consciousness, just as he understated the resilience of capitalism, its ability, that is, to increase the exploitation of labour and at the same time improve the workers' living standards. In short, Marx did not foresee the full extent of the increase of the productivity of labour under capitalist auspices, which, in advanced capitalist nations, altered the conditions that had been expected to generate a revolutionary consciousness.

IV

This seems to be contradicted by the existence of the so-called socialist part of the world. In fact, the search for a socialist humanism is directly connected with the existence of socialist countries. These nations, it turns out, display no more humanism than capitalist states and, consequently, are accused of violating their own principles and ignoring their own potentialities. It seems as if the very means to reach socialism pervert the socialist end and that new ways must be found to avoid this dilemma. However, the immediate ends of these nations was not, and could not be, the achievement of socialism but rather capital accumulation, even though it was accumulation under the auspices of the state instead of private capital. Socialism exists in these states only in ideological form as the false consciousness of a non-socialist practice. It has nevertheless been accepted as reality even by the free-enterprise bourgeoisie, because from their particular standpoint, state capitalism equates with socialism merely because it dispenses with private property in the means of production.

Capital formation as the appropriation of surplus-labour in capitalistically less-developed nations presupposes the existence of at least two social classes – the producers and the appropriators, and the relationship between them will be a market relationship between capital and labour. Even if planning and not competition determines the rate of accumulation, the planning is done by the appropriators, not the producers, of surplus-labour. As previously, under private property relations, the producers are 'alienated' from their products. It is the rate of accumulation, decided upon by the state, that is, by a special group of people, which determines the immediate life-conditions of the labouring population. The decisions of the state cannot be arbitrary, for its very existence depends, internally, on a sufficient rate of accumulation and, externally, on a rate sufficiently competitive to secure national existence. Capital accumulation still dominates the producers of capital. Under such conditions, however, the increasing rate of exploitation cannot be immunised through better living standards which make life sufficiently tolerable for a free acquiescence in the prevailing social relations. Exploitation will be secured by authoritarian methods of control. There is no chance for humanism to raise its head.

The capitalist world, unable to transform itself into a socialist society, but still able either to neutralise or subdue the potentially-given social forces that could affect such a transformation, tends towards its own self-destruction. Its partial destruction during two world-wide wars merely prepared the way for its total destruction in a highly-probable nuclear holocaust. The recognition that war can no longer solve the problems that beset the capitalist world does not affect the drift towards war, for the relentless drive for political and economic dominance, either to gain or retain it, is the outcome and sum-total of all the asocial behaviour that comprises social life in capitalism. The political decision-makers are no less trapped in this *cul-de-sac* than the emasculated and indifferent masses. Simply by making the 'right' decisions, in accordance with the specific needs of their nations and the security of their social structure, they may destroy themselves and a large part of the world.

While it is generally granted that war, though improbable, may be released 'accidentally', a concern with humanism must assume that, while war is probable, peace may be maintained 'accidentally'. In that case, there arises the possibility of a new upsurge of anti-capitalist sentiments and activities. The capacity of private capitalism, in its variously diluted forms, to ameliorate the conditions of exploitation is clearly limited. This is apparent in the division of the labouring population in a decreasingly favoured and an increasingly neglected sector. The elimination of human labour that accompanies the further expansion of capital neither wipes out the proletariat numerically, nor kills its desire to live decently. The very expansion of the newly-developing capitalistic system, on the other hand, brings with it the growth of an industrial proletariat and thus the objective conditions of class consciousness. The resumption of the struggle for socialism would also be the rebirth of socialist humanism.

1965

1 Karl Marx, *Economic and Philosophical Manuscripts of 1844*, Moscow, pp 75-76.
2 *Ibid*, p 69.
3 Karl Marx, Friedrich Engels, *The German Ideology*, New York, 1939, pp 7-8.
4 *Ibid*, pp 14-15.
5 Karl Marx, *Grundrisse der Kritik der Politischen Oekonomie*, Berlin, 1953, p 176.

CHAPTER X

Marxism and the New Physics

The conflict between the East and the West, although it involves different ideologies, has little to do with different concepts of physical reality. Ideologies differ because material and social interests differ; 'physical reality', on the other hand, is quite the same for all the combatants. Nevertheless, in both camps, the ideological struggle is carried into the natural sciences – in the East, in the form of a rearguard defence of dialectical materialism; in the West, in the assertion that dialectical materialism is "the real root of the conflict between East and West, because it is the basis of the fanatic belief of Marxists that the world is bound to fall to them spontaneously and inevitably".[1]

Both sides insist, of course, that their scientific interpretations of the external world are free of all ideological encumbrances. While for the Eastern scientists and philosophers the whole of modern physics seems to verify dialectical materialism, for those of the West Marxism appears completely outdated because the idea of determinism has disappeared. The very term 'materialism' is rejected as belonging to the last century. During Marx's lifetime, it is pointed out, "nothing was known of today's relativistic and atomistic physics; matter was at that time what our senses conveyed it to be; physical measurement dealt with sensually perceivable properties of things,"[2] which is no longer true.

Marx, of course, had only the natural science of his period to rely on; but the changes in science since then do not affect his theories. Marx did not coin the term *dialectical materialism* but used the word *material* to designate the basic and primary conditions of all human existence. Hegel's dialectic merely formed the point of departure for Marx's critique of capitalist society. It was important to Marx because of "the enormous historical sense upon which it was founded," and because "it dissolves all conceptions of final, absolute truth, and of a final, absolute state of humanity corresponding to it."[3]

The materialism which Marx encountered was not historical, and the dialectic then in vogue was not materialistic. By pitting Feuerbach against Hegel and Hegel against Feuerbach, Marx developed his own concept of social development, for which Friedrich Engels coined the term *historical materialism.* This materialistic conception of history did not stem from the "physical determinism derived from Newtonian mechanics".[4] On the contrary, it developed, by way of dialectics, in direct opposition to the materialism based on Newtonian mechanics. It excluded the idea of human history being determined by over-riding 'natural laws', whether mechanical or dialectical. Although recognising the inter-relations between men, society and nature, it was, first of all, a theory of men and society.

Unfortunately, however, the persuasive power of historical or dialectical materialism – as it came to be known – was great enough to carry away even Engels, who spoke of its universal validity. While some tolerant critics found this merely amusing,[5] the less well-disposed used this over-zealousness as an excuse to reject the whole of Marxism as just an oddity of German mysticism. But while the notion of the 'universality' of the dialectic process is not defensible, neither is it essential to Marxism, which loses none of its force by omitting it. Marx, at any rate, did not concern himself with the 'dialectics of nature'. However, it is not the ideas of Marx but 'Marxism', as the ideology of the rising European labour movement and of the self-declared 'socialist' states of the Eastern power bloc, that nourishes Western anti-Marxism. And it is for this reason that the struggle between the 'Marxist' East and the anti-Marxist West, however real, tells us nothing about the validity or invalidity of Marxism for our time.

Marxism as Ideology

The pre-capitalist world was agitated by the question of the primacy of spirit or nature. "Those who asserted the primacy of spirit to nature comprised the camp of idealism. The others, who regarded nature as primary, belonged to the various schools of materialism."[6] In opposing both the conditions and the religious ideologies of the feudal past, the revolutionary middle class was materialistic. It considered nature as objectively-given reality and man as determined by natural laws. The natural sciences were to explain his life and actions and, with the function of his brain, his sensations and consciousness. Freed from religious superstitions, science devoted itself to the discovery of natural laws, and Newtonian mechanics served as the basis for a growing conviction that all natural phenomena follow definite causal rules.

Radical middle class materialism lost its ideological urgency with the establishment of the bourgeoisie as the ruling class. The emancipation of natural science from theology could not be extended to the emancipation of society from religion. As Napoleon expressed it: "As far as I am concerned, religion is not the mystery of creation but the mystery of society. Religion connects the idea of equality with heaven and thus prevents the butchery of the rich by the poor. Society depends on the inequality of incomes, and the inequality of incomes, on the existence of religion."[7] The co-existence of science and religion in the uneasy bourgeois world found ideological support in idealistic interpretations of the further results of scientific development.

The early materialists, or natural philosophers (Francis Bacon and Thomas Hobbes) were convinced that through sense experience and through intellectual activities derived therefrom, it would be possible to gain absolutely valid knowledge of the external world. This optimism vanished with John Locke, who saw this knowledge limited by the very intervention of ideas. He thought it valid only to the extent to which ideas were actually in conformity with things. Although sensations and ideas related to the external world, this world itself could not be really known. Immanuel Kant accepted the proposition that ultimates (the thing in itself) are not knowable and that empirical knowledge restricts itself to the subjective forms in which man becomes aware of the objective world. It was for this reason that he saw the need for *a priori* concepts which brought order into experience and made it intelligible. Concepts of time, space and causality were inventions of the human mind and, though not empirically verifiable, were nevertheless necessary to science, philosophy and effective human activity. In its essential structure, the world was, then, a product of the idea. And just as the materialist theory of knowledge became for many materialists the materialist theory of reality, so for many idealists the idealist theory of knowledge became an idealist theory of reality.

In an attempt to carry the materialist representation of the objective world into the process of knowledge itself, Ernst Mach opposed both the new idealism and the old materialism. He insisted "that we cannot make up properties of nature with the help of self-evident suppositions, but that these suppositions must be taken from experience".[8] But, since all knowledge derives from sensations and cannot go beyond sensations, it cannot make statements about objective reality; it can merely fill out the gaps in experience by the ideas that experience suggests. Although he opposed the Kantian point of view, he also rejected mechanical materialism and regarded its objective world of matter, space, time and causality as artificial conceptions. Mach's critical empiricism supported, although unintentionally, a rising idealistic trend in the philosophy of science.

Marxist 'revisionism', i.e. the successful development of labour organisations within the confines of capitalism and the hope, connected therewith, of a purely evolutionary transition from capitalism to socialism, led to the loss of an earlier militant atheism and to an ambiguous acceptance of the rising idealist trend in the form of neo-Kantianism. Radical socialists began to defend the old materialism of the revolutionary bourgeoisie against the new idealism of the established capitalist class and its adherents in the labour movement. For Russian socialists this seemed of particular importance since the Russian revolutionary movement, still on the verge of the bourgeois revolution, waged its ideological struggles to a large extent with the arguments of the Western revolutionary bourgeoisie. The intelligentsia, largely from the middle class, formed the spearhead of the movement and was quite naturally inclined to adopt Western middle class materialism for their own purposes, that is, for the task of opposing the religious ideology that supported Czarist feudalism.

Because, for Ernst Mach, science had its origin in the needs of life, his ideas had a certain appeal to socialists. Some Russian revolutionaries, Bogdanov in particular, tried to combine them with Marxism. They gained some influence in Russia's Socialist Party and Lenin set out to destroy this influence with his book, *Materialism and Empiriocriticism.* The subjective element in Mach's theory of knowledge became, in Lenin's mind, an idealist aberration and a deliberate attempt to revive religious obscurantism. It was Mach's insistence upon the derived, abstract character of the concept of matter which disturbed Lenin particularly, because for him, as for the early materialists, knowledge was only what reflects objective truth; truth, that is, about matter. He thought that reducing objective reality to matter was necessary for the unconditional recognition of nature's material existence outside the mind.

The independent existence of the external world was not denied by Mach. He merely pointed out that our knowledge in this respect is limited because it is limited to sense experience. But Lenin found it "unconditionally true that to every scientific theory there corresponds an objective truth, something absolutely so in nature".[9] For him dialectical materialism had already discovered what nature is and does, if not as yet completely, at any rate approximately. "From the standpoint of modern materialism, or Marxism," he wrote, "the relative limits of our approximation to the cognition of the objective absolute truth are historically conditioned; but the existence of this truth is unconditioned, as well as the fact that we are continually approaching it."[10] With the discovery of the substance and motion of the universe, all that was left to do was to proceed in every separate field of knowledge in accordance with the principles established for nature as a whole. One could then not fail to have scientific practice conform with objective reality, just as the latter was bound to show up in every true scientific endeavour. The difficulty with this is, of course, that it is impossible to apply the criterion of practice to a theory of the universe, not to speak of the fact that nobody knows what nature as a whole is.

It was in this way that Lenin extended historical materialism into dialectical materialism. Nature has had a history and its dialectical pattern of development has been progressive in the sense that it has developed from the inorganic through the organic mind and consciousness. "Matter is not a product of mind," Lenin wrote, "but mind itself is only the highest product of matter."[11] The world was an "eternally moving and developing material mass which reflects a progressive human consciousness".[12] Human history is a product of universal history. In a certain sense, this is true and follows from the admission of the existence of the external world independent of human existence. And it is clear that consciousness presupposes the existence of the brain.

But it is also true, as Marx pointed out, "that the question whether objective truth can be attributed to human thinking is not a question of theory but is a practical question. In practice men must prove the truth, i.e. the reality and power, the 'this-sidedness' of their thinking. The dispute over the reality or non-reality of thinking which is isolated from practice is a purely scholastic question."[13] The atomic theories of the ancient Greeks, for instance, were based not on experimental facts but were part of a speculative cosmic philosophy and were opposed and defeated by other philosophical schools on purely philosophical grounds. This can no longer be repeated, for today's atomic theory is based on experiment and mathematical treatment, on a scientific practice in brief, able to verify the theory's validity. Not mere speculation but the work of chemists and physicists led from the atomic to the nuclear theory, to the new physics and the new philosophy associated with it. All real knowledge of the external world is the product of men's theoretical and practical activity in the actual world. But this knowledge produced by men can never be more than knowledge produced by men; it is not absolute truth. It is only truth about that part of the universe currently accessible to men, on which they can work and verify their theories. And as their knowledge accumulates with historical development, it leads to the continuous modification of knowledge by way of additional knowledge and sometimes to the discarding of theories made superfluous by theories referring to new discoveries.

The decline of the radical Western labour movement and the success of Russian bolshevism brought with it an almost complete identification of a specific Leninist version of Marxism with Marxism proper. Because the Russian Revolution was simultaneously a 'bourgeois' and a 'proletarian' revolution – in the sense that the preconditions for socialism were non-existent while *laissez faire* capitalism was no longer possible – it led to a form of state-capitalism which could be designated as 'socialism' only because it was something other than private-property capitalism. But the functions assigned to private enterprise and competition were now the functions of the bolshevik state. By appropriating part of the social product and allocating productive resources for the construction of a larger productive apparatus and a higher productivity, the bolshevik rulers turned into controllers of labour and capital.

While the capitalist's 'peace of mind' and the necessary acquiescence of the workers require some form of general agreement on the indispensability of capital and private initiative, the new Russian situation needed a different ideology that could make the interests of the controllers and the controlled appear identical. Marxism could somehow satisfy this need because it was formulated during capitalism's *laissez faire* stage. For there were no longer in Russia any capitalists in the traditional sense; and as to the government, it characterised itself as the executive of the ruling working class.

But since only the miserable are inclined to believe in an equal sharing of a miserable situation, the bolshevik 'elite' soon found that income differentiations, by serving as incentives for greater individual effort, could turn into a blessing for all. In order to improve the life of all in the long run, it was necessary to improve that of some immediately. Thus a new class came into being based on control of the state apparatus and nationalised means of production. To hasten productive developments, both the 'positive' incentives of power and income, as well as the 'negative' incentives of forced labour and terrorism were repeatedly advanced. Yet, the more the interests of the controllers and the controlled diverged, the more insistently did ideology proclaim their identity.

Under relatively stable social conditions ideological control may suffice to secure the social *status quo*. Under such conditions, designated as a 'free' or 'democratic' society, a struggle for ideas accompanies the social conflicts, and its class structure is simultaneously denied and admitted. Both the existence and non-existence of class relations, for instance, are incorporated in such concepts as 'social mobility' and 'equal opportunities'. Socialism would eliminate these ambiguities, for if there are no classes there is no way of moving from one class to another, and if there are no privileges there are no equal opportunities to partake of. Russian society, while supporting a privileged minority, necessarily adheres to the concept of 'equal opportunities', but it cannot admit the existence of class relations without destroying its socialist label.

Even if, out of fear of utopianism, Marxian socialism never became explicit, one thing was clear nevertheless: socialism implies a classless, non-exploitative society, and not merely a modified class relationship in a modified capitalism. In Russia, ideology only can claim the absence of class relations. Yet, the ruled cannot help being aware of existing conditions and of their unrelatedness to the state-prescribed ideology. This ideology cannot serve as a substitute for, but is an aspect of, direct physical control – an instrument of police power. The enforced absence of social conflicts finds not support, but merely expression, in the apparent unanimity of ideas.

It was in the name of Marxism and socialism that the bolsheviks came into power, and in their name they destroyed all their enemies. Even their internal struggles for positions and influence within the controlling hierarchy must be expressed in Marxian terms – either as adherence to, or as an alleged deviation from, a once-established 'orthodoxy'. The total unrelatedness of Marxian socialism to Russian conditions makes impossible any questioning or serious discussion of Marxian theory. Lenin's dogmatised 'Marxism' must be accepted as an article of faith. Only in this way can it be fitted into Russian conditions. And it is not only Lenin's use of middle class materialism in defence of 'Marxism' which indicates the half-bourgeois, half-proletarian character of bolshevism and of the Russian Revolution itself. There is also the bolshevik state-capitalist concept of 'socialism', the authoritarian attitude toward organisation and spontaneity, the outdated and unrealisable principle of national self-determination and, finally, Lenin's conviction that only the middle class intelligentsia is able to develop a revolutionary consciousness and is thus destined to lead the masses. The combination of bourgeois materialism and revolutionary Marxism which characterised early bolshevik philosophy reappears with victorious bolshevism as a combination of neo-capitalist practice and socialist ideology.[14]

Science and Society

"In social production," Marx wrote, summing up his materialism, "men enter into definite relations that are indispensable and independent of their will; these relations of production correspond to a definite stage of development of their material powers of production. The sum total of these relations of production constitutes the economic structure of society – the real foundation, on which rise legal and political superstructures and to which correspond definite forms of social consciousness. The mode of production in material life determines the general character of the social, political and spiritual processes of life. It is not the consciousness of men that determines their existence, but, on the contrary, their social existence determines their consciousness."[15]

Marx did not concern himself with the dialectic or any other absolute law of nature because for him "nature fixed in isolation from men – is *nothing* for men".[16] He dealt with society as an "aggregate of the relations in which the producers live with regard to nature and to themselves".[17] Although nature exists independently of men, it exists actually for men only in so far as it can be sensed and comprehended. The labouring process in its various forms, including scientific labour, is the interaction and metabolism between men and nature; it dominates, exploits and alters nature, including the nature of man and society. 'Laws of nature' relate not to 'ultimate reality' but are descriptions of the behaviour and regularities of nature as perceived by men. Perceptions change with the change of knowledge and with social development which affects the state of knowledge. *Concepts* of physical reality relate then not only to nature and men but also indirectly to the structure of society and to social change and are therefore historical.

Although specific social relationships, bound to specific forms of social production, may find ideological reflection in science and affect its activities in some measure; science, like the production process itself, is the result of all previous social development and in this respect is independent of any particular social structure. Concepts of physical reality may be shared by structurally different societies. And just as different technologies may evolve within a particular social structure as, for instance, the current so-called Second Industrial Revolution, so one concept of physical reality may be replaced by another without affecting existing social relationships. Yet, these new concepts are still historical in comparison with earlier concepts of physical reality associated with previous and different modes of production and previous and different social relationships.

Science in the modern sense developed simultaneously with modern industry and capitalism. The rapidity of scientific development parallels the relentless revolutionising of the production process by way of competitive capital accumulation. There is an obvious connection between science, its technological application and the prevailing social relationships. Although modern science is not only quantitatively but also qualitatively different from the rudimentary science of the past, it is a continuation of it nonetheless. Likewise, the science and technology of the hypothetical socialist future – no matter how altered – can only be based on all previous scientific and social development. There is no 'bourgeois science' to be replaced by 'proletarian science'. What a Marxist critique of science is directed against is the class-determined ideological interpretation and class-determined practical utilisation of science wherever and whenever it violates the needs and well-being of humanity.

Although science strives toward some hypothetical ideal objectivity, the application of science is guided by other considerations. Like the utilisation of other productive and human resources, it is subordinated to the requirements of class relations which turn the social production process into capital formation. The utilisation of science for prevailing profit and power principles may not affect internal scientific objectivity, but it affects the direction of scientific exploration. Because there is no 'end' to science and because its fields of exploration are unlimited, science can choose to concentrate upon one or another. The emphasis upon a specific field and a particular direction depends upon the needs, structure and superstructure of a particular society. There was, in the sixteenth and seventeenth centuries, an obvious connection between the concentration on astronomy and the development of world trade. There is an obvious connection between the present emphasis on atomic physics and the current imperialist military struggles.

In Marxist values, man is the measure of all things and science should be science *for* men. As socialism implies the further growth of the social forces of production, it also implies that of science. It intends to add to the principle of scientific objectivity that of social responsibility. And just as it rejects fetishistic capital accumulation, so it rejects 'science for the sake of science'. This fetishistic attitude towards science, supposedly based on an innate human need to search for ultimate reality, is actually only another expression of the lack of sociality in class society and the fierce competition among scientists themselves. The irresponsible, irrational and self-defeating disregard for humanity on the part of many scientists today, who defend their work in the name of science even though it has often no other but destructive purposes, is possible only in a society that is able to subordinate science to the specific needs of a ruling class. The humanisation of science presupposes, however, the humanisation of society. Science and its development is thus a social problem.

Materialism and Determinism

Marxism, not being a theory of physical materialism and not bound to Newtonian determinism, is not affected by the new physics and microphysics. To be sure, Marx had no way of rejecting and no desire to reject the physics of the nineteenth century. What distinguished his historical materialism from middle class materialism was his rejection of the latter's direct confrontation of individual man and external reality and its inability to see society and social labour as an indivisible aspect of the whole of reality. What united Marxism with middle class materialism was the conviction that there is an external world independent of men and that science contributes to the knowledge of this objective reality.

While Marxists accept the positivist emphasis on experience, they reject the notion that sensations are the sole source of experience – a notion which led some people into the self-contradictory sterility of solipsism and others to idealism and the indirect justification of religious beliefs. Although sense perceptions are individuals' perceptions, men extended the range and amplified the powers of their senses in quality as well as quantity. Moreover the "knowledge of an orderly external world on which we can act rationally is derived almost entirely from society. The scraps disclosed in sense perceptions by themselves would make no pattern but fit into the pattern whose outlines society has taught us. Indeed what we perceive with our sense organs is conditioned very largely by our education – by what our elders and fellows have taught us to notice."[18]

The concept of matter now implies something different from what it did a hundred years ago. While for Lenin, and middle class materialism before him, matter, composed of atoms, was the very stuff of nature, and for Mach atoms were a mental artifice not susceptible to sense experience, matter is now regarded as something 'in-between' because "matter as given by our senses appears as a secondary phenomenon, created by the interaction of our sense organs with processes whose nature can be discovered only indirectly, through theoretical interpretations of experimentally observed relationships; in other words, through a mental effort."[19] Matter was once conceived as consisting of indivisible atoms. This concept lost its validity by newly discovered properties of matter such as radio-activity. It was found that "material particles are capable of disappearing while giving rise to radiation, whilst radiation is capable of condensing into matter and of creating particles".[20] Einstein formulated the transformation of mass into energy and now the term, *matter*, when it is used, includes all the physical phenomena of which men are aware. Experimental methods were devised which recorded the effects of atoms and of the elemental particles of which they are composed. These elemental particles may be considered the ultimate units of matter – "precisely those units into which matter decomposes under the impact of external forces. This state of affairs can be summed up thus: all elemental particles are made of the same stuff – namely, energy . . . Matter exists because energy assumes the form of the elemental particles."[21]

These discoveries do not deny the objective existence of physical reality, nor its manifestation in things considered to constitute matter. Whatever science may reveal as properties of nature, and whether or not matter is considered 'real' or 'unreal', as a 'primary' or as 'secondary' phenomena, it exists in its own right and without it no immaterialist would be there to deny its existence. The material world is the world of men, quite independent of the fact – scientifically or philosophically speaking – that the *old concept* of matter is insufficient to account for physical reality.

The equivalence of mass and energy, of light and matter, extended the wave-corpuscle duality – at first discovered for light – to all matter. Like light, material particles can be pictured as either corpuscles or waves, and both pictures are necessary to explain their properties. According to Max Planck's quantum theory radiation is not continuous but, like matter, can be dealt with only in individual units. Emission and absorption of these units involves the principle of probability. The application of quantum mechanics to the problems of atomic structure by Niels Bohr and Werner Heisenberg led to the principle of uncertainty, of indeterminism, and to the concept of complementarity. According to the latter the description of micro-objects, such as electrons, requires both wave and corpuscle models; although mutually exclusive, they also complement one another. The uncertainty principle relates to the impossibility of ascertaining with accuracy both the position and the momentum of a particle simultaneously.

Because in their totality the elementary processes constitute physical reality, the indeterminist, statistical, probabilistic character of quantum physics led to a denial of causality. Not all scientists, however, are willing to recognise acausality as a fundamental aspect of nature. For

Einstein, quantum theory in all its implications seemed only a temporary makeshift – an expression of our ignorance. Max Planck held that the quantum hypothesis will eventually find its exact expression in certain equations which will be a more exact formula of the law of causality. And Heisenberg speculates whether acausality is only a consequence of the separation of observer and observed and is not applicable to the universe as a whole.

However this may be, the problem can only be resolved, if at all, by further scientific work. While some scientists hold that behind the statistical laws of quantum physics there are hidden, but discernable, parameters obeying the laws of classical physics, others think that causality in macroscopic phenomena is itself based on probability laws. While for some, causality once ruled absolutely, now chance rules absolutely for others. Marxism, which does not think in absolutes, accepts the state of physics for what it is, convinced that like any other state previously it, too, is transitory and is not the final end of physical knowledge.

Newtonian mechanics worked well on the macroscopic and human scale of phenomena. The knowledge gained about objective reality through our sense organs and scientific instruments did not perceptibly affect external reality itself. In microphysics, however, the interaction between the observed and the observer affects the observed phenomenon. Sense impressions and instruments imply the transfer of energy (photons) which forms an integral part of the behaviour of the atomic objects under observation. This inescapable situation, deplored by some as the definite borderline to all understanding of objective reality, induced others to state "that science stands between man and nature", and though events in the world of nature do not depend on our observations of them, nevertheless, "in science we are not dealing with nature itself but with the science of nature – that is, with nature which has been thought through and described by man".[22]

While this aspect of quantum physics is used, more often than not, as an argument against philosophical materialism and as evidence in favour of idealism, in a way, and differently expressed, it rather suits Marxism quite well. What stands *between* men and nature also *connects* men and nature. Marxism, for which knowledge of objective reality implies the indivisible inter-relationship between man, society and nature, does not bother with an 'objective reality' apart from that recognisable by men. If there should be no way towards 'absolute' objectivity, that degree of objectivity attainable is the objective reality for men. The recognition that nature and the nature revealed through science may not be the same merely compels us to the largest possible degree of objectivity, quite apart from the question as to whether or not it will lead to an understanding of 'ultimate reality'.

Microphysics is one of many human endeavours and though it led to new concepts of physical reality, it did not alter the human situation in the macroscopic world. The duality "between statistical and dynamic laws is ultimately associated with the duality between macrocosm and microcosm, and this we must regard as a fact substantiated by experiment. Whether satisfactory or not, facts cannot be created by theories, and there is no alternative but to concede their appointed places to dynamical as well as to statistical laws in the whole system of physical theories."[23] Space, time, causality, derived from experience, remain dependable guides to most human activities, quite independently of the over-riding or under-lying relativistic and atomistic theories of reality. It is quite certain that classical mechanics will "remain the instrument best fitted to solve certain questions, questions which for us are of the highest importance, since they relate to our scale of magnitude".[24]

Nothing is altered in this situation if the deterministic interpretation of classical mechanics is also regarded as a fallacy.[25] For causality and determinism do not refer to nature in its totality but to our inter-relationship with nature through which we discover rules and regularities that allow us to expect – and thus to predict – natural events with a degree of probability close to certainty. Although the early ideal of absolutely certain knowledge of the external world vanished in the very quest for scientific objectivity, 'natural laws' which allow for predictability retain their 'absolute' validity on the human scale of experience. And while the understanding of atomic processes implies probability and statistics, the utilisation of this knowledge leads to predictable activities as if based on cause-and-effect relationships. Likewise, "the notions of classical physics provide an *a priori* foundation for the investigations of quantum physics, since we can carry out experiments in the atomic field only with the aid of concepts from classical physics."[26]

Because indeterminism rules in quantum physics, and determination is out of the question "even in the simplest classical science, that of mechanics", Max Born finds it "simply fantastic to apply the idea of determinism to historical events".[27] However, historical materialism, in so far as it claims predictive powers, does not claim that these powers are derived from, or are analogous to, natural processes but that they are based on 'social laws' of development fortified by the evidence of history. To reject 'social determinism' it is necessary to demonstrate its impossibility in society and history, not by analogy with physical processes. By doing the latter, Born does exactly – only the other way around – what pseudo-Marxists were doing when they read 'social laws' of development into nature. If one analogy is bad, so is the other.

Society does not develop and function by chance but through human responses to definite necessities. Man must eat in order to live, and if he must work in order to eat, the work itself leads to a regulated behaviour on his own part and in connection with his obeying of, and his struggle against, natural phenomena and their regularities. When men work in groups and societies, new necessities and new regulations arise out of the social labour process. With the increase of productivity there develops social class relations and social regulations based on them. With the further growth of the productive powers of society the determination of human behaviour by external necessity diminishes while the determination by social arrangements increases. Determination is largely a social product; it is the social development itself which leads – with the recognition of the material and social requirements of production and reproduction – to predictability.

Because of the socially-produced character of social determination, Marx is neither a determinist nor an indeterminist in the usual sense of these terms. "In his opinion history is the product of human action, even while men are the products of history. Historical conditions determine the way man makes subsequent history, but these historical conditions are themselves the result of human actions . . . The basic point of departure is never history, but man, his situation, and his responses."[28]

In known history stages of human and social existence are recognisable through changing tools, forms of production, and social relationships that alter the productivity of labour. Where social production stagnates, society stagnates; where the productivity of labour develops slowly, social change is also tardy. But all previous development is the result of progress made in the sphere of production and it is only reasonable to expect that the future will also depend on it.

This indicates little with regard to the actual transformation from capitalism to socialism anticipated by Marx. It merely predicts that socialism is the next step in the development of the social forces of production, which includes science and social consciousness. Every class structure, according to Marx, both fosters and retards the general development of social production. It fosters it in contrast to previously-existing social relations of production; it retards it by attempting to make existing social relations permanent. Definite social class relations are bound to definite levels of the expanding social forces of production – all the actual over-lapping of old and new forms of social relations and modes of production notwithstanding. In our time, it is the capital-labour relationship, the basis of all social antagonisms, which fetters further social development. But such development requires the abolition of social antagonisms. And since only those able to base their expectations on a classless society are likely to strive towards its realisation, Marx saw in the working class and its needs a force of human emancipation.

Although Marx was convinced of capitalism's inevitable end, he did not commit himself as to the time of its departure. This depended on the actual class struggle and was certain only on the assumption of a continuation of the previous course of social development. Future events can only be based on present knowledge and predictions are possible only on the assumption that the known pattern of past development will also hold for the future. It may not; yet, all knowledge justifies some expectations and allows for actions which themselves will decide whether the expectations were justified or not. When Marx spoke of the end of capitalism, he also thought of the elements of a new society already present and unfolding in the 'womb of the old'. Capitalism had no future because its transformation was already an observable phenomenon. As it developed, it enlarged all its contradictions so that its expansion was at the same time its decay when regarded from a revolutionary instead of from a conservative point of view.

The Ideological War

While there is no connection between Marxism and physical determinism or indeterminism, there is also no real connection between the cold war and the different concepts of physical reality in the East and the West. Indeed, what possible connection could there be between the indeterminacy of nuclear physics and all the social problems that beset the world and give rise to its political movements? These social struggles were disturbing the world before the rise of the new physics and they cannot be abated by either science or philosophy. Political relations between East and West will not improve simply because physicists abstain from ideological interpretations of their work. This work, and its practical application, is the same in the East and the West. Where there is disagreement, it does not matter, i.e. in speculations as to what the physical knowledge of the future may reveal. Some Eastern scientists do not bother to embroider their work with philosophical interpretations; others try to fit it into the scheme of dialectical materialism so as not to violate the state-prescribed ideology in which they may also actually believe, just as Western scientists accept almost generally the ruling idologies of their own society.

At any rate, reality is always stronger than ideology, as is demonstrated by the recurrent need to incorporate the new findings of science and the advancements of technology into the prevailing ideologies. There was a time when Russian dialectical materialists denounced Einstein's relativity theory as bourgeois obscurantism, only, and rather quickly, to come to celebrate it as still another manifestation of dialectical materialism. Space-time, wave-mechanics, the structure of matter, in short, the whole of modern physics has been turned into so many revelations of the dialectics of nature and of its material substance. The principle of 'complementarity', i.e. the abandonment of a conceptually unitary picture of atomic phenomena, has been interpreted as yet another example of dialectical development by way of contradiction and reconciliation, that is, as a struggle between thesis and anti-thesis, bringing forth the synthesis.

As yet, however, the 'synthesis' is only philosophically anticipated by dialectical materialists to satisfy the Leninist criterion of absolute objective truth. Some Eastern physicists (not all) simply claim that the phenomena observed in microphysics with regard to both wave and particle are completely objective, whereas for some Western scientists (not all) they are in part subjective, because of the disturbing and altering interplay between observer and observed, and because wave has the character of a probability wave and is not regarded as an objective entity. Of course, the Russian physicists admit that the sheer objectivity of micro-objects is only partly recognisable but they believe that, in principle, it will be possible to establish their full objectivity by finding ways and means to discount the influence of the observer and his instruments upon the observed micro-objects. The application of atomic energy appears to them as proof of the objective character of atomic phenomena.

For Western physicists, all that matters presently is quantum theory in its present state and the problems to which it gives rise. This, of course, is also true for Russian scientists. And it can at once be admitted that their search for absolute objectivity, whether realisable or not, seems a better working-hypothesis than the subjectivistic resignation to an assumed absolute limit to the understanding of objective reality on the part of some Western physicists. However, atomic energy has been applied on both sides of the 'barricades'; the pragmatic truth of atomic theory has been revealed quite aside from dialectical materialism and bourgeois idealism.

Because Lenin insisted on the objectivity and universal validity of causality and because Leninism is the ruling ideology, it cannot very well be denied by Russian physicists. There is also no real need to do so, for according to dialectical materialism causality does not exclude but implies chance. The indeterminacy in quantum physics, though recognised, is explained as due to experimental techniques and not to a fundamental law of nature. The differences between the Eastern and Western physicists may then be summed up as differences relating not to their work but to additional expectations on the part of Eastern physicists that their work will come to verify the assumptions of dialectical materialism.

These assumptions, however, relate not to the victory of socialism over capitalism, but merely to the re-establishment of causality for the whole of nature and to the re-acceptance of the concept of matter, in its present sense, as the sole basis of all existing phenomena including the human mind. Of course, in a certain sense, such expectations may be regarded as an expression of a general optimism associated with the rise, success and expected triumph of bolshevism and its ideological concomitant, Leninism. Still, it is difficult to see how dialectical materialism in physics could determine the political decisions of people one way or another or could be regarded an instrument of class struggle.

Ideologies are weapons, but in the age of the atom bomb they are no longer decisive or even very important weapons. As little as the Western nations trust in the 'rationality' and the 'naturalness' of their socio-economic relations, just as little do the Eastern 'Marxists' put their trust in the dialectical course of history – not to speak of that in nature – as the means to final victory. Both sides rely, first of all, on their material might. It can only be to the good, of course, when material might finds ideological support, for which reason successful ideologists in both camps find themselves in comfortable income brackets. But their professional rating of the meaning and power of ideologies is only an over-rating of their own importance.

1960

1 Max Born, The Concept of Reality in Physics. *Bulletin of the Atomic Scientists*, Chicago, 1958. Vol.XIV, No.8, p.320.
2 *Ibid.*, p.319.
3 F. Engels, *Ludwig Feuerbach*, New York, 1945, p.22.
4. M. Born, *The Concept of Reality in Physics*, p.320.
5 B. Croce, *Lebendiges und Totes in Hegels Philosophie*, Heidelberg, 1909.
6 F. Engels, *Ludwig Feuerbach*, p.31.
7 Alphonse Aulard, *Histoire Politique de la Révolution Française; Origines et Développement de la Démocratie et de la République(1789–1804)*, Paris, 1901, p.734.

8 E. Mach, *The Science of Mechanics*, London, 1942, p.27.
9 *Materialism and Empiriocriticism*, New York, 1927, p.107.
10 *Ibid.*, p.107.
11 *Ibid.*, p.63.
12 *Ibid.*, p.109.
13 Marx's Theses on Feuerbach in F. Engels, *Ludwig Feuerbach*, p.73.
14 A more extensive criticism of Lenin's scientific and philosophical ideas is to be found in *Marxism and Philosophy*, by Karl Korsch, and *Lenin as Philosopher*, by Anton Pannekoek.
15 *Critique of Political Economy*, Chicago, 1904, p.11.
16 *Economic and Philosophical Manuscripts of 1844*, Moscow, p.169.
17 *Capital*, Chicago, Vol.III, p.952.
18 V.G. Childe, *Society and Knowledge*, New York, 1956, p.97.
19 M. Born, *The Concept of Reality in Physics*, p.319.
20 L.d. Broglie, *Physics and Microphysics*, New York, 1960, p.68.
21 W. Heisenberg, From Plato to Max Planck. *Atlantic Monthly*, Boston, November, 1959, p.113.
22 W. Heisenberg, *From Plato to Planck*, p.112.
23 M. Planck, *A Survey of Physical Theory*, New York, 1960, p.64.
24 E. Borel, *Space & Time*, New York, 1960, p.182.
25 See: M. Born, *Voraussagbarkeit in der klassischen Mechanik*. Physikalische Blatter, 1959, Heft 8.
26 W. Heisenberg, *From Plato to Max Planck*, p.112.
27 *The Concept of Reality in Physics*, p.320.
28 A.G. Meyer, *Marxism: The Unity of Theory and Practice*, Cambridge, 1954, p. 10.

CHAPTER XI

Monopoly Capital

The authors of *Monopoly Capital*[1], Paul A. Baran and Paul M. Sweezy, attempt to overcome "the stagnation of Marxian social science" by shifting the focus of attention from competitive to monopoly capital. The Marxian analysis of capitalism, they say, "still rests on the assumption of a competitive economy", which has, however, in the meantime, undergone a qualitative change by turning into monopoly capitalism. Marx, the authors relate, "treated monopolies not as essential elements of capitalism but rather as remnants of the feudal mercantilist past which had to be abstracted from in order to attain the clearest possible view of the basic structure and tendencies of capitalism" (p.4). Their own book tries to remedy this situation and to do so by using Marx's own "powerful analytical method".

Marx's analysis of capitalist development is based on the labour theory of value and surplus-value. However, market relations, Baran and Sweezy point out, "are essentially price relations" and in their view "the study of monopoly capitalism, like that of competitive capitalism, must begin with the workings of the price mechanism" (p.53). For Marx, price relations derive from value relations and the study of capitalism must therefore *begin* with value relations. The value analysis of capitalism disregards competition, for in the social aggregate all prices equate with total value. Contrary to what Baran and Sweezy say, the Marxian analysis does not rest on the assumption of competitive capitalism but on the abstract concept of total capital. If this concept is at all valid, it is so regardless of whether the actual capital structure is competitive, monopolistic or both.

Marx lived in a highly competitive capitalism, to be sure, and he knew that prices, not values, determine market events – even though market events are themselves circumscribed by the social relations as value relations. The descriptive parts of *Capital* refer to capital competition and to the elimination of competition by way of competition, i.e. to the centralisation and concentration of capital. What Baran and Sweezy might possibly mean by their assertion that Marx neglected monopoly – i.e. administered instead of competitive prices, and a tendency toward stagnation rather than expansion – is that Marx did not use the term *monopoly* in its bourgeois sense in opposition to competition. His theory of capital competition is at the same time a theory of monopoly, and monopoly, in this sense, always remains competitive, for a non-competitive monopoly capitalism implies the end of market relations such as sustain private-property capitalism.

Of course, during capitalism's heyday there is more competition than during its early or late stages. "When capital is still weak," Marx pointed out, "it tends to lean on the crutches of past modes of production. As soon as capital feels itself strong, however, the crutches are thrown away and capitalism moves in accordance with its own laws of motion. But as soon as it begins to feel itself as a barrier to further development and is recognised as such, it adapts forms of behaviour through the harnessing of competition which seemingly indicate its absolute rule but actually point to its decay and dissolution."[2] In other words, the prevalence of monopoly characterises the infantile and the senile stages of capital development. Appearances to the contrary notwithstanding, when, instead of being a form of competition, monopoly eliminates competition, capitalism finds itself on the way out.

For Baran and Sweezy, the asserted 'fundamental structural change' from competitive to monopoly capitalism demands an alteration in the laws derived from Marx's 'competitive model', as, for instance, that of the falling rate of profit. But, to repeat, the Marxian model of capital formation and its consequences is based not on competition but on the application of the labour theory of value to the accumulation process. Although capital accumulation is actually a competitive process, the falling rate of profit does not depend on competition but on the shifting value relations of capital expansion.

To recall this law: according to Marx, capital invested in means of production advances relatively faster than capital invested in labour-power. Because surplus-value is surplus-labour time, the reduction of labour time relative to the growing mass of unproductive capital leads to a fall of the rate of profit, since this rate is 'measured' on total capital, i.e. on both the capital invested in means of production, or constant capital, and that invested in labour-power, or variable capital.

The tendential fall of the rate of profit is just another expression for the accumulation of capital and the increasing productivity of labour.

Marx speaks of a *tendency* of rates of profit to fall because the same causes "which bring about an absolute decrease of surplus-value and profit on a *given capital*, and consequently in the percentage of the rate of profit, produce an increase of the absolute mass of surplus-value and profit appropriated by the total capital".[3] This is so, because "while any aliquot part, any hundred of the social capital, any hundred of average social composition, is a given magnitude, for which a fall in the rate of profit implies a fall in the absolute magnitude of profit just because the capital which serves as a standard of measurement is a constant magnitude, the magnitude of the social capital, on the other hand, as well as that of the capital in the hands of the individual capitalists . . . varies inversely to the decrease of its variable portion".[4]

Notwithstanding the tendential fall of the rate of profit "there may be an absolute increase in the number of labourers employed by capital . . . an absolute increase of the mass of surplus-value absorbed, and consequently an absolute increase in the mass of the produced profit. And this increase may be progressive. And it may not only be so. On the basis of capitalist production, it *must* be so, aside from temporary fluctuations".[5] All that this requires is that "capital grows at a faster rate than the rate of profit falls".[6] It is the accumulation process itself which nullifies the immediate practical importance of the declining rate of profit.

According to Marx, however, accumulation is characterised by: "First, the increase of surplus-labour, that is, the reduction of the necessary labour time required for the reproduction of labour-power; secondly, the decrease of the labour-power (the number of workers) employed in general for the purpose of setting in motion a given capital."[7] These occurrences are mutually conditioned by one another and affect the rate of profit in opposite ways. While the rate of surplus-value rises in one direction, the number of labourers falls in the opposite direction. "To the extent that the development of the productive powers reduces the paid portion of the employed labour, it raises the surplus-value by raising its rate; but to the extent that it reduces the total mass of labour employed by a certain capital, it reduces the factor of numbers with which the rate of surplus-value is multiplied in order to calculate its mass."[8]

And thus, while the fall of the rate of profit is checked by accumulation it cannot entirely be prevented, for there are definite limits beyond which the absolute labour-time cannot be extended and the necessary labour-time, i.e. the labour-time falling to the workers, cannot be any further shortened in favour of surplus-labour time. To speak in extremes: the absolute working-time during any one day cannot exceed 24 hours, and the necessary labour-time cannot be reduced to zero. The compensation of the relative reduction in the number of workers by their increased exploitation cannot go on ' forever '. Whatever the mass of labour-power in the real capitalist world, in relation to the progressively faster growing constant capital it must become a diminishing quantity. Thought out to its 'logical end', a continuously accelerating capital expansion will change the latent decline of the rate of profit into its actual decline because of a lack of surplus-value with respect to the swollen mass of total capital. At such a point, reality would correspond to Marx's *model* of capital accumulation.

There is a point of accumulation where the decreased variable capital cannot find compensation in an increase of surplus-value large enough to yield sufficient profits on total capital. At this point the rate of profit falls below what is necessary to continue the expansion process. The arrival of this point in concrete reality is not predictable, but the tendency in this direction explains for Marx the recurrent crises and the increasing difficulty of overcoming periods of capital stagnation through changes in the conditions of production which raise the rate of surplus-value. However, as long as capital accumulates it does so because it is still able to increase the mass of surplus-value. Under such conditions there is no point in rejecting the theory of the falling rate of profit because of an observable increase in the mass of surplus-value; this does not affect Marx's theory.

Baran and Sweezy think it necessary to *substitute* "the law of rising surplus for the law of falling profit", apparently unaware of the fact that for Marx, too, and for all practical purposes, a rising surplus-value cancels the actual fall of the rate of profit. By engaging in this superfluous task, Baran and Sweezy say they are not "rejecting or revising a time-honoured theorem of political economy", but are simply "taking account of the undoubted fact that the structure of the capitalist economy has undergone a fundamental change since this theorem was formulated" (p.72). For them, the mere 'change' from competition to monopoly sufficed to set aside Marx's immanent law of capital expansion. The 'proof' for this assertion is the apparent abundance of surplus-value in the United States. Assuming, for the moment, that Baran and Sweezy are right, they would still only repeat what Marx himself pointed out, namely, that a sufficient rate of exploitation temporarily bars the fall of the rate of profit.

Baran and Sweezy not only substitute "the law of rising surplus for the law of falling profit", but also *surplus* for surplus-value. "We prefer the concept 'surplus' to the traditional Marxian 'surplus-value'," they say, "since the latter is probably identified in the minds of most people familiar with Marxian economic theory as equal to the sum of profit-interest-rent." It is true, they continue, "that Marx demonstrates that surplus-value also comprises other items such as the revenues of state and church, the expense of transforming commodities into money, and the wages of unproductive workers. In general, however, he treated these as secondary factors and excluded them from his basic theoretical schema" (p.10). According to Baran and Sweezy, such "procedure is no longer justified", and they express the hope that their change of terminology, the substitution of surplus for surplus-value "will help affect the needed shift in theoretical position" (p.10).

Because for Marx "the relation between wage-labour and capital determines the entire character of the capitalist mode of production",[9] his capital analysis is in terms of value and surplus-value. Even the division of surplus-value into profit, interest and rent disappears in his value analysis. The best points in *Capital*, Marx wrote to Engels, "are 1) the twofold character of labour, according to whether it is expressed in use-value or exchange-value (all understanding of the facts depends upon this); and 2) the treatment of surplus-value independently of its particular form of profit, interest, ground rent, etc."[10] By observing the relation of surplus-value to total capital, Marx succeeded where Ricardo had failed, namely, in recognising in the falling rate of profit an immanent law of capital accumulation; a law, which for Marx, "was the most important of political economy".[11] If there is no point in considering interest and rent in the value analysis of capital development, there is even less in considering the additional items enumerated by Baran and Sweezy into which surplus-value is divided in capitalist society – except that this distribution will affect the rate of accumulation in case too much surplus-value is consumed instead of being capitalised.

Even in Baran and Sweezy's definition of *surplus* as constituting "the difference between what society produces and the costs of producing it", (p.9) we still have only value and surplus-value. If surplus-value is now simply called 'surplus' by Baran and Sweezy, it is because "in the actual economy of monopoly capitalism only part of the difference between output and cost of production appears as profit" (p.76). But this was equally true for competitive capitalism. The substitution has been made because Baran and Sweezy have switched from Marxian to bourgeois economic analysis, which does not operate with class terms such as value and surplus-value but with the amalgam national income, the concept of 'effective demand', and the Keynesian remedies for capital stagnation. It would indeed be a strange kind of 'Marxism' which paid more attention to the distribution of surplus-value among the capitalists and their retainers than to the division of the social product between labour and capital. But if there is just income and just 'surplus' instead of surplus-value, there is of course no falling rate of profit as a consequence of the value relations of capital production and no immanent barrier to profit production. If there is stagnation nonetheless, it is due not to the production relations as capital-labour relations, but to something else and, in Baran's and Sweezy's view, to the monopoly structure of present-day capitalism.

In Baran's and Sweezy's view, the difficulties of monopoly capital are caused not by a lack of profit but by an unabsorbable 'surplus'. The magnitude of the 'surplus' in the United States, they point out with the aid of Joseph D. Phillips, "amounted to 46.9 per cent of Gross National Product in 1929 and reached 56.1 per cent in 1963. But the portion of the surplus which is usually identified with surplus-value, i.e. profit, interest and rent, declined sharply in the same period. In 1929 this property-income was 57.5 per cent of total surplus, and in 1963 it was only 31.9 per cent." In view of these facts, Baran and Sweezy think that "not only the forces determining the total amount of surplus need to be analysed but also those governing its differentiations and the varying rates of growth of the components" (p.11).

Whatever these statistics may be worth, and they are admittedly not worth much, they do not relate to the Marxian problem of the determination of the rate of profit, but to the capitalist problem of the division of recorded income – other than wages – among the various interest groups living on the surplus-product. They simply tell us what is obvious, namely, that in a few capitalist nations the productivity of labour has enormously increased in order to allow for a great amount of waste-production as well as for higher living standards even under conditions of relative capital stagnation. They also indicate that government requires and receives an ever greater share of the Gross National Product. Apparently, all is well with capitalist society as far as the rate of exploitation is concerned. Only the utilisation of the 'surplus' provides difficulties and requires such obnoxious items as advertising, government expansion, armaments, imperialism and war.

Looked at from Marx's theory of the falling rate of profit, Baran and Sweezy write, "the barriers of capitalist expansion appeared to lie more in a shortage of surplus to maintain the momentum of accumulation than in any insufficiency in the characteristic modes of surplus utilisation" (p.13). But under monopoly capitalism and "with the law of rising surplus replacing the law of the falling tendency of the rate of profit, and with the normal modes of surplus utilisation patently unable to absorb a rising surplus, the question of other modes of surplus utilisation assumes crucial importance" (p.114).

According to Baran and Sweezy, the normal modes of surplus utilisation are capitalist consumption and investment – augmented by unavoidable expenses of the circulation process and by necessary but unproductive activities. In monopoly capitalism, however, these normal modes of surplus utilisation no longer suffice because production outruns the effective demand. And since 'surplus' can no longer be absorbed it will not be produced. The normal state of monopoly capital is thus stagnation. "With a given stock of capital and a given cost and price structure, the system's operating rates cannot rise above the point at which the amount of surplus produced can find the necessary outlets. And this means under-utilisation of available human and material resources. Or to put the point in slightly different terms, the system must operate at a point low enough on its profitability schedule not to generate more surplus than can be absorbed" (p.108). What Baran and Sweezy have thus far said is that it does not pay 'monopoly capital' to increase production beyond the point where it ceases to be profitable. This was equally true for 'competitive capitalism', as the recurrent periods of depression testify. Only, what used to be a period of stagnation within the business cycle has seemingly become the normal state of affairs. Because periods of stagnation are crisis conditions, one could say that the temporary crisis has become permanent.

The unabsorbable 'surplus', of which Baran and Sweezy speak, does not really exist because production stops at the point of loss of profitability. Instead, there are unused human and material resources. It is, then, not an actual 'surplus' which troubles monopoly capital but merely a *potential surplus*, which could be, but is not, produced. Monopoly capital, Baran and Sweezy write, "left to itself, that is to say, in the absence of counteracting forces which are no part of what may be called the 'elementary logic' of the system, would sink deeper and deeper into a bog of economic depression" (p.108). And on the basis of their theory it could not be otherwise, for if monopoly capital is no longer able to 'absorb' the 'surplus' it is capable of producing, any further increase in the productivity of labour, which would enlarge the 'surplus' still further, would force monopoly capital into still more extensive restrictions of production. With the resultant growth of idle resources, capital accumulation, that is, the capitalist mode of production, would come to an end.

For all practical purposes it is quite immaterial whether a lack of effective demand is made to explain a restriction of production, or a lack of profitability is seen as the cause for a restriction of production and a consequent lack of effective demand. In the one case the problem is approached from the market angle and in the other from that of production, but in both there is restriction of production. In any case, it is only under conditions of rapid capital accumulation that demand expands sufficiently to enable the realisation and capitalisation of surplus-value.

Because productivity increases even in the absence of accumulation, it is quite independent of the production process as a capital-expansion process. With accumulation a going concern, however, the increasing productivity of labour goes hand in hand with the value-expansion of capital. Constant and variable capital in their value form are inextricably intertwined with the material conditions of production, i.e. the means of production and labour power. Marx distinguished between the value composition and the material (technical) composition of capital. Between the two, he wrote, "there is a strict correlation. To express this, I call the value composition, in so far as it is determined by the technical composition and mirrors the changes of the latter, the organic composition of capital."[12] The concept of the organic composition of capital points to the *identity* and the *difference* between the material and value production and repeats, on the larger social scale, the concept of value as the identity and the difference of use- and exchange-value – the basic contradiction of capital production. For Marx, it is a discrepancy between material and value production which leads to difficulties in the accumulation process, but which also allows for its resumption and expansion through changes in the material-technical conditions of production which raise the productivity of labour and therewith the rate of surplus-value and profit. Where and when this is no longer possible, investments will be unprofitable and consequently will not be made.

According to Marx, moreover, the profitability of any particular capital depends on the profitability of the capitalist system as a whole. The latter is an unknown quantity. The only indication as to whether it is rising or falling is given by market events. It is, then, the state of the market which decides for any particular capital whether it should expand, contract or leave production at a given level. To increase their shares of a given market, or to maintain their profitability in a shrinking market, the different capitals will try to cheapen their production in order to maintain or increase their competitive ability. They do so all along; but under conditions of economic contraction, weaker capitals succumb more quickly to stronger ones, and the changes in the sphere of production are accompanied by changes in the market sphere. Capital will not only be more productive but also more concentrated and centralised. Fewer capitalists will have a larger market to themselves, and though this change 'for the better' is due to changes in the conditions of production, it appears, and is recognised, as a change in market conditions, as the restoration of an effective demand allowing for the resumption of the accumulation process.

For Baran and Sweezy, however, capitalist problems are exclusively market problems. Not the *production* but the *realisation* of the 'surplus' is capitalism's current dilemma. A lack of effective demand relative to the production potential leads to unused resources. It is clear, in that case, that if production were less effective the demand would be relatively greater. And since the rising 'surplus' and the lacking demand are one and the same phenomenon, the one cannot serve as an explanation for the other; rather, this two-sided but single phenomenon is itself in need of explanation. Obviously, if monopoly capital were able to sell a larger product it would do so. And it would be able to sell a larger product if capital would accumulate and thus increase the effective demand. But capital does not expand because it would not be profitable. The complaint about the lack of demand is then, actually, a complaint about insufficient profitability.

In Baran's and Sweezy's exposition it is the sheer capacity to produce which enforces the restriction of production. This theory disregards the value-character of capitalist production. The 'surplus' is seen not as surplus-value but simply as surplus production. In capitalism the increasing mass of commodities (as use-values) appear, however, as exchange-values. Since the mass of exchange-value declines with the growing productivity of labour, capital accumulation requires a faster growing mass of use-values. It is only through the growing capacity to produce that total exchange-value is enlarged and capital accumulated. In fact, the capacity to produce increases particularly in crisis situations in order to effect a resumption of the accumulation process. It is precisely the *compulsion* to increase the capacity to produce which points to the reality of the tendential decline of the rate of profit. It is also the only available means to arrest this decline. It is then the exchange-value of the surplus products, not the products themselves, which must be related to the value of total capital in order to determine the sufficiency or insufficiency of profitability. Since the capitalist capacity to produce relates not to a definite quantity of commodities but to the exchange-value of this quantity, Baran and Sweezy would have to prove their position not with reference to the increasing capacity to produce commodities but with an increasing capacity to produce exchange-value.

In capitalism all 'surplus' is surplus-value or it is not a surplus but a loss. According to Baran and Sweezy, 'monopoly capital' prevents the loss by limiting the 'surplus' through the limitation of production. In reality, however, capital, no matter what its structure, relentlessly attempts to increase surplus-value under conditions of either a full or a partial use of productive resources. When resources remain idle it is not because they are too productive but because they are not productive enough. The increasing rate of obsolescence indicates the quickening pace in which means of production lose their profit-producing capacity. It is often only the most efficient productive apparatus which will secure the profitability of capital. Moreover, insatiable as it is in its quest for profits, capital goes out of its way to extract surplus-value from all the corners of the world in order to augment the profits made at home.

Why this enormous appetite for surplus-value and profit when, according to Baran and Sweezy, 'monopoly capital' is already choking on the available 'surplus'? Actually, there can never be enough surplus-value and profit, because of the diminishing profitability in the course of capital expansion. The surplus-value embodied in commodities is surplus-labour time. Whatever the 'surplus' in its physical form, with respect to the capitalist system it is just a definite quantity of surplus-labour time – part of the total labour time. No matter how much the 'surplus' may be increased in its commodity form, the surplus-labour time diminishes with the diminishing total labour time in the course of the rising organic composition of capital. It is not the mass of commodities as a growing 'surplus' which determines the rate of profit, but the value relations between 'dead' and 'living' labour; that is, the changing relationship between constant and variable capital – modified by the rate of exploitation. The rate of profit can fall in spite and because of a 'rising surplus', seen as just a mass of commodities. In that case, the 'surplus' itself expresses the fall of the rate of profit in its concrete manifestations in the crisis of over-production, or, more recently, in the semi-permanent underutilisation of productive resources. Both situations indicate that the rate of profit on capital is such as to discourage, or even exclude, additional capital investments on a scale large enough to bring forth an effective demand which would assure the realisation of surplus-value on a larger production.

To think once more in extremes: assume that a thoroughgoing

automation of production reduces the variable capital to an insignificant part of the total capital. The productivity of labour would then turn, so to speak, into the 'productivity of capital'. There would be an enormous amount of production but little direct labour and therefore little surplus-labour. Because the displaced working population would still be there, it would have to be supported out of the automated production; capital would feed labour instead of labour feeding capital. The conditions of capitalism would have been completely reversed. Value and surplus-value production would no longer be possible.

It is for this reason, of course, that such a situation cannot come to pass within the framework of capitalism. For so long as exchange-value is the goal of production, labour-time quantities remain the source and measure of capitalist wealth. "Although the very development of the modern means of production," Marx wrote, "indicates to what a large degree the general knowledge of society has become a direct productive power, which conditions the social life and determines its transformations,"[13] capitalism's particular contribution to this state of affairs consists of no more "than in its use of all the media of the arts and sciences to increase the surplus-labour, because its wealth, in value form, is nothing but the appropriation of surplus-labour time."[14]

Marx's model of capital accumulation represents a closed homogeneous system in which the rising organic composition of capital results in the fall of the profit when the limits of surplus-value extraction are reached. If a highly industrially-advanced country such as the United States – which underlies the whole reasoning of Baran and Sweezy – could be considered a closed system, then, in the Marxian view, its rate of profit should fall with its increasing organic composition of capital, unless offset by an increased rate of surplus-value expressed in an accelerated capital expansion. But it is not a closed system, and is thus able not only to slacken its rising organic composition of capital, by way of capital exports, for instance, but, via the world market, to increase its profits through the importation of profits from abroad. However, capital exports have not significantly hindered the rise of the organic composition of capital, and profit imports have thus far not been large enough to explain America's apparent profit sufficiency. In the main, it is the increasing productivity of labour which accounts for her increased production.

Considering the world as a whole, however, it is self-evident that it does not suffer from 'surpluses' but from 'shortages'. The 'potential surplus' of 'monopoly capital' is more than matched by the actual lack of everything in the capital-poor nations. The overproduction of capital in one part of the world confronts the undercapitalisation in another.

Considering capitalism as a whole – as a world market system – the 'surplus' disappears and instead there is a great lack of surplus-value.

For capitalism as a whole, of course, the organic composition is not high enough to account for a rate of profit too low to induce further rapid capital expansion. But the accumulation process is at the same time a capital concentration process, and just as it tends to play the accumulating capital into fewer hands in each nation, so does it concentrate the world capital into a few countries. For it is the value-expansion of the existing capital that matters, not its extension into space, and the latter takes place only to the extent that it enhances the value-expansion of the concentrated and dominating capitals. Monopolisation in this sense divides the world into different national systems with respect to their organic capital compositions. If capitalism could expand generally, if the accumulation process would not simultaneously be a capital concentration process, the 'potential surplus' in a few industrially advanced nations, even if turned into an actual surplus, would hardly suffice to take care of the capitalisation needs of world capitalism. The contradiction of capital production erects barriers to its expansion long before the abstract borders of Marx's theory of capital development find some kind of approximation in reality.

Marx predicted that capitalism, while once rapidly developing the social powers of production, would come to fetter them, and that its further existence would then necessitate not only periods of crises and stagnation but the outright destruction of capital. The inability of capitalism to capitalise world production is evident in the 'potential surplus' in capitalistically advanced nations and in the increasing misery in the rest of the world. From the market point of view, this inability appears as a profit-realisation problem. While 'monopoly capital' is unable to sell what it is potentially capable of producing, the rest of the world, due to the retardation of its productive powers, cannot buy for lack of surplus-value. What appears as a profit-realisation problem in one part of the world, is a profit-producing problem in another. Considering the system as a whole, however, it is a general lack of surplus-value which accounts for its slow rate of expansion.

In principle, it is not different in any particular capitalist country. The increasing disuse of productive resources resulting from a lack of profitability can only increase the dearth of profits relative to the capitalist accumulation needs. Insofar as the unused resources represent constant capital, they lose their capital character through their disuse, i.e. they do not function as surplus-value-producing capital. To the extent that capital loses its capital character, the profitability of total capital – whatever it may be – will be impaired, and the surplus-value, however great, will be smaller than it would be under conditions of full use of productive capacity.

In Baran's and Sweezy's view, however, "monopoly capital . . . tends to generate ever more surplus, yet fails to provide the consumption and investment outlets required for the absorption of the rising surplus and hence for the smooth working of the system" (p.108). What makes 'monopoly capital' so extraordinarily profitable? "Declining costs," Baran and Sweezy say, "which imply continuously widening profit margins" (p.71). This was of course true throughout capitalist development and explains this development. According to Baran and Sweezy, however, there is a difference with respect to 'monopoly capital', which, in distinction to 'competitive capital', is no longer a 'price taker' but a 'price maker' (p.54), and "owing to the nature of the price and cost policies of the giant corporations, there is a strong and systematic tendency for surplus to rise" (p.79). In brief, it is simply by administered prices, that is, by keeping them artificially high while costs are lowered, that 'surplus' is piled up.

At one point in Baran's and Sweezy's exposition, a 'surplus' arises because the economy's capacity to produce grows too rapidly. Now, it is due to the imperfection of competition under monopoly conditions. Through increasing productivity and the power to make its own prices, 'monopoly capital' succeeds in securing and enlarging its profits even under conditions of relative capital stagnation. Because, by and large, the existing productive apparatus is more than adequate to take care of the given 'effective demand', there is no point in making significant new capital investments. Depreciation charges largely suffice to finance the technical innovations of, and the additions to, the productive apparatus, which, with a slow rate of expansion, is effective enough to provide an increasing national income and an even faster rise of profits. While production, productivity and profits soar, the rate of investments declines. In short, the capacity to produce a growing 'surplus' diminishes the accumulation of capital.

Capitalistically, however, the growth of production and productivity makes 'sense' only when it enlarges the existing capital. Insofar as it is not consumed, surplus-value must become additional capital. There would be no point in increasing production if the rate of accumulation were to diminish. The rate of accumulation is the determining, not the determined factor with regard to production. The basic reason for the expansion or contraction of the economic system is to be found in capital-labour, or wage-profit, relations – not in the technical capacity to produce. Ignoring this basic social relationship, Baran and Sweezy make possible the capitalistically impossible by combining an increasing 'surplus' with a diminishing rate of accumulation.

They can do so only, however, by accepting the current illusion that income-transfers and expenses can be counted as income so long as they are government transfers and expenses. They even go one better by extending this curious idea to private capital; not only by asserting that monopoly profits enlarge the social 'surplus', but by discovering a way of accumulating capital by way of advertising. As regards monopoly profits secured by price manipulations, it should be clear that they can be gained only through corresponding profit-losses on the part of the non-monopolistic capital. No matter what the structure of capitalism, there is, at any given time, a definite amount of national and international income derived from surplus-value. If 'monopoly capital' is able to enlarge its share of this total by selling far above the average rate of profit, it can do so only at the expense of capitals unable to do likewise; consequently, the latter have to divide among themselves a correspondingly smaller part of the total income falling to total capital.

Monopoly profits reduce the competitively established average rate of profit and therewith lead to the progressive decline of the quantity of profits transferable to monopoly capital. In the not-so-long run, the extraction of monopoly profits is a self-defeating process, bound to affect negatively both the monopoly-rate and the competitive rate of profit. Only under conditions of rapid capital expansion would it be possible to maintain monopoly profits without reducing simultaneously the *absolute* rate of profit of competitive capital. Conditions of stagnation, under which Baran's and Sweezy's 'monopoly capital' operates, exclude this possibility.

If 'monopoly capital', as Baran and Sweezy say, tends to generate 'ever more surplus', why should it still insist upon price policies which diminish the profits of competitive capital? But, then, Baran and Sweezy also say that 'monopoly capital' does not really generate a 'surplus', for it stops producing before a 'surplus' arises, as illustrated by the growing idle resources. Nonetheless, even though there is no 'surplus', in their view, a fierce competitive struggle ensues for the realisation of the 'surplus', which, due to the monopoly character of capital, is now waged by salesmanship rather than by price-cutting. Although there is no real, but only a potential 'surplus', capital's rationale derives, just the same, "from the simple fact that the obverse of 'too much' on the supply side is 'too little' on the demand side; instead of cutting back supply they aim at stimulating demand" (p.110).

Conceptually, Baran and Sweezy write, the sales effort "is identical with Marx's expenses of circulation. But in the epoch of monopoly capital, it has come to play a role, both quantitatively and qualitatively, beyond anything Marx ever dreamed of" (p.114). The sales effort, they go on to say, "turns out to be a powerful antidote to monopoly capitalism's tendency to sink in a state of chronic depression" (p.131), for it "absorbs, directly and indirectly, a large amount of surplus which otherwise would not have been produced" (p.142). By increasing the 'effective demand', advertising increases the level of income and employment, so that "the direct impact of the sales effort on the income and output structure of the economy is similar to that of government spending financed by tax revenue" (p.126). Finally, "with regard to investment opportunities, advertising plays a role similar to that which has traditionally been assigned to innovations. By making it possible to *create* the demand for a product, advertising encourages investments in plants and equipment which otherwise would not take place" (p.126).

According to this theory, advertising accomplishes a number of contradictory things; while it is an expense of circulation, it also is a creator of income, and while it 'absorbs' part of the 'surplus', it also enlarges the 'surplus' by inducing new investments. Obviously, a lot of people make their living by selling and advertising, while others lose part of their incomes by paying higher prices – prices which include the costs of advertising. This has always been so, but, according to Baran and Sweezy, its quantitative extension under 'monopoly capital' gives it a qualitative difference, i.e. if the expense is large enough it becomes a form of additional income. Because consumption is increased through exhortations, the enlarged consumption leads to increased production and investments. This is, of course, Keynes' increasing 'propensity to consume' as a possible medium for an expanded production under conditions of decreasing investments. But while Keynes' suggestion (unrealisable within capitalism) relates to total national income, Baran and Sweezy relate it only to the 'surplus', that is, to that part of social production which falls to the capitalists.

Advertising penetrates the whole market, not only that part which caters to capitalist consumption. Everybody is advised to spend more even though, according to Baran and Sweezy, it is only the 'surplus' which has to be gotten rid of. The 'surplus' is there (and is as large as it may be) because the costs of production, that is, the income of the workers, is as small as it is in comparison with the 'surplus'. To have that 'surplus' means to have correspondingly low costs of production, for which reason it would not do to increase the 'propensity to consume' by way of higher wages. Unless taken from the workers, there is no 'surplus', and the latter, in order to be such, must first be realised on the market. If not realised there is no 'surplus' but a loss. Capitalists intensify their sales efforts so as to avoid losses, not to get rid of the 'surplus'. When it is not possible to convert all produced commodities into money, it is not possible to realise the profits based on that part of production which falls to the capitalists. The 'sales effort' finds its emphasis not in an increasing 'surplus' but in the market situation as a whole as determined by a declining rate of accumulation.

Advertising cannot 'create' anything but advertisements. New products, catering to new wants, are not advertisements, even though they may be advertised. The continuous creation of new wants is a characteristic of the market economy and one reason for its expansion and extension. Advertising as such cannot increase the 'effective demand' and, via this demand, enlarge production. Capital must accumulate in order not only to remain competitive but to retain its capital-value. Capitalists cannot consume all of their profits, for by doing so, they would soon cease being capitalists. Advertising cannot affect this compulsive need to accumulate, and accumulation determines the 'effective demand' with respect to consumption goods from this quarter. No advertising could enlarge the *objectively determined* 'effective demand', although it may affect it in favour of one or another product, or one or another seller of identical commodities. Advertising can affect the distribution of the available surplus-value, but it cannot add to its size, for it is itself only a part of the available total surplus-value.

Baran's and Sweezy's curious reasoning with respect to advertising rests on the illusion that production outside the 'self-limiting' confines of 'monopoly capital', i.e. production which is actually undertaken but would not be forthcoming were it not for advertising and government purchases, could actually benefit 'monopoly capital', and, by creating income and employment, the whole of society. There is, then, after all, a growing 'surplus' which does not need to issue into protracted stagnation, and full employment combines with an 'absorption' of the 'surplus' through government – and advertising – agencies. What remains regrettable in Baran's and Sweezy's view, however, are the irrational uses to which the larger part of the 'surplus' is put by both these agencies.

The 'surplus' in evidence in the 'affluent society' is, then, not a 'surplus' produced by monopoly capital but in spite of it. It is in fact brought forth, as Baran and Sweezy point out, by government purchases which increase the 'effective demand' and thus prevent crisis conditions. The crisis is set aside by the "colossal capacity to generate private and public waste" (p.3). To waste the 'surplus' is one way of 'absorbing' it, however, and as there are no limits to the generation of waste, there is no need for a 'surplus' to arise and thus also no 'surplus-utilisation' problem. Particularly not, because, in Baran's and Sweezy's view, the waste does not reduce the profits of 'monopoly capital', for it constitutes that part of the 'surplus' over and above the 'surplus' realised as profit. Just as the 'sales effort' absorbs "a large amount of surplus which would otherwise not have been produced", so "government plays a similar role but on a larger scale" (p.142). When idle resources are put to work, "they can produce not only necessary means of subsistence for the producers but also additional amounts of surplus. Hence if government creates more effective demand, it can increase its command over goods and services without encroaching on the income of its citizens" (p.143).

By treating surplus-value as 'surplus', Baran and Sweezy manage to look upon capitalism as if it were something other than itself. "The size of the surplus," they write, "is an index of productivity and wealth, of how much freedom a society has to accomplish whatever goals it may set for itself" (p.9). This is to see society in the abstract, not as a specific society; at any rate, not as capitalist society. In the latter, the means of production belong to a specific class – not to the government and not to the 'citizens'. The idle resources – even in their idleness – remain capitalist property. Unless confiscated, they can be utilised by government only through its purchases, and the money used in these transactions must first be extracted from private capital either by taxation or through borrowings. Financed in this manner, government-induced production does not increase the quantity of *marketable* commodities and can thus not be turned into exchange-value and, consequently, not into surplus-value. No matter how much employment and income it may generate, the *final product* of government-induced production, such as public works of a useful or wasteful nature, is not a marketable product, whereas the real income in capitalist society has to be realised via the circulation of commodities. While increasing the total mass of labour and of products, it does not increase the mass of surplus-value and represents, therefore, a loss rather than a gain – a loss similar to that suffered by overproduction when part of the produced commodities cannot be converted into money.

According to Baran and Sweezy, "the vast and growing amounts of surplus absorbed by government in recent decades are not deductions from what would otherwise be available to corporations and individuals for their private purposes" (p.147). However, Baran and Sweezy, themselves, have pointed out that that portion of the surplus usually identified with surplus-value declined sharply from 1929 to 1963. To recall, while property-income was 57.5 per cent of total surplus in 1929, it was only 31.9 per cent in 1963. According to these statistics, the 'surplus' absorbed by government grew faster than that falling to property owners. The reduction of surplus-value has some connection with the growth of government expenses, or, in Baran's and Sweezy's terms, with the 'absorption' of 'surplus' by government.

To be sure, Baran and Sweezy maintain that this property-income would not have been any greater without government-induced production. This is most probably so, because government-induced production is enlarged to compensate for the declining private production, in order to ameliorate the social consequences of prolonged crisis conditions. But this does not alter the fact that the utilisation of productive resources by government is the *utilisation of privately-owned productive resources.* And as the government has nothing to give in exchange but the money it extracts out of the economy, the utilisation of private productive resources by government equates – as far as private capital is concerned – with their non-utilisation in their previous state of idleness.

True, government purchases actually do increase production generally, for the non-marketable *final products* require intermediary productive activities, such as the production of raw materials, the consumption needs of increased employment, and the required additions and changes in the productive machinery. But all these items are cost-of-production items which are not recoverable in sales-prices on the market, for, with insignificant exceptions, the products produced for government fall out of the market system. Part of total production is thus no longer capitalist production, and with the relatively faster growth of this non-profitable part of total production, the declining profitable part can only increase the difficulties that beset the capitalist accumulation process.

Still, Baran and Sweezy insist that government absorption of 'surplus' is in addition to, not subtracted from, private surplus. Even more: "Since a larger volume of government spending pushes the economy nearer to capacity production, and since up to this point surplus grows more rapidly than effective demand as a whole, it follows that both the government and the private segments of surplus can and indeed typically do grow simultaneously" (p.148). And so it seems; but it does not show up in the rate of capital expansion, only in the size of the Gross National Product, of which a growing part is no longer profitable. This fact is hidden, however, by the money-veil that covers capitalist production and exchange, and quite successfully so, since even critics of 'monopoly capital' are taken in by it.

"If what government takes would otherwise not have been produced at all," Baran and Sweezy write, "it cannot be said to have been squeezed out of anybody. Government spending and taxing, which used to be primarily a mechanism for transferring income, have become in large measure a mechanism for creating income by bringing idle capital and labour into production" (p.150). It is through this 'new mechanism' that "what the government takes in taxes is an addition to, not a subtraction from, private surplus" (p.149). The government has not succeeded, however, in convincing the capitalists that this is actually so, for, now as before, capital does object to the increase in taxes and the growth of the national debt as being detrimental to its own profitability and accumulation requirements.

What does the government actually do by bringing together labour and idle capital for the production of non-marketable goods? Taxes are a part of realised income through market transactions; if taken from capital they do reduce its profits, regardless of whether or not these profits would have been consumed or reinvested into additional capital. If not, idle capital in its money form would exist as a private hoard. As such it cannot function capitalistically; but neither can it function capitalistically when taken by government to finance the non-profitable production of public works and government waste. Instead of a capitalistically-useless money hoard there is then a capitalistically-useless production of goods and services. There is a difference, however: whereas without taxation capital would be in possession of a money hoard, with taxation – for purposes of public spending – capital is actually expropriated to the extent of the otherwise possible money hoard.

When used for government purchases, taxes taken from capital flow back to the capitalists in form of government contracts. The production resulting from these contracts is being paid for by the capitalists through their taxes. Getting their money back through government orders, the capitalists provide the government with an equivalent quantity of products. It is this quantity of products which the government 'expropriates' from capital. The size of this quantity determines the extent to which production has ceased being capital production, and the growth of production by way of taxation indicates the decline of the capitalist system as a profit-determined private enterprise system. Not only is this type of production non-profitable, it is made possible only through that part of total production which is still sufficiently profitable to yield taxes large enough to extend government production by way of taxation. With the decline of profitability it becomes increasingly more difficult to expand production in this particular way.

But government can borrow additional funds. These funds also flow back to the capitalists as payments for production contracted by government. The expense of government-induced production piles up, in part, as the national debt. The increase of the debt is held to be quite harmless as long as the national income increases faster than the debt. The growing national debt is then usually compared with the growing national income, which substantiates the claim that deficit-financing will be accompanied by a rising national income. This claim rests, however, on a curious way of accounting, for, actually, the growing national debt cannot be related to total national income, but only to that part of the total which has not been injected by government into the economy. It is by counting an *expense* as an *income* that the illusion arises that a growing national debt is neutralised by a rising national income.

Unless the national debt is actually recovered through additional income in the private sector of the economy, that is, *additional income apart from that injected into the economy by government*, the 'income' derived from the latter procedure remains, as far as capital is concerned, a mere government expense. This 'expense' consists of the government's utilisation of privately-owned productive resources for non-profitable purposes. It is a partial 'expropriation' of capital, even though the 'expropriated' capital was no longer able to function capitalistically on its own behalf. But that does not prevent the capitalists from demanding compensation for the government's use of *their* productive resources. The possibility of honouring the government debt depends on the future profitability of private capital. Unless this profitability actually materialises, the debt cannot be honoured and today's additional income becomes tomorrow's loss of income. The whole matter is a case of 'counting one's chickens before they are hatched', and given the tendential decline of the rate of profit in the course of capital expansion, there will be no chickens.

Immediately, of course, government-induced production increases income and employment beyond what it would be without this intervention. There is more production, albeit largely waste-production, and part of this production Baran and Sweezy regard as a 'surplus'. This 'surplus', however, does not contain surplus-value, but exists as an unavoidable expense of surplus-value production. "Given the inability of monopoly capitalism to private uses for the surplus which it can easily generate," they write, "there can be no doubt that it is to the interests of all classes – though not of all elements within them – that government should steadily increase its spending and its taxing" (p.151). If this is so, it will of course not only increase the production of waste, but slowly and surely destroy the private-enterprise system. In the first place, government spending must be restricted to production and services that do *not compete* with those of private capital, for otherwise it would reduce the 'effective demand' within the private sector of the economy to the same extent to which it increases the 'effective demand' through government-induced production. In order not to destroy private capital, government-induced production must remain non-profitable production. In the second place, government-induced production must remain small relative to total production so as not to deprive too much of the capital resources of their capital character, i.e. of being profit-producing means of production. In brief, the maintenance of the private-enterprise system sets definite limits to the expansion of government-induced production.

Not so, however, in Baran's and Sweezy's opinion. Even America's "ruling class attitude toward taxation and government spending," they write, "has undergone a fundamental change . . . To the Big Businessman . . . government spending means more effective demand, and he senses that he can shift most of the associated taxes forward onto consumers or backward onto workers" (p.149). He not only 'senses' this but actually does so, which, however, can only mean that while he secures his own profitability, he reduces the 'effective demand' through higher prices. This procedure, however, is precisely the way by which part of the expense of government spending is spread over all of society. While part of the expense of government-induced production piles up as the national debt, another part is continuously distributed over the whole of the economy and being paid for in higher prices by means of inflation.

The businessman's positive attitude toward government spending, in so far as it exists, is determined by the profit requirements of his particular business. Why should he understand the capitalist economy any better than Baran and Sweezy, who, even by considering the economy as a whole and not merely a particular business within it, come to the conclusion that government spending would solve the economic problems of capitalism and of all its classes? But while the businessman has the excuse, at least, of his flourishing business, Baran and Sweezy have no excuse, because the 'prosperity' created by way of government spending is a false prosperity, capable of postponing, but not of abolishing, crisis conditions.

The individual businessman is not concerned with the nature of the 'effective demand' which he supplies. To him, it makes no difference whether it stems from government or from private spending. Likewise, the financiers do not care whether loans are made to private entrepreneurs or to government, so long as they are secure and yield the desired rate of interest. To the individual it also makes no difference whether he is employed in the production of waste or in that of marketable commodities. In practice, no distinction is made between the public and the private sector of the economy, and in both all transactions are money transactions. In money terms, production of waste is just as, or even more, lucrative, than the production of commodities, and – until finally repudiated – the accumulation of the national debt appears as the accumulation of capital. Considering society as a whole, however, it is only the private sector which brings forth surplus-value and profit. All the social layers which live on surplus-value, as well as the expansion of *capital as capital*, depend on this surplus-value, which, however much it may be increased through the growing productivity of labour, is at the same time also decreasing through the relatively faster growth of the non-profitable rather than the profitable sector of the economy.

There is no denying, of course, that in a few nations and for a considerable time, capital has been able to prevent the rise of depressions such as plagued the world prior to World War Two. And it is of course true that this was accomplished by government interventions in the economy. It is thus of great importance to consider whether or not these interventions have actually set aside the laws of capitalist development as set forth by Marx. Undertakings such as Baran's and Sweezy's are fully justified, only, in their case, they sail under a false flag by claiming to avail themselves of Marx's own 'powerful analytical method'. This is precisely what they do not do. Of course, Marx's 'analytical method' may seem to have lost its relevance because of the modifications brought about by monopoly capital and government interventions into the economy. But here appearances are misleading and, in any case, would not suffice to destroy Marx's theory of the immanent laws of capital accumulation.

The modifications of the capitalist system can just as well be interpreted as political reactions to uncontrollable economic events, which, like other 'countertendencies' to the dominating trend of capital expansion, serve, for a time, to maintain social stability through a pseudo-prosperity based on waste production. "If military spending were reduced once again to pre-Second World War proportions," Baran and Sweezy point out, "the nation's economy would return to a state of profound depression" (p.153). In other words, the economy is still in a state of depression, countermanded by expenditures which by no stretch of the imagination can be called an accumulation of capital. Without the accumulation of capital, however, the capitalist system can only contract, and it contracts the faster, the more its production becomes unprofitable. Unless the whole of capital should be nationalised to be utilised for other than private-enterprise ends, government interventions in the economy are necessarily limited by the need to secure the profitability of the dominating private capital. When these limits are reached they will cease countermanding the capitalist crisis.

1966

1 Monthly Review Press, New York, 1966.
2 *Grundrisse der Kritik der Politischen Ökonomie*, Berlin, 1953, p.544.
3 *Capital*, Kerr edition, Vol.III, p.259.
4 *Loc. cit.*
5 *Ibid.*, p.255.
6 *Ibid.*, p.261.
7 *Ibid.*, p.289.
8 *Ibid.*, p.290.
9 *Ibid.*, p.1025.
10 Marx-Engels, *Selected Correspondence*, Moscow, p.232.
11 *Grundrisse*, op. cit., p.634.
12 *Capital*, op. cit., Vol.I, p.67.
13 *Grundrisse*, op. cit., p.594.
14 *Ibid.*, p.595.

CHAPTER XII

Workers' Control

According to socialist theory, the development of capitalism implies the polarisation of society into a small minority of capital owners and a large majority of wage-workers, and therewith the gradual disappearance of the proprietory middle class of independent craftsmen, farmers and small shop-keepers. This concentration of productive property and general wealth into always fewer hands appears as an incarnation of 'feudalism' in the garb of modern industrial society. Small ruling classes determine the life and death of all of society by owning and controlling the productive resources and therewith the governments. That their decisions are controlled, in turn, by impersonal market forces and the compulsive quest for capital does not alter the fact that these reactions to uncontrollable economic events are also their exclusive privilege.

Within the capital-labour relations which characterise the prevailing society, the producers have no direct control over production and the products it brings forth. At times, they may exert a kind of indirect control by way of wage struggles, which may alter the wage-profit ratio and therewith the course or tempo of the capital expansion process. Generally, it is the capitalist who determines the conditions of production. The workers have to agree in order to exist, for their only means of livelihood is the sale of their labour power. Unless the worker accepts the exploitative conditions of capitalist production, he is 'free' only in the sense that he is free to starve. This was recognised long before there was a socialist movement. As early as 1767, Simon Linguet declared that wage-labour is merely a form of slave labour. In his view, it was even worse than slavery. "It is the impossibility of living by any other means that compels our farm labourers to till the soil whose fruits they will not eat, and our masons to construct buildings in which they will not live. It is want that drags them to those markets where they await masters who will do them the kindness of buying them. It is want that compels them to go down on their knees to the rich man in order to get from him permission to enrich him . . . What effective gain has the suppression of slavery brought him? . . . He is free, you say. Ah. That is his misfortune. The slave was precious to his master because of the money he had cost him. But the handicraftsman costs nothing to the rich voluptuary who employs him . . . These men, it is said, have no master – they have one, and the most terrible, the most imperious of masters, that is *need.* It is this that reduces them to the most cruel dependence."[1] Two hundred years later this is essentially still the same. Although it is no longer outright misery which forces the workers in the advanced capitalist nations to submit to the rule of capital and to the wiles of capitalists, their lack of control over the means of production, their position as wage-workers, still marks them as a ruled class unable to determine its own destiny.

The goal of socialists was then and still is the abolition of the wage system, which implies the end of capitalism. In the second half of the last century a working class movement arose to bring about this transformation through the socialisation of the means of production. Profit-determined production was to be replaced by one satisfying the actual needs and ambitions of the associated producers. The market economy was to make room for a planned economy. Social existence and development would then no longer be determined by the uncontrollable fetishistic expansion and contraction of capital but by the collective conscious decisions of the producers in a classless society.

Being a product of bourgeois society, however, the socialist movement is bound to the vicissitudes of capitalist development. It will take on varying characteristics in accordance with the changing fortunes of the capitalist system. It will not grow, or it will practically disappear, at times and in places which are not conducive to the formation of proletarian class consciousness. Under conditions of capitalist prosperity it tends to transform itself from a revolutionary into a reformist movement. In times of social crisis it may be totally suppressed by the ruling classes.

All labour organisations are part of the general social structure and, save in a purely ideological sense, cannot be consistently anti-capitalistic. In order to attain social importance within the capitalist system they must be opportunistic, that is, take advantage of given social processes in order to serve their own but as yet limited ends. It does not seem possible to slowly assemble revolutionary forces in powerful organisations ready to act at favourable moments. Only organisations which do not disturb the prevailing basic social relationships grow to any importance. If they start out with a revolutionary ideology, their growth implies a subsequent discrepancy between their ideology and their functions. Opposed to the *status quo* but also organised within it, these organisations must finally succumb to the forces of capitalism by virtue of their own organisational successes.

At the end of the century, traditional labour organisations – socialist parties and trade unions – were no longer revolutionary movements. Only a small left-wing within these organisations retained its revolutionary ideology. In terms of doctrine, Lenin and Luxemburg saw the need to combat the reformist and opportunist evolutionism of the established labour organisations and demanded a return to revolutionary policies. While Lenin tried to accomplish this through the creation of a new type of revolutionary party, emphasising centrally-controlled organised activity and leadership, Rosa Luxemburg preferred an increase in proletarian self-determination generally, as well as within the socialist organisations, through the elimination of bureaucratic controls and the activisation of the rank-and-file.

Because Marxism was the ideology of the dominant socialist parties, opposition to these organisations and their policies expressed itself also as an opposition to Marxian theory in its reformist and revisionist interpretations. Georges Sorel[2] and the syndicalists were not only convinced that the proletariat could emancipate itself without the guidance of the intelligentsia, but that it had to free itself from middle class elements that usually controlled political organisations. Syndicalism rejected parliamentarianism in favour of revolutionary trade union activity. In Sorel's view, a government of socialists would in no sense alter the social position of the workers. In order to be free, the workers would have to resort to actions and weapons exclusively their own. Capitalism, he thought, had already organised the whole proletariat in its industries. All that was left to do was to suppress the state and property. To accomplish this, the proletariat was not so much in need of so-called scientific insight into necessary social trends as of a kind of intuitive conviction that revolution and socialism were the inevitable outcome of their own continuous struggles. The strike was seen as the workers' revolutionary apprenticeship. The growing number of strikes, their extensions and increasing duration pointed towards a possible *General Strike*, that is, to the impending social revolution.

Syndicalism and such international offspring as the *Guild Socialists* in England and the *Industrial Workers of the World* in the United States were, to some extent, reactions to the increasing bureaucratisation of the socialist movement and to its class-collaborationist practices. Trade unions, too, were attacked for their centralistic structures and their emphasis upon specific trade interests at the expense of proletarian class needs. But all organisations, whether revolutionary or reformist, whether centralisers or federalists, tended to see in their own steady growth and everyday activities the major ingredient for social change. As regards Social Democracy it was the growing membership, the spreading party apparatus, the increasing number of votes in elections, and a larger participation in existing political institutions which were thought of as growing into the socialist society. As regards the *Industrial Workers of the World*, on the other hand, the growth of its own organisations into *One Big Union* was seen, at the same time, as "forming the structure of the new society within the shell of the old."[3]

In the first twentieth century revolution, however, it was the unorganised mass of workers which determined the character of the revolution and brought into being its own, new form of organisation in the spontaneously arising workers' councils. The Russian councils, or soviets, of the 1905 Revolution, grew out of a number of strikes and their needs for committees of action and representation to deal with the industries affected as well as with legal authorities. The strikes were spontaneous in the sense that they were not called by political organisations or trade unions, but were launched by unorganised workers who had no choice but to look upon their workplace as the springboard and centre of their organisational efforts. In the Russia of that time political organisations had as yet no real influence on the mass of workers and trade unions existed only in embryonic form. "The soviets," Trotsky wrote, "were the realisation of an objective need for an organisation which has authority without having tradition, and which can at once embrace hundreds of thousands of workers. An organisation, moreover, which can unify all the revolutionary tendencies within the proletariat, which possesses both initiative and self-control, and, which is the main thing, can be called into existence within 24 hours." . . . [Whereas] "parties were organisations *within* the proletariat, the soviets was the organisation *of* the proletariat."[4]

In essence, of course, the 1905 Revolution was a bourgeois revolution, supported by the liberal middle class to break Czarist absolutism and to advance Russia via a Constituent Assembly towards the conditions that existed in the more developed capitalist nations. In so far as the striking workers thought in political terms, they largely shared the programme of the liberal bourgeoisie. And so did all existing socialist organisations which accepted the necessity of a bourgeois revolution as a precondition for the formation of a strong labour movement and a future proletarian revolution under more advanced conditions.

The soviet system of the Russian Revolution of 1905 disappeared with the crushing of the revolution, only to return in greater force in the February Revolution of 1917. It was these soviets which inspired the formation of similar spontaneous organisations in the German Revolution of 1918, and, to a somewhat lesser extent, the social upheavals in England, France, Italy and Hungary. With the council system a form of organisation arose which could lead and coordinate the self-activities of very broad masses for either limited ends or for revolutionary goals, and which could do so independently of, in opposition to, or in collaboration with, existing labour organisations. Most of all, the rise of the council system proved that spontaneous activities need not dissipate in formless mass-exertions but could issue into organisational structures of a more than temporary nature.

The Russian Revolution of 1905 invigorated left-wing oppositions in the socialist parties of the West, but as yet more with respect to the spontaneity of its mass strikes than the organisational form these actions assumed. But the reformist spell was broken; revolution was again seen as a real possibility. However, in the West it would not be a bourgeois-democratic but a pure working class revolution. But even so, the positive attitude toward the Russian experience was not as yet transformed into a rejection of the parliamentary methods of the reformist parties of the Second International.

II

The prospect for a revival of revolutionary policies in the West proved at first illusory. Not only the 'revisionists' within the socialist movement for whom, in the words of their foremost spokesman, Eduard Bernstein, "the movement was everything and the goal nothing", but also so-called orthodox Marxists no longer believed in either the desirability or the necessity of social revolution. While they were still sticking to the old goal – abolition of the wage system – this was now to be reached in piecemeal fashion through the legal means offered by the democratic institutions of bourgeois society. Eventually, with the mass of voters favouring a socialist government, socialism could be instituted by government decree. Meanwhile, trade union activity and social legislation would alleviate the lot of the workers and enable them to partake in the general social progress.

The miseries of *laissez faire* capitalism not only produced a socialist movement but also various attempts on the part of workers to ease their conditions by non-political means. Apart from trade unionism, a cooperative movement came into being as a medium of escape from wage-labour and as a vain opposition to the ruling principle of general competition. The precursors of this movement were the early communist communities in France, England and America, which derived their ideas from such utopian socialists as Owen and Fourier.

Producers' cooperatives were voluntary groupings for self-employment and self-government with respect to their own activities. Some of these cooperatives developed independently, others in conjunction with the working class movements. By pooling their resources, workers were able to establish their own workshops and produce without the intervention of capitalists. But their opportunities were from the very beginning circumscribed by the general conditions of capitalist society and its developmental tendencies, which granted them a mere marginal existence. Capitalist development implies the competitive concentration and centralisation of capital. The larger capital destroys the smaller. The cooperative workshops were restricted to special small-scale industries requiring little capital. Soon, the capitalist extension into all industries destroyed their competitive ability and drove them out of business.

Consumers' cooperatives proved to be more successful and some of them absorbed producers' cooperatives as sources of supply. But consumers' cooperatives can hardly be considered as attempts at working class control, even where they were the creation of working class aspirations. At best, they may secure a measure of control in the disposal of wages, for labourers can be robbed twice – at the point of production and at the market place. The costs of commodity circulation are an unavoidable *faux frais* of capital production, dividing the capitalists into merchants and entrepreneurs. Since each tries for the profit maximum in its own sphere of operation, their economic interests are not identical. Entrepreneurs thus have no reason to object to consumers' cooperatives. Currently, they are themselves engaged in dissolving the division of productive and merchant capital by combining the functions of both in the single production and marketing corporation.

The cooperative movement was easily integrated into the capitalist system and, in fact, was to a large extent an element of capitalist development. Even in bourgeois economic theory it was considered an instrument of social conservatism by fostering the savings propensities of the lower layers of society, by increasing economic activities through credit unions, by improving agriculture through cooperative production and marketing organisations, and by shifting working class attention from the sphere of production to that of consumption. As a capitalistically-oriented institution the cooperative movement flourished, finally to become one form of capitalist enterprise among others, bent on the exploitation of the workers in its employ, and facing the latter as their opponents in strikes for higher wages and better working conditions. The general support of consumers' cooperatives by the official labour movement – in sharp distinction to an earlier scepticism and even outright rejection – was merely an additional sign of the increasing 'capitalisation' of the reformist labour movement. The widespread network of consumers' cooperatives in Russia, however, provided the Bolsheviks with a ready-made distributive system which was soon turned into an agency of the state.

The division of 'collectivism' into producers' and consumers' cooperatives reflected, in a sense, the opposition of the syndicalist to the socialist movement. Consumers' cooperatives incorporated members of all classes and were seeking access to all markets. They were not opposed to centralisation on a national and even international scale. The market of producers' cooperatives, however, was as limited as their production and they could not combine into larger units without losing the self-control which was the rationale for their existence.

It was the problem of workers' control over their production and products which differentiated the syndicalists from the socialist movement. In so far as the problem still existed for the latter, it solved it for itself with the concept of nationalisation, which made the socialist state the guardian of society's productive resources and the regulator of its economic life with respect to both production and distribution. Only at a later stage of development would this arrangement make room for a free association of socialised producers and the withering away of the state. The syndicalists feared, however, that the state with its centralised controls would merely perpetuate itself and prevent the working population's self-determination.

The syndicalists envisioned a society in which each industry is managed by its own workers. All the syndicates together would form national federations which would not have the characteristics of government but would merely serve statistical and administrative functions for the realisation of a truly collectivist production and distribution system. Syndicalism was predominant in France, Italy and Spain but was represented in all capitalist nations; in some with modifications as in the already noted *I.W.W.* and the *Guild Socialists.* Not only with respect to the final goal, but also in the everyday class struggle, syndicalists differed from parliamentary socialists and ordinary trade unions by their emphasis on direct actions and by a greater militancy.

Although the concern with final goals was premature, it affected nonetheless the actual behaviour of their propagators. The rapid bureaucratisation of the centralised socialist movement and trade unions deprived the workers in increasing measure of their self-initiative and subjected them to the control of a leadership which did not share their living and working conditions. Trade unions lost their early connection with the socialist movement and degenerated into business-unionism, solely interested in wage-bargaining and, where possible, in the formation of job monopolies. The syndicalist movement was bureaucratised to a far lesser extent, not only because it was the smaller of the two main streams of the labour movement, but also because the principle of industrial self-control affected the everyday class struggle as well.

To speak of workers' control within the framework of capitalist production can mean only control of their own organisations, for capitalism implies that the workers are deprived of all effective social control. But with the 'capitalisation' of their organisations, when they become the 'property' of a bureaucracy and the vehicle of its existence and reproduction, it follows that the only possible form of direct workers' control vanishes. It is true that even then workers fight for higher wages, shorter hours and better working conditions, but these struggles do not affect their lack of power within their own organisations. To call these activities a form of workers' control is a misnomer in any case, for these struggles are not concerned with the self-determination of the working class but with the improvement of conditions within the confines of capitalism. This is, of course, possible so long as it is possible to increase the productivity of labour at a rate faster than that by which the workers' living standards are raised.

The basic control over the conditions of work and the surplus-yields of production remain always in the hands of the capitalists. When workers succeed in reducing the hours of their working day, they will not succeed in cutting the quantity of surplus-labour extracted by the capitalists. For there are two ways of extracting surplus-labour – prolonging the working day and shortening the working time required to produce the wage-equivalent by way of technical and organisational innovations. Because capital must yield a definite rate of profit, capitalists will stop producing when this rate is threatened. The compulsion to accumulate capital controls the capitalist and forces him to control his workers to get that amount of surplus-labour necessary to consummate the accumulation process. He will try for the profit maximum and may only get the minimum for reasons beyond his control, one of which may be the resistance of the workers to the conditions of exploitation bound up with the profit maximum. But that is as far as working class exertions can reach within the capitalist system.

III

The workers' loss of control over their own organisations was, of course, a consequence of their acquiescence in the capitalist system. Organised and unorganised workers alike accommodated themselves to the market economy because it was able to ameliorate their conditions and promised further improvements in the course of its own development. Types of organisations effective in such a non-revolutionary situation were precisely reformist socialist parties and centrally-controlled business unions. The enlightened bourgeoisie, too, saw the latter as instruments of industrial peace by way of collective agreements. Capitalists no longer confronted the workers but their representatives, whose existence was based on the existence of the capital-labour market, that is, on the continued existence of capitalism. The workers' satisfaction with their organisations reflected their own loss of interest in social change. The socialist ideology was no longer supported by real working class aspirations. This state of affairs came dramatically to light in the chauvinism which gripped the working classes of all capitalist nations at the outbreak of the First World War.

Left-wing radicalism had been based on what was designated by their reformist adversaries as the 'politics of catastrophe' . The revolutionists expected not only deteriorating living standards for the labouring population but also economic crises so devastating as to call forth social convulsions which would, in the end, lead to revolution. They could not conceive of revolution short of its objective necessity. And in fact, no social revolution occurred except in times of social and economic catastrophe. The revolutions released by World War One were the result of catastrophic conditions in the weaker imperialist powers and they raised, for the first time, the question of workers' control and the actualisation of socialism as a real possibility.

The Russian Revolution of 1917 was the result of spontaneous movements in protest to increasingly unbearable conditions in the course of the unsuccessful war. Strikes and demonstrations escalated into a general uprising which found the support of some military units and led to the collapse of the Czarist government. The revolution was backed by a broad stratum of the bourgeoisie and it was from this group that the first provisional government was formed. Although the socialist parties and trade unions did not initiate the revolution, they played a greater part in it than had been the case in 1905. As in that year, so also in 1917, the soviets did not intend, at first, to replace the provisional government. But in the unfolding revolutionary process they encompassed increasingly greater responsibilities; practically, power was shared by the soviets and the government. The further radicalisation of the movement under deteriorating conditions and the vacillating policies of bourgeois and socialist parties soon gave the Bolsheviks a majority in the decisive soviets and led to the October *coup d'état* which ended the bourgeois-democratic phase of the revolution.

The growing strength of the Bolsheviks within the revolutionary movement was due to their own unconditional adaptation to the real goals of the rebelling masses, that is, the end of the war and the expropriation and distribution of the landed estates by the peasants. Already on his arrival in Russia in April, 1917, Lenin made clear that for him the existence of the soviets superseded the quest for a bourgeois-democratic regime. It was to be replaced by a republic of workers' and peasants' councils. Yet when Lenin demanded preparation for the *coup d'état,* he spoke of the exercise of state power not by the soviets but by the Bolsheviks. Since the majority of the soviet delegates were Bolsheviks, or supported them, he took it for granted that the government formed by the soviets would be a Bolshevik government. And this was the case, of course, even though some left Social-Revolutionaries and left Socialists were given positions in the new government. But to continue the Bolshevik domination of the government, the workers and peasants would have to continue to elect Bolsheviks as their deputies in the soviets. For that there was no guarantee. Just as the Mensheviks and Social-Revolutionaries, once in the majority, found themselves in a minority position, so things could change again for the Bolsheviks. To retain power indefinitely meant to secure for the Bolshevik Party the monopoly of government.

However, just as Lenin equated soviet power with the power of the Bolshevik Party, so he saw in the latter's government monopoly only the realisation of the rule of the soviets. After all, there was only the choice between a parliamentary bourgeois state and capitalism and a workers' and peasants' government which would prevent the return of bourgeois rule. Considering themselves the vanguard of the proletariat, and the latter the vanguard of the 'people's revolution' , the Bolsheviks wished to do for the workers and peasants what they might fail to do for themselves. Unguarded, the soviets were quite capable of abdicating their power positions for the promises of the liberal bourgeoisie and their social-reformist allies. To secure the 'socialist' character of revolution demanded that the soviets remain Bolshevik soviets, even if this should require the suppression of all anti-Bolshevik forces within and outside the soviet system. In a short time, the soviet regime became the dictatorship of the Bolshevik Party. The emasculated soviets were only formally retained to hide this fact.

Although the Bolsheviks won with the slogan, 'All power to the soviets', the Bolshevik government reduced its content to that of 'workers' control'. Proceeding at first rather cautiously with its socialisation programme, the workers were not expected to administer but merely to oversee the industrial enterprises that were still in the hands of the capitalists. The first decree on workers' control extended this control "over the production, storing, buying and selling of raw materials and finished products as well as over the finances of the enterprises. The workers exercise this control through their elected organisations, such as factory and shop committees, soviet elders, etc. The office employees and the technical personnel are also to have representation in these committees . . . The organs of workers' control have the right to supervise production . . . Commercial secrets are abolished. The owners have to show to the organs of workers' control all their books and statements for the current year and for the past years."[5]

Capitalist production and workers' control are incompatible, however, and this makeshift affair, whereby the Bolsheviks hoped to retain the aid of the capitalist organisers of production and yet to some extent satisfy the yearnings of the workers to take possession of industry as the peasants had done of the land, could not last very long. "We did not decree socialism all at once throughout the whole of industry," Lenin explained a year after the decree on workers' control, "because socialism can take shape and become finally established only when the working class has learned to run the economy . . . That is why we introduced workers' control, knowing that it was a contradictory and partial measure. But we consider it most important and valuable that the workers have themselves tackled the job, that from workers' control, which in the principal industries was bound to be chaotic, amateurish and partial, we have passed to workers' administration of industry on a nationwide scale."[6]

But the change from 'control' to 'administration' turned out to entail the abolition of both. To be sure, just as the emasculation of the soviets required some time, for it required the formation and consolidation of the Bolshevik state apparatus, so the workers' influence in factories and workshops was only gradually eliminated through methods such as shifting the controlling rights from the soviets to the trade unions, and then transforming the latter into agencies of the state controlling the workers instead. Economic collapse, civil war, peasant opposition to any socialisation of agriculture, industrial unrest and partial return to the market economy, led to various contradictory policies, from the 'militarisation' of labour to its subordination to the revived free enterprises, in order to secure the Bolshevik government at all costs. The government's dictatorial policies confronted not only its capitalist and political enemies but the workers as well. The basic need was a greater production and because mere exhortation could not induce the workers to exploit themselves to the same or greater extent that they had suffered in the old regime, the Bolshevik state took on the functions of a new ruling class to reconstruct industry and to accumulate capital.

Lenin perceived the Russian Revolution as an uninterrupted process leading from the bourgeois to the socialist revolution. He feared that the bourgeoisie proper would rather accept a compromise with Czarism than risk a thorough-going democratic revolution. It was, then, up to the workers and poor peasants to lead the impending revolution, a point of view shared by other observers of the Russian scene, such as Trotsky and Rosa Luxemburg. In the context of World War One, Lenin approached the Russian Revolution from an international point of view, envisioning the possibility of its westward extension, which might provide the opportunity to destroy Russian bourgeois rule at the very point of its inception. It was then essential to hang on to power, regardless of compromises and violation of principles which this might involve, until a Western revolution complemented the Russian Revolution and allowed for a form of international cooperation wherein Russia's objective unreadiness for socialism would be a less weighty factor. The isolation of the Russian Revolution eliminated this perspective. To remain in power under the actually ensuing conditions meant to accept the historical role of the bourgeoisie but with different social institutions and a different ideology.

Of course, to hang on to power was already necessary if only to save the Bolsheviks' own necks, for their overthrow would have meant their deaths. But aside from this, Lenin was convinced that the capitalisation of Russia under the auspices of the state was more 'progressive' and therefore preferable to leaving her development to the liberal bourgeoisie. He was also convinced that his party could do the job. Russia, he once said, "was accustomed to being ruled by 150,000 landlords. Why can 240,000 Bolsheviks not take over the same task?" And so they did, by constructing a hierarchical authoritarian state and its extension into the economic sphere, insisting all the while that economic control by the state meant economic control by the proletariat. Just the same, the foundation of socialism, Lenin declared, "calls for absolute and strict *unity of will*, which directs the joint labours of hundreds, thousands and tens of thousands of people . . . How can strict unity of will be assured? By thousands subordinating their wills to the will of one. Given ideal class-consciousness and discipline on the part of those taking part in the common work, this subordination would be quite like the mild leadership of a conductor of an orchestra. It may assume the sharp form of a dictatorship, if ideal discipline and class-consciousness are lacking. But be that as it may, *unquestioning subordination* to a single will is absolutely necessary for the success of processes organised on the pattern of large-scale machine industry."[7] If this statement is taken seriously, class-consciousness must have been totally lacking in Russia, for control of production and of social life in general took on dictatorial forms exceeding anything experienced in capitalist nations and excluding any measure of workers' control down to the present day.

All this does not alter the fact, however, that it was the soviets which overthrew both Czarism and the bourgeoisie. It is not inconceivable that under different internal and international conditions the soviets might have retained their power and prevented the rise of authoritarian state-capitalism. Not only in Russia, in Germany, too, the actual content of the revolution was not equal to its revolutionary form. But while in Russia it was mainly the general objective unreadiness for a socialist transformation, in Germany it was the subjective unwillingness to institute socialism by revolutionary means which largely accounted for the failure of the council movement.

In Germany, opposition to the war expressed itself in industrial strikes, which, due to the patriotism of Social Democracy and the trade unions, had to be clandestinely organised at the workplace through committees of action that coordinated various enterprises. In 1918, workers' and soldiers' councils sprang up all over Germany and overthrew the government. The class-collaborationist labour organisations found themselves forced to recognise and enter this movement, if only to dampen revolutionary aspirations. This was not difficult because the workers' and soldiers' councils were composed not only of communists, but socialists, trade-unionists, non-politicals and even adherents of bourgeois parties. The slogan 'All power to the workers' councils', was therefore self-defeating as far as the revolutionists were concerned, unless, of course, the character and composition of the councils should come to change.

However, the great mass of the workers mistook the political for a social revolution. The ideology and organisational strength of Social Democracy had left its mark; the socialisation of production was seen as a governmental concern, not as the task of the working class itself. Though rebellious, the workers in the main were such only in a social-democratic reformist sense. 'All power to the workers' councils' implied the dictatorship of the proletariat, for it would leave the non-working layers of society without political representation. Democracy, however, was understood as general franchise. The mass of workers desired both workers' councils *and* the National Assembly. They got them both: the councils in a meaningless form as part of the Weimar Constitution – but with it also the counter-revolution, and, finally, the Nazi dictatorship.

It was not different in other nations – Italy, Hungary and Spain, for example, where workers gave expression to their revolutionary inclinations through the formation of workers' councils. It thus became obvious that workers' self-organisation is no guarantee against policies and actions contrary to proletarian class interests. In that case, however, they will be superseded by traditional or new forms of control of working class behaviour by the old or newly-established authorities. Unless spontaneous movements, issuing into organisational forms of proletarian self-determination, usurp control over society and therewith over their own lives, they are bound to disappear again into the anonymity of mere potentiality.

IV

All that has been said relates to the past and seems to be without relevance to either the present or the near future. As far as the Western world is concerned, not even that feeble world-revolutionary wave released by World War One and the Russian Revolution was repeated during the course of World War Two. Instead, and after some initial difficulties, the Western bourgeoisie finds itself in full command over its society. It boasts of an economy of high employment, economic growth and social stability which excludes both the compulsion and the inclination for social change. Admittedly, this is an overall picture, still marred by some as-yet-unresolved problems, as evidenced by the prevalence of pauperised social groups in all capitalist nations. It is expected, however, that these blemishes will be eradicated in time.

It is not surprising then that the apparent stabilisation and further expansion of Western capitalism after World War Two led not only to the demise of genuine working class radicalism but also to the transformation of the reformist social-democratic ideology and practice into the ideology and practice of the mixed economy's welfare-state. This event is either celebrated or bewailed as the integration of labour and capital and the emergence of a new, crises-free socio-economic system, combining in itself the positive sides of both capitalism and socialism while shedding their negative aspects. This is often referred to as a post-capitalist system in which the capital-labour antagonism has lost its former relevance. There is still room for all kinds of changes within the system, but it is no longer thought to be susceptible to social revolution. History, as the history of class struggles, has seemingly come to an end.

What is surprising are the various attempts which are still being made to accommodate the idea of socialism to this new state of affairs. It is expected that socialism in the traditional concept can still be reached despite the prevalence of conditions which make its appearance superfluous. Opposition to capitalism having lost its base in the exploitative material production relations, finds a new one in the moral and philosophical sphere concerned with the dignity of man and the character of his work. Poverty, it is said,[8] never was and cannot be an element of revolution. And even if it were, this would no longer be true because poverty has become a marginal issue, for, by-and-large, capitalism is now in a position to satisfy the consumption needs of the labouring population. While it may still be necessary to fight for immediate demands, such struggles no longer bring the entire order into radical question. In the fight for socialism more stress must be laid upon the qualitative rather than the quantitative needs of the workers. What is required is the progressive conquest of power by the workers through 'non-reformist reforms'.

Workers' control of production is seen as such a 'non-reformist reform' precisely because it cannot be established in capitalism. But if this is so, then the fight for workers' control is equivalent to the overthrow of the capitalist system and the question remains how to bring this about when there are no pressing needs to do so. There is also the question of the organisational means to be employed to this end. The integration of existing labour organisations into the capitalist structure has been possible because capitalism was able to provide the majority of the working class with improving living conditions, and if this trend were to continue there is no reason not to assume that the class struggle will cease being a determinant of social development. In that case – man being the product of his circumstances – the working class will not develop a revolutionary consciousness, will not be interested in risking its present relative well-being for the uncertainties of a proletarian revolution. It was not for nothing that Marx's theory of revolution based itself on the increasing misery of the working class, even though this misery was not to be measured solely by the fluctuating wage-scale of the labour market.

Workers' control of production presupposes a social revolution. It cannot gradually be achieved through working class actions within the capitalist system. Where it has been introduced as a measure of reform, it turned out to be an additional means of controlling the workers via their own organisations. The legal work councils in the wake of the German Revolution, for instance, were mere appendices of trade unions and operated within their restricted activities. Although attempts were made to substitute councils for trade unions, the latter were able, with the aid of the employers and the state, to assert their control over the shop committees. This relationship did not change with the rebirth of the council system after World War Two, then implemented by a so-called co-determination law, which was to give labour a voice in decision-making with regard to production and investments. But the spirit of all this labour legislation may be surmised from Article 49 of the German Works Constitution of 1952: "Within the framework of the applicable collective agreements, employer and works council collaborate in good faith, working together with the trade union and employer associations represented in the enterprise, for the good of the enterprise and of its employees and under consideration of the common welfare. Employer and works council must not do anything which might endanger the work and the peace of the enterprise. In particular, employer and works council must not carry out any measures of labour struggle against each other. This does not affect the labour struggles of parties entitled to conclude collective agreements."[9]

Co-determination did not and does not affect the employer's sole determination over his property, i.e. his enterprise and production. What it was meant to imply was the right of workers' representatives to make suggestions to management – in theory, even regarding the use of profits. But suggestions need not be accepted and, actually, there is no evidence that suggestions running against capitalist interests were ever heeded by management. To be meaningful, co-determination would have to be co-ownership, but that would be the end of the wage system. Co-determination itself merely allows for the usual activities carried on by trade unions, such as wage agreements, plant regulations, and grievance procedures by which industrial peace is maintained.

What has been said about workers' control in Germany, can be repeated, with some unimportant modifications, for any other capitalist nation which legalised shop stewards, works committees and similar forms of workers' representation within the industrial enterprises.

These measures do not point to an unfolding industrial democracy but are designed to safeguard existing production relations and reduce their immanent frictions. They are not a way toward but away from social change. But even social revolutions may not lead to workers' control when workers fail to secure their hold over the means of production and relegate their power to governments as the sole organisers of the social transformation process. This was the case in Russia and, with some modifications, it became the model for the East European 'socialist states' which emerged as a consequence of World War Two. Yugoslavia, however, seems to be an exception, for there it was the government which offered the workers' councils managerial functions and a measure of control over their production.

Although the Yugoslav Communist government remains the ultimate source of all power, after its break with Russia it decided on a policy of economic decentralisation by a return to market relations and the consequent autonomy of individual enterprises under the control of workers' councils. The latter took on competitive entrepreneurial and managerial functions within the framework of a state-determined general developmental plan. Within definite limits set by the government, the councils and managing boards elected by them, make decisions regarding the regulation of work, production plans, wage schedules, sales and purchases, the budget, credit, investments and so forth. A director, appointed by a mixed commission of workers' councils and local governments, presides over each enterprise, managing its everyday activities with respect to workers' discipline, hiring and firing, job assignments and the like. He has the right to veto decisions made by the workers' councils should they conflict with state regulations.

Government regulations of a rather complicated nature circumscribe the self-regulatory powers of the workers' councils. They are partly introduced by government decree and partly by local authorities in conjunction with the workers' councils. A system of taxation determines that part of the individual enterprise's income over which it may itself dispose and therewith its range of decision-making as regards investments and wages. Profits are siphoned off by government to cover its own expenses and to invest in government enterprises. The government determines the general rate of increase of personal incomes, but, while demanding adherence to a minimum wage, it allows for incentive-wages and bonuses to increase the productivity of labour. The social security system diminishes the workers' gross income by more than half. Investments or disinvestments are determined by the profitability principle and are steered in the desired direction by price, interest and credit policies. In brief, in so far as possible under these conditions, overall control of the economy remains in the hands of the government despite the limited self-control on the part of the workers' councils. While the latter cannot affect the decisions of government, the government sets the conditions within which the councils operate.

What is far more important than the relationship between councils and government, however, is the objective impossibility of establishing genuine workers' control of production and distribution within the market economy. It comes up against the same dilemma which harrassed the early cooperative movement, even though, in distinction to the latter, it cannot be destroyed by private capital competition if the government decides otherwise. "The workers forming a cooperative in the field of production," wrote Rosa Luxemburg, "are faced with the contradictory necessity of governing themselves with the utmost absolutism. They are obliged to take toward themselves the role of the capitalist entrepreneur – a contradiction that accounts for the usual failure of production cooperatives, which either become pure capitalist enterprises or, if the workers' interests continue to predominate, end by dissolving."[10] Operating in a competitive market economy, the Yugoslav workers have to exploit themselves as if they were still exploited by capitalists. While this may be more palatable, it does not change the fact of their subordination to economic processes beyond their control. Profit production and capital accumulation control their behaviour and perpetuate the misery and insecurity bound up with it. Yugoslav wages are among the lowest in Europe; they can increase only as long as capital increases faster than wages. The measure of control granted the workers' councils promotes anti-social attitudes because fewer workers have to yield larger profits in order to raise the incomes of those employed. Workers are unemployed because their employment would not be profitable, i.e. yield a surplus above their own reproduction costs. They roam all over capitalist Europe in search for work and payments denied them in their own 'market-socialism'. The integration of the national into the capitalist world market subjects the working class not only to self-exploitation and to that of a new ruling class, but to the exploitation of world capitalism by way of trade relations and foreign capital investments. To speak of workers' control under these conditions is sheer mockery.

While there cannot be socialism without workers' control, neither can there be real workers' control without socialism. To assert that the gradual increase of workers' control in capitalism is an actual possibility merely plays into the hands of the widespread demagoguery of the ruling classes to hide their absolute class-rule by false social reforms dressed in terms such as co-management, participation or co-determination. Workers' control excludes class-collaboration; it cannot partake in but instead abolishes the system of capital production. Neither socialism nor workers' control has anywhere become a reality. State-capitalism and market-socialism, or the combination of both, still find the working class in the position of wage workers without effective control over their production and its distribution. Their social position does not differ from that of workers in the mixed or unmixed capitalist economy. Everywhere, the struggle for working class emancipation has still to begin and will not end short of the socialisation of production and the abolition of classes through the elimination of wage labour.

It can hardly be expected, however, that a working class, satisfied with the social *status quo*, will engage in power struggles in preference to wage struggles for higher incomes within the prevailing system. Although improvements in proletarian living conditions in advanced capitalist nations are highly exaggerated, they have nevertheless been sufficient to extinguish working class radicalism. Even though the 'value' of labour power must always be smaller than the 'value' of the products it creates, the 'value' of labour-power may imply different living conditions. It may be expressed in a twelve- or a six-hour day, in good or in bad housing, in more or less consumption goods. At any particular time, however, the given wages and their buying power determine the conditions of the labouring population as well as their complaints and aspirations. Improved conditions become the customary conditions, and continued acquiescence of the workers requires the maintenance of these conditions. Should they deteriorate, it will arouse working class opposition in the same way that deterioration of less-affluent conditions did previously. It is then only on the assumption that prevailing living standards can be secured and perhaps improved that the social consensus may be maintained.

Though apparently supported by recent experiences, this assumption is not warranted. But to assert its lack of validity on theoretical grounds[11] will not affect a social practice based on the illusion of its permanency. There are indications, however, that the capitalist crises mechanism is reasserting itself despite various modifications of the capitalist system. In view of America's persistent economic stagnation and the levelling-off of West European expansion, a new disillusionment has already set in. With the diminishing potency of government-induced production, the capitalist need to secure its profitability regardless of the ensuing social instability increases. The new economic innovations reveal themselves as being capable of postponing, but not of overcoming, capitalism's built-in crisis-mechanism. This being so, it is only reasonable to assume that when the hidden crisis becomes acute, when the pseudo-prosperity leads to real depression, the social consensus of recent history will make room for a resurgent revolutionary consciousness – the more so as the growing irrationality of the system becomes obvious even to social layers that still benefit by its existence. Apart from pre-revolutionary conditions existing in almost all under-developed nations, and apart from the seemingly limited, yet unceasing wars, waged in different parts of the world, a general unrest underlies and undermines the apparent social tranquility of the Western world. From time to time there is a breaking out into the open as in the recent upheavals in France. If this is possible under relatively stable conditions, it is certainly possible under general crisis conditions.

The integration of traditional labour organisations into the capitalist system is an asset to the latter only so long as it is able to underwrite the promised and actual benefits of class collaboration. When these organisations are forced by circumstances to become instruments of repression, they lose the confidence of the workers and therewith their value to the bourgeoisie. Even if not destroyed, they may be overruled by independent working class actions. There is not only the historical evidence that lack of working class organisations does not prevent organised revolution, as in Russia, but also that the existence of a well-entrenched reformist labour movement can be challenged by new working class organisations, as in the Germany of 1918, and by the shop steward movement in England during and after the First World War. Even under totalitarian regimes, spontaneous movements may lead to working class actions that find expression in the formation of workers' councils as in Poland and in the Hungary of 1956.

Reforms presupposes a reformable capitalism. So long as it has this character, the revolutionary nature of the working class exists only in latent form. It will even cease being conscious of its class position and identify its aspirations with those of the ruling classes. But when capitalism is forced by its own development to recreate the conditions which lead to the formation of class consciousness, it will also bring back the revolutionary demand for workers' control as a demand for socialism. It is true that all previous attempts in this direction have failed, and that new ones may fail again. Still, it is only through the experiences of self-determination, in whatever limited ways at first, that the working class will be enabled to develop toward its own emancipation.

1967

1 *Théorie des lois civiles, ou Principes fondamentaux de la société*, pages 274, 464, 470.
2 G. Sorel, *Reflections on Violence*, 1906.
3 *Preamble of the Industrial Workers of the World.*
4 *Russland in der Revolution*, Dresden, 1909, pp.82, 228.
5 J. Bunyan and H.H. Fisher, *The Bolshevik Revolution*, Stanford, 1934. p.308.
6 V.L. Lenin, *Questions of the Socialist Organisation of the Economy*, Moscow, p.173.
7 *Ibid.*, p.127.
8 By André Gorz, for example, in his *Strategy for Labor*, Boston, 1964.
9 Quoted in A. Sturmthal, *Workers' Councils*, Cambridge, 1964, p.74.
10 R. Luxemburg, *Reform or Revolution*.
11 See: P. Mattick, *Marx and Keynes, The Limits of the Mixed Economy*.